contaminating

THEATRE

contaminating

THEATRE

Intersections of Theatre, Therapy,

and Public Health

Edited by Jill Mac Dougall

and P. Stanley Yoder

Northwestern University Press
Evanston, Illinois

Northwestern University Press
Evanston, Illinois 60208-4210

Printed in the United States of America

ISBN 0-8101-1534-4 (cloth)
ISBN 0-8101-1535-2 (paper)

Library of Congress Cataloging in Publication Data

Contaminating theatre : intersection of theatre, therapy, and
    public health / edited by Jill Mac Dougall and P. Stanley Yoder.
        p. cm. — (Psychosocial issues)
        ISBN 0-8101-1534-4. — ISBN 0-8101-1535-2 (pbk.)
        1. Drama in health education. 2. Drama—Therapeutic use.
    I. Mac Dougall, Jill R., 1942– . II. Yoder, P. Stanley. III. Series.
    RA440.5.C67 1998
    615.8'515—dc21   98-7121
                                                              CIP

The paper used in this publication meets the minimum requirements of the American National Standard for Information Sciences—Permanence of Paper for Printed Library Materials, ANSI Z39.48-1984.

Contents

Introduction

Jill Mac Dougall and P. Stanley Yoder

The Art of Healing/Healing through Art

Healers and artists share a long history as distrustful bedfellows. Despite their alliance in ritual healing and therapy, health and theatre are frequently separated into categories labeled science and art. Western assumptions tend to drive a wedge between health—most frequently represented as freedom from disease obtained through biomedical technology, optimal living conditions, and "good" behavior—and theatre, often seen as an aesthetic and gratuitous display of symbols, a play of mirrors that entertains or manipulates the audience. If the healer's theatrical means are uncovered, (s)he might well be considered a quack. If the performer is unmasked as facilitator or therapist, (s)he risks losing the status of artist. It appears that natural ties between art and healing must be severed for each to maintain an artificial purity.

In the West, particularly in North America, the image of the physician practicing the art of healing has given way to the image of the diagnostician prescribing medicines suggested by the results of laboratory tests. Ironically, as biomedicine increases its capacity to manage chronic diseases, the limits of its capacity to extend life have become more visible. In this context of biomedical claims for greater control over the body, a movement toward reinstating healing as an art and the arts in healing has developed. In addition, the search continues unabated for modes of healing that lie outside biomedicine.

At first blush it would seem that the medical scientist, engaged in the continual search for a "magic bullet" and armed with military images for representing the combat against disease, has little in common with the artist seeking to communicate new visions for enriching our daily existence. The physician promises expanding control over the body, while the artist offers openness and self-discovery. Doctors are highly paid professionals who wield considerable political clout, while artists often finance their artistic productions by working at other jobs. In a world obsessed with control, in a technological society that claims that we can regulate the environment, the weather, and our own state of health or illness, the biomedical approach resonates with the dominant images of popular culture also projected through technological magic.

We cannot forget, however, that the physician and the artist share working through the individual body on a basic level where illness and healing somehow occur. That may explain, in part, the recent success of the arts in the healthcare movement. It is in the domain of the social body as the origin of sickness that the capacities of healer and artist diverge dramatically. Artists respond to the afflictions of the collective body such as environmental decay, poverty, drug abuse, and violence by directly addressing the social context and creating public forums to seek solutions, whereas physicians tend to pull back into biotechnology and to medicalize social problems.

In the gap between what is biomedically possible to control and what escapes control, art as healing has resurfaced. Three paradigms emerge from this context:

1) "Disease art," as it has been facetiously dubbed by high-art critics, is the direct conversion of experiences of illness into commercially viable artistic products, such as in choreographer Bill T. Jones *Still/Here* or director Joseph Chaikin's recent work.

2) The Arts in Healthcare Movement, where artists work in clinical settings to aid patients and in university settings to develop interpersonal skills or raise awareness of the healing potential of the arts, is

rooted in a tradition that englobes drama and dance therapy. As stated in the journal *High Performance,* which devoted its Winter 1996 issue (19:4) to this topic, the Society for Arts in Healthcare lists twenty-nine founding members, is firmly implanted in programs such as Duke University's, and is spreading across the nation.

3) Arts in Public Health Education is an overarching concept of preventive medicine that encompasses multiple theories and practices. These range from TIE (Theatre in Education) methods used in AIDS awareness workshops among American high school students to mass communications theories employed in international development projects.

Active Contaminations

This collection of essays at the intersection of theatre, therapy, and public health overlaps these three paradigms while setting itself apart as a fourth possibility. Freely borrowing from established models, Contaminating Theatre recognizes theatre as the most political of the arts and performance as an immediate social exchange, and willfully incorporates healing and prevention into an activist tradition. Contamination implies the passive and the active reception of external elements, the interpenetration of constructed disciplines, and the acknowledgment of the inevitable seepage between social reality and pure art or pure medicine that occurs when working through the live and problematic medium of theatre.

A panel entitled "A Healthy Art" at the 1993 American Theatre in Higher Education conference brought together five of the contributors to the present anthology and planted its initial germ. In a wrap-up discussion social therapist David Dan and activist theatre director Maureen Martineau discovered a connection in the way their projects were defined negatively as art or therapy. When Dan undertook *A Piece of Wood* with the patients and staff of the mental health clinic where he worked, he was told by the clinic's funders that this might be theatre but not therapy. The main reason given was that no fee was demanded of the patients involved in the process. When Martineau and the Québécois company Théâtre Parminou produced *Les Bleus amoureux* exploring the issue of domestic violence, they were met with a tepid reception by local theatre critics and government funders who argued that, whatever the quality of the production, the social and therapeutic orientation of the piece annihilated its claim to art. This might be therapy but not theatre.

From this exchange emerged the core issues driving this anthology. Who traces the borders and defines the canons of what constitutes acceptable therapy or acceptable theatre? In the contemporary world of hypercapitalism, is healthcare a pure dollars-and-cents commodity? Is theatre a self-contained art existing outside of its sociopolitical context? What happens when the boundaries separating the roles of the therapist, the social worker, the health educator, the actor, and the spectator are tested or infected?

Speaking from a breadth of disciplines, themes, and transnational perspectives, the eight essays of this collection are steeped in cross-disciplinary impurity and fluid roles. Emerging from variant research fields that include psychology and social therapy, anthropology and communication studies, drama and performance studies, cultural and feminist criticism, the theoretical approaches are hybrid. Bibliographic references reveal theories of Western theatre, drama therapy, interactive theatre for social change, communications for development, cultural criticism. The tools of analysis, as well as the styles and formats of the presentations, reflect the diversity of the contributions.

What is shared by all the works is the material grounding of theatre/health experiences in an ongoing tradition of social activism. Anchored in the specific praxis of each contributor working with divergent populations—inner-city adolescents in New York or California, therapists in training at a Montreal University or clients of a Philadelphia mental health clinic, a radio audience in Zambia or a live audience of workers in Zairean mining towns—the anthology reflects the contamination that inevitably occurs in performance when ideals and objectives are pitted against the immediate reality of the context and the audience.

Ironically, most of these experiences come out of an activist tradition, yet many were funded by governmental organizations. Joan Holden, of the renowned San Francisco Mime Troupe, remarks on the irony of a protest theatre collaborating with bureaucrats in a state-funded antitobacco campaign directed toward San Francisco teenagers. This collaboration/contamination between government agencies and activist theatres should not be surprising since both ostensibly seek change for the common good. It is not the ideals defining the overall objectives that differ but the immediate goals in the nitty-gritty implementation and the ultimate reading of the experience. As Stanley Yoder and Kwaleleya Ikafa's research on an AIDS-awareness radio drama in Zambia points out, theatre practitioners are wary of overarching definitions of efficacy. Because they are bound to process and must work in the changing and fluid present of each performance, theatre practitioners are often much more cautious than public health agencies in defining objectives and evaluating results.

Although all of the contributions touch on methodology and evaluation, none prescribe. This is not a manual nor a self-congratulatory appraisal of results. Rather, it is a grappling with the issues driving the praxis of the contributors and the contaminations this implies, an active investigation into the sociopolitical nature of theatre working toward health. Because these contributions speak from a variety of specific sites and because they all focus on microprocesses and on multiple voices involved in the planning, producing, and evaluating of each experience, they offer a wide-ranging view of the potential for theatre in the sphere of public health.

This collection proposes theatrical strategies to the health educator or therapist. To the student of theatre it offers ways of using her art outside of the restricted and often ideologically dubious commercial theatre circuits. In the contemporary world we all share—marked by dramatic contradictions between communication technologies and our frequent inability to understand each other, between the potential for minimally healthy conditions for the planet and an increased hypercapitalism with its inevitable third-worlding of an expanding majority across the globe—Contaminating Theatre is a modest proposal of a medium for change.

Contributions

The first two contributions to this anthology are authored by longtime members of two companies rooted in the activist theatre that thrived in North America in the 1960s and 1970s. Both the Théâtre Parminou, of Quebec, and the San Francisco Mime Troupe are established theatres that have survived two to three decades by continually reappraising their work in the light of their current context and the social issues marking those contexts. In the two projects presented, public health emerges as a social issue of the 1990s.

In "Art Scarred by Reality" Maureen Martineau and Jill Mac Dougall, director and translator, respectively, of *Les Bleus amoureux,* analyze a Parminou play on domestic violence. The essay follows the evolution of the production, which treats the abuse of women from the perspective of the abusers. Exploring the work from the actors' initial research in collaboration with social workers to its performances in a traditional theatre venue, in community centers, and in prisons, this essay announces many of the core issues of Contaminating Theatre: the tension between the notion of pure art and art "tainted" by social reality, the creation of a context to explore an issue rather than dictate solutions, the gaps and links between the ideal of transformation shared by therapists and theatre practitioners, and the actual production of measurable change.

Introduced by playwright Joan Holden, of the San Francisco Mime Troupe, and health educator Mele Smith, of the San Francisco Tobacco Free Project, the second contribution is the complete script of *Revenger Rat Meets the Merchant of Death.* The play uses the SFMT's comedic social satire style to attack the manipulative tactics of tobacco advertisers to capture the prospective market of teenage smokers. Produced in collaboration with the San Francisco Health Department and performed in the city's high schools, the play describes the rise and demise of a cartoon hero named Revenger Rat and his designer/creator at the hands of the "merchants of death." In her introduction, Holden sketches the evolution of *Revenger,* from conception—marked by her initial reticence to approach the topic—to audience reception. She touches on the problems of creating a theatrical language that does not preach, but seeks to reach a high school audience directly.

The two contributions that follow are case studies of performances observed from the outside but directed from inside the community immediately concerned with the problem at hand. As an activist theatre practitioner and scholar, Lucy Winner explores interventions in another group of urban teenagers—New York inner-city high school students—that address the immediately life-threatening problems of AIDS and peer violence. Stanley Yoder, as international health consultant, and Kwaleleya Ikafa, as principal agent directing the piece, share the construction, reception, and evaluation of a Zambian AIDS-awareness radio drama series sponsored by a development agency and produced by local artists in the mother tongue of the target community.

Winner's "Adolescence and Activism" is based on the work of the SPARK Peer Players, a company of young actors working with the New York City Board of Education, and Teatro Vida, adult actor/facilitators who conduct workshops in inner-city classrooms and create theatre-in-the-moment according to the themes, characters, and narratives suggested by the students. Through personally implicated witnessing of live performances and their immediate impact, the author conveys the dynamic potential of an *inter-activist* theatre that invites a group of peers to voice their views and take hold of their problems rather than to submit passively to lessons dictated from above.

Yoder's analysis of the *Nshilakamona* radio series—written and directed by Ikafa working with a cast of community theatre artists—reveals how even radio can be used as an interactive medium. The essay describes the genesis of *Nshilakamona* from its inception as a public health development project through its popularization among Zambian listeners to the evaluation of the project's educational impact. The radio series, a cross between a soap opera and a sitcom, revolves around two urban families living in the era of AIDS. Parallel to the comedy/drama portrayed in the serial fiction runs the comedy/drama of its actualization, marked by the episodic tension between health educators in the U.S. and dramatists in Zambia, and by the street demonstration organized by listeners protesting the brazen behavior of some of the characters and the frank exposure of sexual activities on the public airwaves.

The next two chapters treat theatre as a psychotherapeutic tool, but in very different contexts and from variant perspectives. As a social worker, David Dan directed a theatre project with the clients and staff of a community mental health center. As a drama teacher, Muriel Gold developed a method to train family therapists. This exchanging of roles evident in the practitioners' positions is also a motor of the experiences analyzed.

Dan's text describes the year long process of creating *A Piece of Wood* initiated with a reading of Collodi's nineteenth-century original social satire and a critique of the Disney version of Pinocchio. As the project evolved, patients and staff began interpreting their lives in relation to the narrative and also to renegotiate the boundaries of therapeutic relationships. Woven through the author's telling of this particular tale are two issues central to this anthology. The first is the reciprocal "contamination" of stories and roles in the interactive process that runs counter to the current trend toward mental health treatment as a cost-effective commodity. The other is the very notion of "becoming real" underlying the Pinocchio allegory and the theatrical process that ironically allowed a heightened awareness of daily reality and the revelation of inner reality.

Gold's Fictional Family method also employs theatrical fiction and persona creation as a revelatory mechanism. Her essay touches on the reciprocal relationship between theatre and psychology, acting and therapy, before describing a university workshop conducted with family therapy interns. Acting within the collectively created fictional family, the participants try out new roles that allow expression of personal conflict distanced from their own family nucleus and explore subtext to discover how interpersonal relationships can be affected by incongruent messages.

The final two chapters of this anthology cross the fields of theatre, therapy, and public health to investigate the problems and dynamics of a Contaminating Theatre. Although the two research practices vary radically in context and purpose, both Mady Schutzman's and Jill Mac Dougall's essays touch on the value and limits of interactive theatre in the challenging of social norms and the quest for health. Analyzing workshops and performances in university settings as well as in the field, both problematize the notion of health and healing as embedded in wider political contexts and immediate interchanges.

Through three projects conducted with students, Schutzman's "Ads and Ills" addresses the pathologizing of the body in contemporary consumer society. Allying Boal's Theatre of the Oppressed techniques with feminist theories, the author's workshops use advertising iconography to explore issues of gender, sexuality, and "female disorders." In an attempt to trouble the seductive power of media images and norms of consumer behavior, the work moves from the classroom to the shopping mall. The analysis reappropriates the notion of hysteria to critically examine what constitutes health and the dysfunctional effects of ads invading the individual and social body.

Mac Dougall's research also incorporates interactive theatre techniques that, although ostensibly designed for public health education, frequently prove subversive. "*Kwash* and Other Ventures in Contaminating Theatre" explores performance as a two-way medium in health communication projects conducted in two widely divergent settings: Zairean popular theatre and North American universities. Through *Kwash,* a Mwondo Théâtre piece on childhood malnutrition produced in collaboration with local pediatricians and through acting and facilitating workshops with healthcare professionals, this essay critiques vertically controlled lessons of healthy behavior as unrealistic because they abstract health from the sociopolitical context and as impoverishing because they prohibit the circulation of ideas. Instead, the author envisions a theatre that invites reciprocal contamination in the active production of positive change.

Poster by François Gingras.

Art Scarred by Reality:

Les Bleus amoureux (*Blues and Bruises*),

A Théâtre Parminou Intervention

on Domestic Violence

Maureen Martineau and Jill Mac Dougall

In a television documentary on Native Canadian art, an Inuit sculptor expressed an intriguing definition of art, which resonates with that of Michelangelo: art is imprisoned in the stone; the artist's job is to liberate it. This metaphor evokes a struggle with an external force, the matter itself, a struggle that ultimately delivers the symbolic inner core. Transposed to the theatre, an art that continually interacts with its primary material—social reality—the sculptor's image is illuminating. It is very far from the romantic notion of a "divine muse" whispering in the ear of the poet and even farther from the modern notion of the quasi-divine individual artist. The contemporary theatre *auteur* seeks to reveal his or her personal vision. The individual creator signing the work *is* the work, its matter, its builder, and its cipher; the objective is not to reveal but to transcend material reality.

In the collective, activist praxis of the Théâtre Parminou the artist is more like the Inuit sculptor chipping away at the surface of social reality to uncover its inner logic and absurdities. Images, narratives, characters, drama emerge from the raw material. Sifting through the material, the artist questions the signs that emerge and investigates his or her own assumptions. The fiction does not spout forth from the artists' imagination but is discovered as the work progresses. It is as if a precious clue to a vast puzzle lay beneath each problematic nexus of the social fabric. The Parminou refers to its work as *théâtre d'intervention*, which underscores the contextual nature of the plays and workshops intervening in an ongoing process of social change. Production involves a reciprocal contamination of social problems and aesthetics.

The debate of art versus social reality would be a moot point for the Parminou were it not for the fact that the company's material existence depends in part on being defined as an artistic product in the eyes of government funders and cultural ideologists. The Canadian government, following the lead of its neighbor to the south, is reducing services to its citizens. The arts are inevitably the first to fall under the ax. For the funders a reduced budget has implied stricter parameters of what constitutes pure art on the one hand and, on the other, of reducing art to a commodity. The relation of art to material and social reality is an old debate. Hackneyed as the arguments on both sides might be, the current waging of the debate testifies to the tension alive in our society. That we evolve in a society of dis-ease is a fact of daily existence. As artists we choose either to retreat into the world of art or to confront that reality, however problematic the encounter or uncertain the outcome.

The following study revolves around one Parminou production, *Les Bleus amoureux* (*Blues and Bruises*),[1] based on one social problem of our environment, domestic violence. After introducing the Parminou, this essay describes the evolution of *Les Bleus* from its inception through its public performances. Investigating the symbiotic fields of the context and the theatrical agenda in the research, narrative, staging, acting, and diverse audience reactions to a play that depicts a therapeutic process, we will circle back to the problematic relationship between art and social reality.

The Théâtre Parminou, or Coopérative des travailleurs et travailleuses de théâtre des Bois-Francs (Cooperative of Theatre Workers of the Bois-Francs Region), celebrated its twentieth anniversary in 1994. Born in the effervescent social movement that swept through Quebec in the 1970s, the company's mission has been to create popular theatre directly engaged in pertinent problems marking the immediate social environment of the audience and the actors. Started by a group of young actors trained in the professional schools of Montreal and Quebec City, the Parminou elected to establish its home base in Victoriaville, a small town of forty thousand situated between the two major cities of Quebec, and to seek a regional audience outside of the traditional "theatre market" centers.

Structured as a self-managed cooperative, the Parminou creates original works in small ensembles, which allows the preparation and touring of several productions simultaneously. Currently six full-time members collaborate with some fifty freelance artists and staff assistants each season. The company has produced over 150 shows, given more than four thousand performances, and reached over a million spectators in widely diverse contexts. One of the major characteristics of the work is its ambulatory quality. Venues range from theatres, public halls, and work sites to picket lines, demonstrations, and public squares. Productions range from brief interventions of fifteen minutes to over two-hour performances that extend into audience discussion.

Outside of state grants from the Québécois provincial—and, until recently, Canadian federal—cultural agencies, productions have been funded in collaboration with cosponsors from governmental and non-governmental agencies. Frequently the company receives requests to design plays for organizations such as a union of hospital employees or an agricultural cooperative. These *spectacles de commande* (made-to-order shows) may be produced for a single event, as in the case of *Bonne fête des mots* (Happy Words Day), which reached four thousand students and educators gathered for a literacy conference, or they may be performed for several smaller groups to treat a specific work-related problem.

Whether invited to address a particular issue or initiating a reflection on an issue, as in the case of *Les Bleus amoureux,* the Parminou always works closely with appropriate cosponsors during all steps of the process, from the initial research—discussion, documentation, workshops—to the organization of the tour. This collaboration is essential not just in securing the material foundations of the production but in building relationships with the targeted audience, circumscribing the issues driving the piece, and even developing its style and imagery.

The images with which people characterize their milieu and its problems are inseparable from what they wish to convey. For example, in a workshop discussion with hospital employees on the deterioration of their working conditions, nurses described the maternity ward in terms of an assembly line: "I might as well be working in a potato chip factory"; "When I'm scrubbing them for the delivery room, I could swear I was working in a car wash." The potency and inherent humor of these metaphors provide a graphic look inside the subject's world and raw material for theatrical processing through improvisations and writing.

Over the years the company has experimented with a variety of popular and activist theatre performance styles. It has borrowed and adapted techniques and formats from commedia dell'arte, circus clowning, stand-up comedy, Epic Theatre, Theatre of the Oppressed, as well as farcical and musical traditions specific to Quebec. Frequently, masks and broad physical characterizations have been juxtaposed to a more intimate style of acting. The Parminou dramaturgy has incorporated traditional narrative and the fragmentary temporality of the television medium. Each production seems to demand its own format and aesthetics. Linked together these productions describe the continuing evolution of a distinct Parminou style. However, the primary objective is not to formulate aesthetic rules but to continue questioning social aberrations in our environment. In this effort the collaborators—the sponsors and eventually the audience—become cocreators in shaping each performance.

The Start of the Blues

The instigation for producing a play on domestic violence came not from an outside contract offer but from a member of the Parminou who wished to explore theatrically the issues behind domestic violence. Motivated by some of the members' interest in the theme and by the social urgency of the problem,[2] the company sought out prospective partners. Although the Parminou wished to reach a general audience with this piece, the question of intervening in a concerted effort with those most directly concerned was fundamental. Thus the company approached the Association des ressources intervenant auprès des hommes violents (ARIHV), an association of twenty organizations across Quebec specializing in counseling and therapy for male perpetrators of domestic violence. The first performances were scheduled within a campaign designed to inform the general public about the existing resources in Quebec to help perpetrators of domestic violence. The Canadian Ministry of Health and Welfare agreed to finance partially the project.

The next step was to sit down with members of the ARIHV to identify the target audience and the verb that most precisely defined this intervention. The choice of a verb is always crucial in determining the objectives and the form of a piece. From the beginning the objective was to shed light on the shadowy zones of the problem, to explore the underlying causes of domestic violence from the perspective of the man living the conflict. The guiding verb of the intervention was *interpeller,* or "to call out to," which better reflected the goals than "to demonstrate that," "to raise consciousness," "to sensitize men to," or "to sensitize women to." The verb *interpeller* harbored a cry, a desire to meet the other, and implied a brief contract of reciprocal trust. The expression provided not only a goal but also an impetus in the creative process.

The production was first shaped from the improvisational workshops set up with ten social workers who treat perpetrators of domestic violence. Because of the confidential nature of therapy and the actors' professional limits, this intermediary population constituted the initial cocreators. Mindful of avoiding verbose analytical narratives, the social workers were invited to theatrically reconstruct therapeutic work situations. At the same time, in-house improvisational workshops began, in which the actors addressed their own experiences and their relation to family violence. A tenuous synchronic link between the therapists, the invisible or virtual perpetrators, and the actors was created in the grappling with conflicts often leading to domestic violence. And—capital for the project—possible avenues of change were explored.

The second force impacting on the production came from outside the intimate experimental space. At that time the mass media was bombarding the public with numerous articles and television documentaries on domestic violence. The narrative most frequently depicted was that of an abused and traumatized woman who fervently wished to, but could not, leave the relationship. All notion of agency or change was excluded in these horror stories marked by the paralysis of the victim and the sterile culpability of the perpetrator. Although this reinforced the Parminou's decision to center the play on the perpetrators, the narratives of these women contributed to an understanding of how the victims of abuse viewed themselves, and ultimately to the way they would speak through the production: "I was nothing anymore. He threatened me constantly. 'Air head. You've got no brains.' One day he tried to make his threat come true. He ran after me with a knife screaming 'Bitch, I'm gonna cut your head off. Then everybody'll see you've got nothing on your shoulders.' "[3] From the language abused women choose to express their distress and the violent images employed to denigrate them, certain forms began to emerge. The erasure of the subject through the terror of being physically reduced to nothing led the Parminou to opt for an all-male cast. Two actors—Réjean Bédard and Yves Séguin—began to create the roles of Mario and Pierre, two clients of a group therapy. They were later joined by Raymond Arpin, who played Alain, the social worker. Maureen Martineau, the only woman directly involved in the creation of this piece, assumed the role of director. The set designer, François Roux, collaborated in the mise-en-scène.

By eliminating the stage presence of the wife or child, the pitfall of perpetrating violence through its enactment was also avoided. The wives of the two characters undergoing therapy would remain allusions emerging through the men's narratives and their interactions. One way of visually representing the absent other appeared naturally in the role plays of the therapy sessions—which became "play within the play" sequences—and in openly theatrical constructions where one actor would demonstrate, in Brechtian fashion, the woman featured in the other character's stories. Even these reenactments of arguments would be highly stylized. The recurrent realization of the Other as a product of one's own narrative, and the absence of a determined victim of abuse, created a climate of uncertainty that demanded the character continually confront himself.

Another means of representing the absent other was through material objects. Since the abused are reduced to the status of an object, they would be symbolized by props: a tricycle that is tripped over and then dragged across the room as if it were a child; a closed door that is pleaded with and furiously pounded on; a dress pinned against the wall; a suitcase that is clutched desperately. Seen from the perspective of the abuser, the persona of the abused is manifest in the object. The dress is caressed then ripped; lovingly removed from the suitcase then smothered. The suitcase becomes the sign of her departure and her longed-for return home.

The force of this symbolic language lies in its relationship to the reality from which the metaphors are drawn. Because the artistic imagery embodies the real, it remains dynamic. The power of the art is to allow the audience to enter the world of domestic violence through the symbolic and to gain an understanding within the protection of the theatrical frame. Theatre allows simultaneous identification with and distance from the emotions driving the play. The positioning of the self inside and outside of the drama creates the disengagement necessary to understand the process of violence vicariously experienced. The impact of the communication—the "calling out" objective orienting the production—is determined by the simultaneous experience of emotional distress, which can be paralyzing, and aesthetic pleasure, which can be liberating.

Spatial and Narrative Structures

The structure and the aesthetics of *Les Bleus* emerged from research workshops with the members of the ARIHV and the production unit's improvisations and writing. The backbone of the dramatic narrative and the theatrical structure of the production grew out of the insights the social workers shared of their work. The evolution of the play would follow the process of a small therapy group, but the artists wanted to avoid soap-opera psychological realism or a literal representation of a therapy group. On a practical level this would have required more than three actors. On an artistic level the terrain of exploration was not the surface discourse, but the underlying mechanics and symbolics of the process.

The ambiguous sentiments of the subject in therapy are present in the title, *Les Bleus amoureux* (literally "loving blues"). In Québécois French *les bleus* evokes the same state of nostalgia, longing, and depression we hear in the American English phrase "I've got the blues." On a more physical level the word *bleus* also means "bruises." The oxymoronic juxtaposition of a blue mood, graphic bruises, and love translated the emotional confusion of the agents involved in spousal abuse. Love—or rather, childhood deprivation of love and a fear of losing the loved object—is one of the principal motors of domestic violence. The title also contains a playful irony that would run through *Les Bleus* despite the gravity of the issues.

The poetics of the title were performed through the music, which punctuated key scenes or interrupted the flow of the narrative, and through the spatial design. Aside from a door and two chairs, nothing realistically mimed the room where a therapy group might meet. The stage was a set of platforms at odd angles, evoking a sort of no-man's-land, a destructured universe, the chaotic terrain of the subject. Appropriately, the entire set was painted a mottled blue.

The impressionistic indeterminacy of the space contrasted with the prosaic quality of the objects—a tricycle, a suitcase, a party dress or a nurse's uniform—and the actors in street clothes. The costumes discreetly signified the professions of the three protagonists: Alain, the social worker, in casual dress, as if he were at home in this environment; Mario, the blue-collar worker, also dressed casually, in jeans and a sweatshirt; Pierre, the business man, armored in suit and tie until he appears in a loud sport shirt toward the end of the piece, when he proclaims his liberation.

The actors' physical incarnation of the characters grew in parallel to the protagonists' narratives. Just as the abstract set contrasted with the specific visual characteristics of the three men, the overall temporality of the piece was nonrealistic and contrasted with the individual histories related by Pierre and Mario. Instead of representing the time frame of an actual therapy, the structure of four seasons in an indeterminate time was adopted. The seasons might symbolize steps in the therapeutic process or cyclic regeneration. Music and a young boy's voice offstage introduced each cluster. The child, whom we gradually discover is Mario's son, serves as a link to the next generation and signifies change. Set in this cyclic temporality is the representation of the erratic forward/backward movement of a therapeutic process.

The notion of a steadily progressive improvement was dispelled in the segmenting of the play. The four scenes corresponded to four seasons and four moments in the characters' journey together:

Summer: Mario's depression/Pierre's denial
Autumn: Mario's remission/Pierre's confession
Winter: Mario's relapse/Pierre's acceptance
Spring: Mario's responsibility/Pierre's escape

The scenes do not flow one from the other but suggest shifts and interruptions within the subject or outside of the therapy sessions. Each scene constituted in itself a dramatic nexus, a movement defined by exposition, rupture, change.

Embedded in this nonlinear representation of the therapeutic process is the narrative of the two perpetrators and their struggle to confront their own responsibilities as protagonists of their personal dramas. Pierre's and Mario's stories of what led them to therapy—as well as "what happened last night," fragments from their childhood, and what is likely to happen tomorrow—describe a trajectory that is full of gaps and does not necessarily lead to a happy ending.

Pierre is in therapy under court order. He is an executive in his late forties who has sacrificed much of his personal life to professional success. His pride in his economic position and ability to control both his family and his firm is challenged when his wife returns to a nursing career. His efforts to regain control over his wife, Carole, degenerate into psychological terrorism and physical abuse. He accuses her of "painting herself up like a whore" and sleeping with young male nurses on night shifts. He punctures her tires so she cannot go to work, and when she storms in one morning to confront him, he strikes her in the face. Until a painful enactment of the violent scene, Pierre maintains he was acting in self-defense. Although there is a glimmer of self-recognition in this scene and a playback sequence with his father's image exhorting him to be like a man, to be like the stone of his name (Pierre = Peter = rock), Pierre's recovery remains problematic. At the play's end he has replaced the wife with a young woman who works in his firm. He experiences the end of his requisite term in therapy as a liberation and chooses not to continue with the group.

Mario's story, on the other hand, suggests he will remain in contact with the therapist even though his wife—after repeated attempts to reverse the couple's dynamics—divorces him. Mario is a thirty-year-old factory worker who has struggled to make ends meet for his family. He is in therapy because his wife has left and will not return until he gets help. She runs a small daycare center and is raising their four-year-old son. Like Pierre, Mario is initially bent on controlling his household. He is enraged by the disorderly state of his domestic space and takes it out on his wife and child. It is the boy who eventually brings his father to confront his own responsibility in perpetuating a climate of terror. Contrary to Pierre's authoritarian father image, Mario's memory of his father, revealed in a role play, is that of a defeated and silent man who left the child raising to an embittered mother. The play's ending suggests that Mario will continue to process his own history and develop his relationship with his son while taking responsibility for his own actions.

Both Pierre's and Mario's narratives are marked by a shifting between denial and recognition of responsibility, between incrimination of outside forces—their wives, their environment, alcohol, or other exterior demons—and self-loathing or fear of inner demons. Toward the beginning of the play both men shake off the notion of personal responsibility in the events that have brought them to therapy. As is illustrated in the following excerpt, Mario maintains that his wife is constantly pushing him over the edge and Pierre blames his wife for having disrupted the family.

PIERRE: Oh, she'll come back. I know her. I'm sure she's sorry she brought this
    all on. Of course she's a little shook up, but she knows it was an accident.
    She knows me. She knows I'm not a violent man.

ALAIN: Yet you beat her?

PIERRE: Oh come now, I didn't really beat her.

MARIO: A little kick isn't a beating.

PIERRE: Beating is a strong word for a little push.

ALAIN: You prefer "assault." Okay, you both assaulted your wives.

MARIO: Listen, when a woman pushes you over the edge . . .

PIERRE: When she provokes you . . .

MARIO: When she won't listen . . .

PIERRE: When she just won't understand . . .

MARIO: A man loses his temper, that's normal.

PIERRE: You can't get rid of violence.

MARIO: We all have it in us, it's natural.

PIERRE: It's just part of our nature.

MARIO: We're men, after all.

ALAIN: Give me your definition of a man.

   Pierre and Mario hesitate.

MARIO: A man's somebody who pisses standing up.

PIERRE: He's the one who opens the ketchup bottle.

Stymied to define the nature of virility—and how this might correlate with the "naturalness" of male violence—the two men turn to "demon rum" or the inner demon theory. Pierre pounces on a discovery: all his problems with his wife Carole result from his drinking too many martinis, which he resolves to stop. Mario first attributes his Monday-morning blues, the time he most abuses his wife, Sylvie, to watching hockey all day on Sunday television, then to his work situation and his fear of losing his job. Ultimately, both men recognize their need to confront themselves rather than exterior circumstances. This first takes the form of an inner monster to whom they relinquish control. "It's like a volcano erupting inside," says Pierre when he finally breaks down. "I'm afraid of myself," screams Mario, "something inside me."

Constructing the characters' narratives involved deconstructing individual justifications perpetuating domestic violence and suggesting openings to break the chain of violence. Contingent to the myths of violence as intrinsically male or due to uncontrollable forces was the myth of violence as a loss of control. Whatever passions are at work in the act, violence demonstrates a will to control. The following dialogue demonstrates Pierre's need to control. When the therapist asks whether his wife might consider coming back, he responds as if he had foreseen everything:

PIERRE: No, she won't budge. I didn't really expect her to. I told myself I'd put all I had in our meeting. It was my last chance, double or nothing. It was nothing. But I wasn't too upset. You have to go on, you have to forget the past. And there are plenty of other women around. . . . Actually I have a little thing going with one of my colleagues.

ALAIN: So you were betting on two games at once, weren't you?

PIERRE: There's nothing wrong in thinking of myself for a change, is there?

MARIO: There's something wrong in trying to manipulate Carole with your crying. How did you do it? An onion hidden in your pocket? Or have you rehearsed so much you can cry when you want?

PIERRE: Oh stop riding me, would you?

MARIO: You can't take what you give out?

ALAIN: Okay, Mario, relax. Pierre, tell us about your new girlfriend.

PIERRE: Françoise? I met her at a dinner given by the Chamber of Commerce. She's thirty-eight, divorced, no children. She lives alone, near Westmount. Her ex works at the National Bank on Saint-Denis. But it's over between them. They never see each other.

ALAIN: She told you all this at a business dinner?

PIERRE: Not exactly.

MARIO: Or did you conduct a little investigation?

PIERRE: I have to know what I'm getting into.

MARIO: Jeez, you must spend a fortune on private eyes.

ALAIN: What would Françoise say if she knew?

PIERRE: She knows I had problems in my first marriage and that I'm in therapy.

ALAIN: What are you afraid of?

PIERRE: Of being burned again, of losing . . .

MARIO: Of losing face, of losing control?

PIERRE: No, not of losing control in any case. I have that licked.

ALAIN: Pierre, suppose it works out with Françoise, suppose you decide to live together, then six months later she tells you she has a new lover.

PIERRE: That would mean she'd been stringing me along, making a fool of me the whole time.

ALAIN: What would you do?

PIERRE: I'd probably smash her face in.

MARIO: You call that being in control?

PIERRE: Of course not. I was only kidding. But there is a limit to what a man can take.

Building the characters' narratives took into account four overlapping principles. First, that domestic violence results less from the loss of control than the desire to control others. Repetitive spouse abuse is not due to an occasional fit of anger or a drug-induced "I was drunk, therefore I was not myself" state. Second, whatever the causes embedded in childhood or the social context, the perpetrator of domestic violence must recognize his own responsibility to break the pattern. Third, therapy offers no miracle cures.

Its rewards are gleaned only from what the client brings to and takes from the therapy workshop. Last—and most important for the acting, the style, and the purpose of *Les Bleus*—the subject, like the therapy itself, is not an autonomous and static entity but a dynamic interactive process.

Performing the Blues

Anyone familiar with the Parminou's work recognizes that this excursion into the world of therapy and psychology was a radical departure from the sociocritical, commedia dell'arte–inspired style of characterization marking most of the repertory. As in every production, *Les Bleus* demanded the reinvention of a performance style. The sensitive and challenging nature of the problem under examination made artistic choices particularly difficult. It was important to individualize the characters and capture their inner struggle while creating socially positioned subjects. It was crucial to draw the audience into "true-life" narratives while revealing the strange, even absurd underside to that reality and provoking the desire to transform. Ultimately, several techniques meshed in the characterization and performance style of the piece. The use of action verbs as subtext, the development of social *gestus* and other Brechtian techniques, and the use of role plays—which afforded distance and ironic humor—combined in performing this particular version of the blues.

In this play most of the action takes place within the characters, in the conflict that pits them against their own violence, which they often perceive as a demonic alien. The protagonist's confrontation with himself is at the heart of the drama. To guide the actors and create the strategic games the protagonist plays to avoid self-discovery, the dialogue was decoded to uncover the imperative verbs driving the words:

PIERRE: **[Hide]** I told you it was an accident. I was asleep. She attacked me.
   I hit her in self-defense.

ALAIN: You hit her? I thought you'd pushed her.

PIERRE: **[Search]** Hit, pushed, whatever.

ALAIN: It's important you remember exactly what happened.

PIERRE: She came in the house screaming at the top of her lungs.

ALAIN: So you heard her coming?

PIERRE: [**Attack**] The whole neighborhood could hear. She gets hysterical when anything goes wrong.

ALAIN: So you knew it was your wife coming toward you. It couldn't have been someone else, your son for example?

PIERRE: [**Control**] Philippe? Lord, no. He would never raise his voice with me, he wouldn't dare. I've at least taught *him* some respect.

ALAIN: So you were sure it was Carole who jumped on you?

PIERRE: [**Defend**] She didn't jump. I protected myself in time. I stood up and I hit her.

This stripping down of speech allowed the actor to express the interior struggle of the character and inform the audience of the tactical negotiations hidden from the character himself. The brief pause in which the actor grasps the internal strategy verb is an interruption in the naturalistic flow of the dialogue. It is an indication that the subject—the actor or the character—is facing a choice. The forces operating in the conflicted subject become palpable, and the problem can be projected beyond the reified character in therapy for woman abuse.

Another means of pushing the problem into the public domain—rather than dismissing it as the personal problem of Mario, Pierre, or whatever other client in therapy—was to highlight physical attitudes. Particular attention was paid to the characters' body language and positioning vis-à-vis each other and to the Brechtian concept of *gestus*. Whatever the individual psychological makeup or the intensity of the interior drama, each character bears the sign of a social role relating to the social system in which he evolves. Mario would like to break down doors and break out of the working class—always threatened by unemployment—in which he seems trapped. His rage bubbles just under the surface. Pierre, on the other hand, has reached the top of the ladder by straitjacket conformity to the role of the executive in control. Mario is all in flailing limbs. Pierre's movements are stiff, like the stone of his name. He recoils from any physical contact with the other men. The characters' embodiment includes both particularities establishing them as credible individuals and social attitudes describing them as more universal prototypes evolving in a network of social exchange and transformation.

The potential for a simultaneous identification with the character and the refusal of his alienating reality was present in the recurrent shifts between naturalistic and openly theatrical styles that reminded the audience of the presence of the actor and the overall frame of the theatre. This *Verfremdungseffekt* or "making strange" effect of Brechtian theory suggests the exoticizing of the audience's contextual reality. Ideally, the spectators become tourists in their own culture and are confronted with the bizarre nature of what passes for the real. This concept called "alienation effect" in English seeks in fact to dis-alienate, that is, to remove reality from its assumed naturalness and predetermined moorings, and to incite the individual to change.

Small epiphanic moments in which reality was suddenly revealed in its constructed—thus subject to change—nature emerged in the role-play scenes of *Les Bleus*. These were of two types: the role plays built into the group therapy fiction and the overtly theatrical portrayal of events or mind distortions played in counterpoint to one of the character's narratives. One example of the latter type was the rapid-action, flashback renditions of Pierre's "self-defense" narrative that follows the excerpt cited above.

PIERRE: . . . I stood up and I hit her.

ALAIN: A reflex, self-defense?

PIERRE: It's instinctive.

ALAIN: Wait, let's go over this again.

   Alain plays Carole and Mario takes Pierre's role in the following enactment. The aggression is pictured in freeze frames as it is described.

ALAIN: Okay. You're in bed. Your eyes are wide open because you can hear Carole screaming. She comes toward you. You turn around, right? You stand up, you look at her, and you punch her in the face. Was it like that, Pierre?

PIERRE: I was only defending myself.

   The following speech is punctuated by rapid motion frames.

ALAIN: One more time. You're lying down. Carole's coming, you're awake, you know it's her. You stand up, you look at her, then. . . .

PIERRE: Yes, I knew it was her, yes, I was awake, yes, I was standing up, yes, I knew where I was hitting.

The staged deconstruction of the action accompanies the unraveling of the character's testimony. In other attempts to portray or revise the men's narratives, the actor playing the therapist takes on the role of absent characters in the protagonists' minds, such as Pierre's wife, Carole. Rendered object himself, the actor submits to Pierre's rage:

PIERRE: Well, she came home very late. Once again. She'd been working the four to midnight shift at the hospital for weeks. She knows I hate that, but she does it on purpose. She was getting all dolled up.
Alain puts on Carole's nurse's uniform.
You should see how she puts on her makeup just to go to work.
Alain offers lipstick and eye shadow to Pierre. Imagining his wife, Pierre begins to furiously paint Alain's eyes and mouth like a clown.
A whore. I've tried to tell her, but she doesn't get it. It's disgraceful for a woman her age to paint her face like a whore.

In another scene, Mario's account of a relapse, which leads to his wife's final departure but also to his personal recovery, is played out by the other two actors and the inanimate objects.

ALAIN: You both agreed on a budget?
MARIO: Okay, I decided.
ALAIN: So then . . .
MARIO: So then she goes and buys steak on a Wednesday! I was so pissed . . .
Then she says "If you're not happy, you should just do the shopping yourself." I answered her back.
Music. The actor playing Pierre whacks a chair which falls on the floor. Mario sees the scene in playback.
Then the kid starts screaming.
Pierre grabs the tricycle and shakes it.
Then Sylvie runs to the bedroom and I can hear her rummaging in the drawers.
Alain holds up the suitcase. Pierre runs to the suitcase and yanks it away as if he were grabbing the woman to hold her back.
Sylvie! She's packing again.
Pierre throws the suitcase on the ground. It opens and the dress falls out.
I don't want her to leave. Sylvie, stay here.
Pierre picks up the dress and holds it pinned against the door.
ALAIN: Were you holding her tightly?

MARIO: Yes.

Pierre shakes the dress, banging it repeatedly against the door.

ALAIN: Were her feet touching the ground?

MARIO: *No!*

ALAIN: Suppose another man were doing that to your wife, how would you react?

MARIO: Stop.

ALAIN: Would you let him get away with it?

MARIO: Stop. Stop it.

Mario gets on the tricycle and, with obvious clumsiness, pedals over to the door.

Stop, Daddy, stop. I don't want you to hurt Mommy.

Pierre drops the dress and steps aside. Mario gets off the tricycle and picks up the dress. Holding it close, he pleads with the dress.

I'm sorry. Please forgive me. I shouldn't have. . . . I'm sorry. . . . Come eat now. You know I love steaks. We'll go get some hot chocolate after dinner. Please . . .

ALAIN: [*slowly pulling the dress from Mario's embrace*] What made you stop beating her?

MARIO: It was Mathieu. He was so scared, so small. He's only four and he took all his courage to . . . defend his mother [*sobbing*] . . . to defend his mother from me.

In this sequence the character becomes a split subject, viewing his own actions through the eyes of another. It is the embodiment of his son looking at him that confirms Mario's resolve to change, whether or not his wife stays with him. Pierre experiences the same kind of self-recognition by speaking through Carole's voice:

Alain hands Pierre Carole's uniform. Pierre puts it on. Music.

PIERRE/CAROLE: It was last year. I was in the far left lane because I was late for work. I was speeding and all of a sudden I couldn't steer. I held control of the car long enough to pull over. I called the garage. My right-front tire had blown out.

Two days later, same thing, except I was going over the bridge and it was very slippery because it had been raining a lot. The car spun around and I found myself facing on-coming traffic. I swerved out of the way of a truck. I pulled over to the side of the bridge. I was shaking like a leaf. The cops came right away. I called the garage and my mechanic found another nail in the tire. He said "Lady, either your kids are real devils or someone wants to turn them into orphans. Your tires are being punctured."

I couldn't think of anybody who'd want to kill me. But everything clicked together when the mechanic said that. Pierre was sick enough to puncture my tires.

I managed to get to work that day. I even came back home that evening. I felt like calling him and saying his wife had died. I wonder how he would have reacted.

The music stops.

PIERRE: I didn't want to kill her, for God's sake, I never wanted to kill her. I just wanted to scare her.

In all of the sequences cited, the personification of props and the objectifying of the actor, the stylized movements, the wearing of another's costume or assuming the first-person voice of another are openly theatrical conventions that allow the actor to represent absent characters as well as the process of the protagonist's self-recognition. Yet, curiously, the most theatrical moments of the performance—and the most revealing of the theatrical nature of the events portrayed—appeared best in the role plays built into the fiction. The scenes where the therapist attempts to have his clients role-play with each other are also the most amusing scenes of the play.

MARIO: They're laying people off at the factory.

ALAIN: Are you afraid you'll lose your job?

MARIO: Let's just say they're breathing down our necks.

ALAIN: Did you talk to Sylvie about it?

MARIO: I don't want to worry her.

ALAIN: Why don't you try to tell her? [*to Pierre*] Play his wife.

PIERRE: Pardon? Play his wife? Uh . . . okay . . . [*grossly overacting as Sylvie*] Well now, Mario. How are things going at the factory?

MARIO: [*to Alain*] You've got to be joking.

ALAIN: Mario, your wife asked you how work's going.

MARIO: [*mumbling*] They're laying people off.

PIERRE: Are you going to lose your job?

MARIO: Let's just say they're breathing down our necks.

    Silence. Mario stares at the ground while Pierre seems to be
    searching for a reply.

PIERRE: Umm . . . I . . . I don't know what to say.

MARIO: My wife sure as hell would have plenty to say if I told her I might lose
    my job.

PIERRE: Well, what do expect me to do? I don't have a script.

ALAIN: Let's try this. Pierre you play Mario.

PIERRE: Mario? Me?

ALAIN: Yes, yes, you're very good at this.

PIERRE: [*flattered*] Really?

ALAIN: And you, Mario, you play your wife.

MARIO: Oh, shit.

ALAIN: Okay Mario, you're Sylvie. Go ahead.

MARIO: [*reluctantly playing Sylvie*] So how are things at work?

PIERRE: [*confidently playing Mario*] They're laying people off.

MARIO: [*as Sylvie*] Are you going to lose your job?

PIERRE: [*as Mario*] They're breathing down our necks.

MARIO: [*as Sylvie*] I knew it!

PIERRE: [*stunned, dropping his role*] Huh? What?

MARIO: [*jabbing his finger at Pierre/Mario*] You have a stupid asshole job,
    they treat you like a stupid asshole, and you accept to be treated like a
    stupid asshole. Conclusion?

PIERRE: I'm a stupid asshole?

MARIO: Exactly.

Behind Alain's attempt to coach the reluctant "actors" of his therapy group—behind Pierre's reference to the lack of a script, Mario's getting into the character, and Pierre's final doubletake—is an ironic commentary on the nature of theatre itself. In this play between actors playing characters playing yet other characters, the theatrical frame is brought to the forefront.

Multiple subjectivity emerges through the use of theatrical devices. The actors slip between the roles of the two protagonists in therapy, their parents, their wives, their children. The synchronic performance of oppressor and victim exposes the inner conflict of the fractured subject. The recall of the theatrical frame in the play-within-the-play sequence allows the audience to experience this confrontation while remaining safe within the walls of the theatre. This is ultimately what differentiates the piece from actual therapy. Although inspired by reality, the fictional nature of *Les Bleus* is repeatedly brought out in the performance. While evoking the emotion of the conflicted subject it allows for a personally disinterested reading of the issues and one's own implication in domestic violence, whether as perpetrator, victim, or witness.

Audience Reaction

In three years *Les Bleus amoureux* was performed over one hundred times in diverse contexts. The three principal venues were an experimental theatre in Montreal, regional prisons, and performances organized in conjunction with the ARIHV in small theatres or community centers throughout Quebec. Although the reactions were not homogenous in any of these contexts—and the audience, even in a prison regime, is by definition atomized—there were observable differences among what we can arbitrarily label the cultural, penal, and community milieux. A comparative reading of the three—as measured by the actors' sense of their exchange with the spectators, postperformance discussions, newspaper reviews, institutional reports, and audience questionnaires—relates directly to the art-versus-social debate underlying this work.

Cultural

The word *cultural* is used here in its most restrictive sense, as it pertains to the world of professional artists, consumers, and ideologists of art, to its canons and critical establishment. Although all the Parminou members are trained and seasoned professional artists, the performances of this activist theatre are generally geared toward a public that does not necessarily frequent either the traditional or avant-garde theatres of the world "cultural capital" of Montreal.

For several years the Canadian Arts Council, which has partially funded the company, had been pressuring the Parminou to produce a show in a Montreal theatre. Company members joined in this wish, because, performing outside of established venues and touring over months in the regions, the Parminou rarely has the opportunity to be covered in the wider-read press or to be seen by professional colleagues who constitute the committees recommending grants. An invitation from the Fred Barry Theatre in Montreal for a three-week run of *Les Bleus amoureux* in the fall of 1992 was welcomed.

An innovative theatre of considerable reputation in the cultural milieu, Fred Barry reaches an audience composed mainly of artists, students, avid theatregoers, and critics. Having long known that this public is more marginal than mainstream, and well aware that the theme was problematic and that no local stars enhanced the marquis, the Parminou did not entertain the ambition of reaching the "Montreal public" via the Fred Barry run. The eighteen performances played for a slim total of eight hundred spectators, whereas when performed only one evening during the same run at a community center a few blocks away the production reached six hundred people.

However minimal the attendance, the performances in the official venue were given far better coverage by the press than the company usually receives. Without exception the reaction of the critical establishment was that this type of theatre did not belong in a theatre. This is not to imply that either the audience or the critics reacted in a uniformly negative fashion. In fact, the critical response was dominantly positive. However, what emerged from even the most laudatory reviews was that a production centered on family violence, or indeed a *théâtre d'intervention,* does not fit into world-of-art slots.

"Intervention theatre is difficult because it leaves little place for art," says Jean Beaunoyer in an otherwise praising review in the popular Montreal daily *La Presse.*[4] "In *Les Bleus amoureux* the Théâtre Parminou serves art as well as activist theatre can," writes Jean St-Hilaire, critic for the Quebec City daily *Le Soleil* in an equally positive review.[5]

These critics seem to offer apologies for complimenting a theatrical enterprise so tainted by social reality. Negative reviewers backed up their opinions by the same sort of "therapy or social activism, but not art" formula. Not-art is a comfortable default category for the critic, as the closing sentences to Marie Labrecque's review in the Montreal weekly *Voir* illustrate: "This public therapy might touch some men who recognize the volcano burning within. So much the better. But lovers of theatre, those who esteem this art is more than a tool in the service of a worthy cause, would do better to seek out information on family violence at their local CLSC."[6] This expulsion of a major social problem from the domain of art and this reduction of the concerned public to "some men" was echoed by a few comments coming from the general public at Fred Barry. Although the reaction to the direction and the acting was highly favorable, the topic left spectators perplexed. The context predisposed the audience to another type of work. Admittedly, it may appear incongruous to present an intervention play on domestic abuse in a Montreal theatre. The audience felt they were being challenged to examine a problem when all they had expected was to spend an evening at the theatre. Or, if they had come specifically to see how the Parminou would treat the issue, they still excluded themselves from the concerned clientele. Although the majority were moved in spite of this—as the questionnaire responses indicated—many concluded that the play belonged on the social rather than on the artistic stage.

Penal

If the Montreal cultural milieu appeared detached from the topic of domestic violence, the prison audience proved, on the contrary, intimately connected to the issues, and this to the point of discomfort. Here the venue also played a crucial role in the reception of the play. Since some of the men had in fact been arrested for assault and battery—or even killing their spouses—*interpeller,* the initial verb driving the intervention, took on its second meaning in French: the disturbingly judicial connotation of "to call in for questioning." And these men were not simply called in; they had been arrested, tried, and incarcerated. In the twenty prison performances the actors found themselves in the uneasy position of putting out a call after the fact. At one performance *Les Bleus* played to an audience with guards patrolling the aisles. There had been a dispute just before the arrival of the actors and the warden had threatened to cancel the performance.

Creating a climate of minimal trust to allow open discussion was naturally difficult in this context. Even soliciting the inmates to attend the performance proved problematic. Word concerning the cause of their detention travels rapidly among prisoners and certain offenses are particularly stigmatizing. These include pedophilia, incest, and conjugal violence. For many detainees the simple fact of attending this performance could label them as wife batterers.

For the men actually serving time for assaulting or murdering their partners the show constantly reminded them of the cause of their detention and the seriousness of their felony. The play could hardly open liberating avenues when they were, quite literally, locked up. The conflict alive in the audience was much more dramatic than the one unfolding onstage. This was palpable to the actors, who felt severely put to the test. The emotional intensity from the coinciding of reality and fiction rendered artistic distancing of the experience virtually impossible.

Interestingly, the prisoners found ways of relieving their own tension and, at the same time, of inadvertently creating *Verfremdungseffekt* disruptions to the theatrical fiction. Literally escaping the room, many made repeated trips to the bathroom. Ignoring theatrical conventions, one detainee walked onto the set and sat down to talk with one of the actors, addressing him as the character and asking him at what time all this would end.

The recurrent invasion of the real had unexpected and disconcerting effects. At the end of the first prison presentation in the Drummondville correctional facilities, a prisoner spoke out during the postperformance discussion. He declared that he shared the name of one of the protagonists and that his son's name was Mathieu, like Mario's son in the play. He was convinced the cast had access to his files and had used his story as a basis for the play. Another prisoner, after a casual discussion with one of the actors following the play, confided that he was in prison for having killed his wife.

The fruitfulness of the postperformance discussion depended a great deal on whether the venue was a maximum- or minimum-security prison, that is, on the gravity of the crime and on the extent the inmates were policed. At the Ste.-Anne-des-Plaines penitentiary, in a ward housing men convicted of crimes of passion, the cast was met with stony silence. The audience would not or could not communicate. Compared to the violent crimes for which these men had been incarcerated, Mario's kicking his wife or Pierre's puncturing his wife's tires appeared as trivial misdemeanors. An exchange across this gulf between the two experiences in the limited time of an afternoon was impossible.

However, these reactions were far from the norm. In general the performances in the penal context did initiate a dialogue. For the most part, responses to the questionnaires indicated the spectators were dialoguing with the actors rather than feeling subjected to sterile denunciations. One of the most encouraging was, "I would like to see this again with my son." Others, however, were a cry of desperation uttered too late: "I need help because I'm a suffering human being and I don't know what to do anymore." Incarceration, if only temporary, frequently compromised the possibility of change that was the goal of the performance.

Community

The initial objective had been to put out a call to spectators, to confront them with the role they might unwittingly play in the cycle of domestic violence, and to suggest avenues of change. It was not to provide counseling, which the Parminou was hardly equipped to do. Considering the purpose of the intervention and the collaboration with ARIHV social workers, it is not surprising that the larger audiences and the most rewarding response came from a regional tour organized with the sponsors.

These audiences were composed of social workers, of men who had been or were currently in therapy for spousal abuse, of women who had been subject to abuse, but also of a general audience attracted by the "people's theatre" reputation of the Parminou or the topic of the play. The postperformance discussions were lively and reciprocally informative exchanges.

Many people used the forum to share their own experiences. Former perpetrators told moving stories of turning their lives around. One man said, "You have to want to change yourself, not to please your wife or whatever, just for yourself." Many women who had been subject to abuse also took the stage to tell their stories of reversing the role of passive victim. These presented a vital counterpoint to the men's narratives. "Domestic violence will cease," said one, "when women stop being afraid."

One of the more interesting issues raised was casting the play from the viewpoint of the male perpetrator. In the questionnaire, although a majority of respondents expressed the wish to hear more of a female viewpoint—and the women's groups consulted during the research period had hotly contested the absence of women's voices for fear the production would become a platform justifying the perpetrators' motivations—the women who spoke publicly said they felt they were in a safe environment because only men were under the spotlight and acts of brutality against women were not literally depicted.

Social workers witnessing the performance, some of whom had initially contributed to the research and documentation, expressed two dominant ideas. First, the work challenged both therapist and client; it incited a rereading of one's own actions. Second, *Les Bleus* deconstructed both the myth of violence as irrevocably locked within an individual's makeup and the myth of therapy as a miracle cure.

All of these reactions speak to the issue of personal responsibility for reversing violent behavior in a society that—as one particularly scathing but astute Montreal reviewer pointed out[7]—regularly exercises violence on men, women, and children. One theatrical intervention could hardly hope to change our society. It could, however, put out a call to individuals to assume responsibility.

Unfinished Business

Alain picks up the props, then moves down stage. The music stops. He speaks directly to the audience.

ALAIN: Pierre never came back, but I ran into him once on the subway about four years later. He was in a hurry, and we didn't talk much. He did tell me he'd remarried. Things seemed to be going well for him.

Mario stayed in contact with the group. He and his wife separated a couple of years ago. They have split custody of their son. Mario stopped by with Mathieu the other day. He's already nine and very proud of going into fourth grade. He's turning into a fine kid.
Lights dim. Music.

BOY'S VOICE *OFF*: In spring everything melts and there's water everywhere. Even the house, because we clean it from top to bottom. My mom scrubs the windows so we can see the buds outside. We pack up our winter clothes, even if it's still cold. My dad says summer will hurry up that way and we'll be warm again. I don't really believe him. I know he's always joking.

I'll spend all Easter vacation with him. I'm glad. Mario and I have a lot of fun together. I call him by his first name, he says I can. I like the name Mario. Mine's Mathieu and my grandfather's Maurice. We all begin with an M. I hope we'll go to sugar camp again. The last time Mario made himself sick on taffy. But I told him on the phone I wouldn't let him eat so much. I have to watch out for him. Sometimes I don't know what he'd do without me.

The music continues as Alain places two chairs at center stage, as if to invite the audience to take a seat.
House lights up as stage lights dim.

The unfinished quality of the play as demonstrated in the last scene contributes to the opening of a forum rather than a dramatic closure. On a narrative level it leaves the stories of Pierre and Mario or Alain and the therapy process suspended in midair; on a performative level the play invites spectators to take the stage. Thus the audience—even in the case of the Montreal spectators who walk away from a problem that does not concern them or the stone-silent maximum-security prisoners who are much too implicated in the problem—collectively writes the ending to each performance. Sometimes the closure is a very anticlimactic cul-de-sac. Sometimes it lifts with collective energy and promises that the performance will carry beyond the walls of the theatre to produce change. In all cases the audience is a responsible participant in the outcome, an actor in the drama of domestic violence and its possible reversal.

Just as the play remains unfinished, the debate of art versus social reality, therapy, or public health is not about to come to an end. In the same week the Labrecque review chastising the "community health" nature of *Les Bleus* appeared, a review entitled "Art and AIDS at the Museum of Contemporary Art: The MCA Takes on the Look of a CLSC" appeared in another newspaper.[8] It criticized the Montreal Museum of Contemporary Art for its *From Media to Metaphor* exhibit on art inspired by the AIDS epidemic—which included works by Robert Mapplethorpe and Keith Haring—and characterized the exhibit as belonging to the world of medicine or social activism rather than the "transcendent" domain of art.[9] The terms used to dismiss the exhibit from what ideologically constitutes "pure art" were remarkably similar to those qualifying *Les Bleus* as a public therapy better belonging in a CLSC. Both the play and the exhibit were defined as more appropriate to a community-service venue than a theatre, museum, or other temple of the arts.

How divorced from social reality art remains in the eyes of its ideologists was brought home in the 1994 refusal of all subsidies from the Canadian Arts Council to the Théâtre Parminou.[10] Nowhere is the "social reality," that is, "not-art" formula better illustrated than in the federal agency's terms supporting their decision. Their letter stipulated that only exclusively artistic endeavors were eligible for their funding. Since its artistic mission cannot be divorced from its social praxis, the Parminou has no claim to funds reserved to "pure art."

For activist theatres the artistic and the social remain inseparable. The scars of social conflict mark our art. We would like to think that art, in its turn, has a role to play in the transformation of social reality. In this North American end of the century, social divisions and dis-ease are likely to increase. We, as theatre practitioners, have a very immediate role to play in bringing art back to the real, in suggesting possibilities for change, and in maintaining simple sanity.

Notes

1. *Les Bleus amoureux,* by Réjean Bédard, Maureen Martineau, François Roux, and Yves Séguin, was translated into English as *Blues and Bruises* by Jill Mac Dougall. Both English and French versions are available, under copyright protection, through the Centre d'essai des auteurs dramatiques, Montreal.

2. Statistics compiled in Quebec indicate that one out of seven women is physically abused by her spouse; between 1987 and 1990 the number of cases reported to the police increased by 83 percent; less than 10 percent of the cases are reported.

3. Paraphrased from a 1992 televised interview, *Le Point* documentary on domestic violence (French language services of Radio Canada).

4. "Du théâtre d'intervention qui émeut," in *La Presse,* 26 Oct. 1992.

5. "Violence conjugale: la thérapie par l'émotion," in *Le Soleil,* Oct. 1992.

6. "Bleu comme l'enfer," in *Voir,* 5–11 Nov. 1992. The Québécois CLSC (Centres locaux des services communautaires) are community-health and social-service centers. Staffed by doctors, psychologists, and social workers, these centers assure numerous services to the population, from general medical care to drug rehabilitation.

7. Gilbert David, "La proie pour l'ombre," in *Le Devoir*, 27 Oct. 1992.

8. Jocelyne Lepage, "Art et sida au Musée d'art contemporain: le MAC prend des allures de CLSC," in *La Presse*, 7 Nov. 1992.

9. This retreat of the conservative critical establishment into an essentialist ART category was well illustrated in the U.S. when the critic Arlene Croce wrote a review (*New Yorker*, December 1994) of Bill T. Jones's *Still/Here*, a choreography based on first-person narratives of people with life-threatening diseases. Perhaps a first of its kind, the review was based on *not* seeing the performance, which would have tainted the author's artistic judgment, because the work, deemed "victim art," was too enmeshed in contemporary reality. For further reflections on art versus social reality see *But Is It Art? The Spirit of Art as Activism*, an anthology edited by Nina Felshin (Seattle: Bay Press, 1995).

10. As of this date the Théâtre Parminou continues to receive funding from the Québécois Ministère de la Culture and to finance its productions with contracts from governmental and nongovernmental social agencies.

Revenger Rat Meets the Merchant of Death, A San Francisco Mime Troupe Production

Introductions by Mele Smith and Joan Holden
Script by the San Francisco Mime Troupe

A Word from Mele Smith, Health Educator, San Francisco Tobacco Free Project[1]

In January 1993 I was thinking about our next two-year plan for the Tobacco Free Project (TFP) in a meeting with Alyonik Hrushow, project director, and Susana Hennessey, project health educator. We were looking for a way to let people know that there was more to tobacco prevention than telling youth not to smoke because "smoking is bad for you." We wanted the message to get at the root cause of the problem: the tobacco industry's marketing of its product to children here and abroad.

The tobacco industry spends over six billion dollars each year—over two hundred dollars a second—advertising and promoting a product that kills when used as intended. The industry claims that its advertising and promotion is targeted at "people who smoke, 21 and older . . . to encourage brand loyalty and brand switching among people who already smoke."

We knew better.

The tobacco industry must recruit thirty-five hundred new smokers a day to replace those that have left the ranks by either quitting or dying. Youth are the prime target for this recruitment since basic economics says that the earlier you hook 'em, the more money you make. This strategy seems to be working, for 90 percent of adults hooked on tobacco started smoking in their teens. As staff of the Tobacco Free Project, funded by the State of California, we wanted to expose the tobacco industry's recruitment of our youth into the ranks of smokers.

Recognizing that theatre is a powerful tool with which to spread information through nontraditional venues, we released a request for proposals for a theatre project to spread the word through schools, community theatres, and parks. The goal of the project was to increase the public's awareness of the tobacco issue and to generate support for tobacco-related prevention policies. The San Francisco Mime Troupe (SFMT) won the bid.

The SFMT delivered a musical play focused on the industry's recruitment of youth that packed a powerful punch aimed directly at the tobacco industry, exposing many of its targeting tactics both in the United States and abroad. From 30 March, 1994 through 30 April, 1994 *Revenger Rat Meets the Merchant of Death* was performed free of charge in eighteen schools and eleven community settings, reaching over six thousand students and two thousand community members.

Results from surveys conducted after the performances at five of the high schools illustrate how well the message of the play was received. Seventy-five percent of those surveyed indicated that the play gave them more information on how the tobacco industry targets youth through its advertising and promotion practices, while a different 75 percent rated the play as an "excellent" or "good" way to learn about tobacco issues as well as "excellent" or "good" in terms of entertainment.

Since the beginning of the antitobacco education and research program and increased taxes on tobacco in California, the number of smokers decreased from 27 percent to 15 percent of adults. The annual consumption of tobacco has decreased by about two billion packs, which represents nearly three billion dollars in lost sales. Although cigarette sales declined after the tax increase took effect, overall teenage smoking has increased by 20 percent over the past few years.

From mid-1994 to mid-1996 there were far fewer state funds available for antitobacco activities in California, and we did not expect to be able to fund *Revenger Rat* again. However, for the first time, in the 1996–97 budget, the tobacco-education account has been fully funded and can collaborate with the SFMT for a second run of *Revenger Rat* with a second script and a concurrent media campaign that will culminate in a policy-maker summit to outline the plan of action to address the tobacco industry's marketing strategies.

Joan Holden on the Creation of *Revenger Rat*

In 1993 the San Francisco public health department's Tobacco Free Project commissioned the SFMT to do a play aimed at youth. Well funded by Proposition 99, the TFP had initiated a sophisticated campaign on billboards and television and smoking rates were actually decreasing in the state. The following year, when *Revenger* was being performed in San Francisco high schools, Governor Wilson would divert most of Proposition 99 money to the state general fund. There would be no more billboards, public-service announcements, or plays. We didn't know then that this might be the last work of its kind.

At the time I was very glad the SFMT got the work, happy for the funding and the chance to perform in high schools, but utterly depressed by the topic: "Smoking Is Bad for You," a boring message to write and certain to bomb with kids to whom it's been preached incessantly since kindergarten.

Then one day I read an article in the *San Francisco Weekly* about rappers going through moral agony over whether to sign with major record labels. I remembered rock bands in the 1960s going through the same thing and I got an idea: young rap artist with revolutionary message is approached by tobacco publicist who wants to use one of his songs for a cigarette commercial. We would avoid the predictable plot about someone getting sick and the central conflict—an artist's dilemma, how far to go for money— would be something I actually wanted to write about. The focus would not be on health but on the tobacco companies manipulating teenagers.

Michael Sullivan, who would eventually play the hero, Neville, improved on the idea. Make him a cartoonist instead of a rapper. A young comic book artist was a more surprising choice and also a direct satire of the immensely successful "Joe Camel" ad campaign. The plot came in a flash: the publicist buys the hero's character, his alter ego; the character begins smoking and millions of kids follow his example; eventually the comic-strip character appears in awful judgment to show his cancered lungs to his creator.

I had given up comic books a few decades before, but I had a great time rediscovering them: the new mainstream work, feminist and African-American comics; and the new underground work, slacker comics and dyke comics. And I had a great source: Spain Rodriguez, creator of *Trashman* and *Big Bitch*, talking head in the movie *Crumb*, and occasional scene designer and poster artist for the SFMT. Spain told me about the McCarthy-era purge of horror comics in the 1950s, so similar to the antiobscenity campaigns today. I asked Spain a question that I find useful when writing about a milieu I don't know well: "What's the worst thing that could happen to you?" He said, "If someone lost my originals."

When we meet Neville in the first scene this has just happened to him. And he's also lost his publisher. Appears Lydia Gutsharp, a tobacco publicist, who offers to print his books in runs of one hundred thousand and distribute them in every corner store and shopping mall in America. Neville is to have complete artistic freedom except for one tiny point: his hero must be smoking a Duke in every panel. Neville's character, his alter ego, is Revenger Rat, in daily life a common but well-informed sewer rat named Rodney. Rodney was born in a toxic-waste dump and suffered one mutation: untruth enrages him, to the point where he grows huge and gobbles up the liar.

Our contract stipulated the scenario had to be approved by the funders. Imagining overpaid, underworked, rigid-minded bureaucrats, I half expected Rodney/Revenger to cost us the commission. All credit for persuading the health commission to approve the project goes to the public servants at the TFP who had first dreamed up the collaboration. Mele Smith, Alyonik Hrushow, and Susana Hennessey laughed all the way through my reading of the scenario.

This was to be a fifty-minute play that could fit into a school assembly period and, now approved, it had to be written fast. I was already working with one collaborator, Ellen Callas, who was busy researching the tobacco industry. I decided I needed two other writers: Nina Siegal (now a reporter for the *San Francisco Bay Guardian*) for the multiracial slacker scene where Neville and his sidekick, Dewey, hang out, and an even younger writer for the high school scene. To become familiar with the milieu we persuaded two teachers to let us interview their students to find out what they thought about smoking. The first contact was a preview of our future audience. The students sat staring at us sardonically, occasionally responding in mono-syllables. The teacher said tactfully afterward, "I've found it's better to try something more interactive." At the next school Ellen led improvisations and the response was much livelier. Three skits emerged, all showing that kids smoke for the same apparent reason as adults: stress. Still, I needed a very young collaborator to get the language right. I recruited Karim Scarlata, a college freshman who had never written dialogue but whom I knew as a funny verbal mimic. For myself I reserved the juicy job of writ-ing Neville and his creation, Revenger Rat.

Revenger winds up sacrificing his life. He forces Neville to draw his sick-ness and death to warn the kids who have followed his example. The tobacco moguls don't realize the subversion—because adults don't read comics—until the last issue hits the stands and it's too late.

I found the perfect fate for Lydia, the publicist who is also a chain-smok-er. In one of those psychic experiences that happens when a play is finally coming together, I met Carolyn Kusack, a local activist and a nurse, at a benefit dinner. When I explained the project she asked, "Have you heard of tobacco-induced cardiovascular syndrome?" I hadn't. "Nicotine constricts the veins, blood doesn't flow. First we cut off their toes, then their feet, then their legs below the knee, then above the knee . . . eventually they die." Each time Lydia appeared she would be missing another piece of her leg. But the ultimate villain of the play, L.B. of Beauregard Tobacco, never pays for his crime. The Merchant of Death remains healthy to the end and deter-mines to capture the Asian market. This is in fact the current strategy of tobacco companies designing campaigns to reach a vast population of potential smokers: Asian women.

We liked our creation, but we were not the audience. Would kids catch the satire? Would they go for Revenger? Would they identify with Neville and his problem? Most of all, could we get past their attitude? Actors who had played high schools told horror stories about audiences who never quieted down, who heckled or loudly ignored the performance. This was not exactly what happened at our first show in a small magnet school, but the kids sat on their hands. They warmed up briefly during the high school scene where director Dan Chumley had assured us a winner by casting Giselle Garcia, a terrific hip-hop dancer. Otherwise our premiere was met by a stony silence. A student I know, the daughter of an actor, passed me as they filed out of the auditorium. "Great show," she tossed me, as theatre kids learn to do. "Then why didn't they laugh?" I asked. She shrugged. I felt the cold clutch of fear; maybe this didn't work. However, first performances, as anyone who has grimly waited for reviews knows, can be off.

The real test would be at our second venue, Galileo, a huge general high school with a majority of immigrant students. The cavernous auditorium shivered and echoed as a thousand kids thundered in. The principal commanded *Quiet*, which is what we got at first. Opening scene, with the tobacco mogul and the publicist, no laughs. Second scene, in the slacker bar, a few promising titters but no reaction to Neville's rap about Revenger. But the high school scene brings the house down. Every character got every laugh. Audible shock at the lesbian subplot we'd thrown in for good measure. Now we had them. Hushed tension when Neville betrays his friend Dewey. Cheers when Revenger appears. Shrieks of disgust rising from a thousand throats when Revenger rips open his chest to display his charred lungs and when Lydia appears missing a limb.

From then on, it went like that. At Wilson, a school with so many problems the Board of Education has since closed it, we had a dream performance. One teacher told us, "I've never seen these kids sit still before." So we've proved our style can work in this population and we're hooked enough to seek out further funds to produce shows for high school audiences. But did we stop anyone from smoking?

I don't know, but I do know we succeeded in bringing home the message of manipulation by the tobacco companies. This didn't come out in the postperformance discussions, which didn't really work. There was never a microphone for audience comments, and the kids who were brave enough and loud enough to make themselves heard usually wanted to talk about acting, not smoking. The questionnaires on the show and the content that the TFP educators passed out were more revealing.

Students, suddenly thrust into the role of appraising adults, proved tough critics. Most rated the production "Good," with "Fair" not far behind. Very few "Outstanding" but also mercifully few "Poor." Asked what they didn't like, many said we had stereotyped high school students. Of course, none minded that we had also stereotyped twenty-somethings, publicists, and CEOs. Most gratifying was the response to the question "What is the main message of the play?" Typical answers:

- The tobacco companies just want us to keep their pockets full.
- Don't get sucked in by good-looking ads that attract our age group.
- People will do anything to support the tobacco industry.
- Smoking messes up your teeth and makes you lose your hair and your legs.

Response to the question "What can local communities do to fight back against the tobacco companies and promote tobacco-free environments and neighborhoods?" was more divided. Many said "Nothing" or "It's impossible." Others were more actively hopeful: "Have a strike . . . Ban the ads . . . Boycott stores that sell cigarettes." One student suggested a three-part plan: "First, put up billboards on how smoking can kill. Second, help people realize that the tobacco industry don't care if people die. Third, start protesting to discontinue the selling and buying of cigarettes." But my favorite response was: "Have more plays like this."

P.S. The note above was written in 1995. In 1996, in the wake of a court battle and widespread political pressure, the governor reversed himself and restored the antismoking campaign funding. The San Francisco Tobacco Free Project commissioned a rewrite and second tour of *Revenger Rat*. The TFP added an item to our assignment. They wanted us to dramatize the effect of tobacco production on the global environment, which gave us a great setting for the opening scene: the rain forest. What follows is the 1997 script.

Note

1. The Tobacco Free Project of the San Francisco Department of Health, Bureau of Health Promotion and Education, was established as a local lead agency of the California Department of Health

Services as part of the statewide campaign to decrease tobacco consumption by 75 percent by 1999. The campaign was initiated as a result of voter passage of Proposition 99, the 1988 Tobacco Tax Initiative, which raised the tobacco tax by 25 cents. Proposition 99 mandated that 20 percent of the generated revenue would go to fund antitobacco health-education programs. As the local lead agency for San Francisco, the TFP is responsible for the development, coordination, and implementation of the Comprehensive Tobacco Control Plan in San Francisco. The San Francisco Mime Troupe's production of *Revenger Rat Meets the Merchant of Death* was financed by the Tobacco Tax Initiative under contract number 89-97927.

Revenger Rat Meets the

Merchant of Death

Script by Joan Holden, Karim Scarlata,
Nina Siegal, Ellen Callas
Songs by Bruce Barthol and Dred Scott

Poster by Spain Rodriguez.

Time: the present

Characters in order of appearance:

Paulo, a guide

Lydia, a publicist

L.B., president of Beauregard Tobacco

A bandleader

Louis, a would-be entrepreneur

Carlos, a pool shark

Roya, a would-be student

Youngstown, a bartender

Dewey, a bicycle messenger

Neville, an artist

High school students: Carina, Jun, Herb,
David, Snappy, Alexandra, Marissa

The vice principal

A scientist

Revenger Rat

The Woman Warrior

ACT ONE

Scene 1: A jungle in Brazil. GUIDE, LYDIA, L.B.

LYDIA: [*Off stage.*] Hey you, wait! Yucky! Ooh! Help, I'm stuck! This mud's so slimy! [*LYDIA enters followed by GUIDE, Paulo.*] Like rubber cement! I told you I have a sore foot. [*A cloudburst, followed by rain.*] And soaked to the skin! [*Slapping mosquitoes.*] Ow! Ow! Ow! Mister, I am not having fun. Get away! Look at these bumps! I paid $5000 for a "week in Paradise" and I end up in hell? I'm supposed to hear monkeys chattering, see jaguars and macaws and tree frogs and three hundred different kinds of butter-flies—there's nothing here but mud and mosquitoes!

GUIDE: Maybe animals hear you coming.

LYDIA: Oh.

GUIDE: Maybe they hide.

LYDIA: Really, you think?

GUIDE: Maybe come out if you sit quiet. [*He starts to light up a cigarette.*]

LYDIA: Hey, no, you're not gonna smoke that?

GUIDE: You want?

LYDIA: Yes—no—get rid of that, hide it, whadaya think I came here for? To purify my lungs. I crushed out my last cigarette on the curb at Kennedy Airport. Two days and eleven hours nicotine-free; don't let me see that.

GUIDE: OK, lady. Just quiet.

LYDIA: I'll try. Gee, the air smells so green. [*Jungle noises.*]

GUIDE: See. Army ants.

LYDIA: In single file, carrying leaves, like umbrellas! Hey, listen—birds! A jun-gle symphony! Look, hanging upside down just like in photo books—a tree sloth! With a baby! Hi, sweetheart! [*Monkey noises.*] Monkeys playing tag! This is the forest primeval. This place could give a person back her love for life. This is why I came: to feel what Eve felt, before she noticed Adam. As if time were new, as if cities had never been built, like there'd never been a deadline, or a market share.

L.B.: [*Off in the distance.*] Lydia. [*Closer.*] Lydia! [*Enters.*]

LYDIA: Or a son of a—

L.B.: Lydia, I found you!

LYDIA: Christ—Two thousand miles up the Amazon! L.B., what the hell are you doing here?

L.B.: Overflying the area, looking at property. I needed to wash, so I landed at the lodge, and there was your name, in the register. Finding you, here—it's a sign, Lydia. We were meant to be a team!

LYDIA: I believed that once.

L.B.: Lydia, I need you, I need your street smarts, your basic instincts. We could build an empire together.

LYDIA: Get lost, L.B. Being here, all of a sudden I know what's important. I don't even think I'll do advertising anymore, and I sure as hell won't advertise tobacco. I quit smoking.

L.B.: I never started. That's a personal choice: we don't have to let it intrude on business. You're not the only one who's reached a watershed, Lydia. I'm forty five years old. All my life I've been second fiddle, bottom banana; even my name—Lester B. Beauregard III? I want something uniquely mine, something to live for. I want Beauregard Tobacco on top! I want Dukes to be number 1, not number 6.

LYDIA: When I went to work for you it was number 36. How many times did I tell you: dump the English aristocrat logo—it's death with the new demographics. Target new markets, bring out brands to match: "Girlfriend, when you need a sister in a smoke." "Malos, asi es bueno!" "Jade, a dynasty of good taste!" Underwrite sports events, neighborhood festivals, set up websites for rock 'n' roll bands.

L.B.: WWW.Dukes.com!

LYDIA: Normally that'd cost you, but I'm on vacation. Paulo, how far to that waterfall?

GUIDE: Not far. I show you.

LYDIA: We're outta here.

L.B.: Maybe it's true what they're saying about you in the business.

LYDIA: Wait, Paulo.

GUIDE: I stay.

L.B.: Sooner or later, it happens to everyone.

LYDIA: What happens? What are they saying?

L.B.: Well, that you've gone stale. Frankly, that you stink of yesterday.

LYDIA: [To GUIDE.] Could I have that cigarette? [Lights up.]

L.B.: You ought to watch that.

LYDIA: Yesterday? Why? Because my campaigns aren't one-week wonders? Because my concepts have staying power? Who started a run for the border? Who united the colors of Benneton?

L.B.: In 1991, or was that '90? I want to reach the youth market.

LYDIA: Youth market? Dukes? Don't make me laugh.

L.B.: Adult smokers die—four thousand every day. Or even worse, quit. Damn tobacco-free propaganda's hitting us where it hurts. The only growth market left is twelve- to seventeen-year-old kids.

LYDIA: You're sick, L.B., sick. What kind of a no-conscience, perverted, sociopath—

L.B.: Your kind. Children: the last virgin market.

LYDIA: *Really* sick. Sell cancer to children?

L.B.: A challenge as big as your talent! I need a song or a slogan—

LYDIA: Words? Dead on arrival. Kids don't buy words. You need an image.

L.B.: Yeah? Tell me more.

LYDIA: You need a character. One that can clobber Joe Camel. Joe's cool, but the weak spot is, also cold—he's remote.

L.B.: I never liked him.

LYDIA: Our character should be someone that lets kids inside. Comic, irreverent.

L.B: Absolutely.

LYDIA: Yet still with heart. Beavis and Butthead with a touch of Barney.

L.B.: Yes!

BOTH: [*Sing.*] "I love you, you love me."

L.B.: Sounds great, but who could come up with it?

LYDIA: Gimme a week. Lydia Gutsharp's last, greatest campaign. After that I'll devote myself to saving the rainforest. Paulo, run back to the lodge: tell 'em pack my bags, warm up the helicopter. [*Stops him.*] Could I get another smoke?

GUIDE: You stop quitting?

LYDIA: Feeds the flame. [*Guide exits. To L.B.*] You go too. I want to say goodbye to the garden of Eden—without the snake. "Looking at property?" Kinda far away for a vacation home.

L.B.: More of a long-term investment. [*Exiting.*] Baby, you're the best!

LYDIA: You bet I am. "Stale," huh? Pinstripe little punks who think you're God's gift to advertising, Ivy League airheads working your way up

Madison Avenue, eat my dust. Okay, new inspiration. Head for the heartland. No, why waste time? Go straight to the hard urban core, the border zone between barrio and bohemia, where youth revolutions begin. [*Monkey noises.*]

Scene 2: A dive bar in San Francisco. Three MUSICIANS, LOUIS, CARLOS, ROYA, YOUNGSTOWN, DEWEY, NEVILLE, LYDIA.

YOUNGSTOWN tending bar, CARLOS and LOUIS shooting pool. MUSICIANS finish transition number. Only YOUNGSTOWN applauds.

BANDLEADER: They call me Rasputin and my band, Age of Disease. This next song is a dedication to my homey, Youngstown, the original nowhere man. He's been bar jockey in this dump since it was the Beat Gong, the Orgasmic Mushroom, and the Leather Rod. If he looks and acts nuts, through and torn up, it's because he *is,* so tip well and he won't poison you by mistake. This is called "Succotash."

Nobody no one
Melanoma from the sun
Sex without your head and then you're done
No hope and dope can't soap away the
Tears I'm cryin' now I'm only tryin' to
Keep my brain from fryin'.
Succotash my life is a disaster. [*Repeat three times.*]

Race into space
Overpopulation in your face
How they get their grit on
We're livin' on a time bomb
The world keeps turnin', Armageddon's gettin' closer
Oppressed get toasted while oppressor gets the toaster.
Succotash my life is a disaster. [*Repeat.*]

YOUNGSTOWN: [*To audience.*] Don't encourage him, he'll just play another song!

ROYA: Absolut on the rocks, baby. Actually, make it straight. It's been one of those days. [*Searches her giant bag for a cigarette.*]

CARLOS: [*To LOUIS.*] Brother, you can't even get the basics straight. It's solid, stripe, solid. [*Sets up balls.*]

ROYA: Bummer. My last cigarette. [*Displays it; it's broken.*]

LOUIS: Yo, that's why I'm here, beautiful baby. I believe I can be of some assistance in this little predicament of yours.

ROYA: Not a chance, Louis. It started with burnt toast. Then I went to State to register and they said I couldn't cuz I missed too many classes last semester. How the hell'm I s'posed to make it to those Amish-houred eight-o'clock classes if I'm shakin' tail until four? Can't afford school without working, can't get a day job cuz I'm in school, can't get to class cuz I work nights!

CARLOS: It's all about odds, mami. Gotta know the odds and work through them. [*He breaks.*]

LOUIS: What you need, I got: free packs of Strikers! [*Unloads a bag of cigarette packs.*]

ROYA: Look at you, fool. Where'd you get all those?

LOUIS: My new entrepreneurial venture. All I gotta do is pass out these ciggies and get my good buddies to fill out these quizzies about their hobbies. This gig is perfect for me: all I gotta do is see my friends, give them presents. It's almost like social work, man. If I get in right with this company, I can move straight to the top coordinating focus groups.

YOUNGSTOWN: Hope you make it, Louis, cuz come January, you couldn't be pushing those in here. That new law. Remember last year, all of a sudden you couldn't smoke in a restaurant? Next year you won't even be able to smoke in a bar. Here. [*LOUIS hands him a pack and a questionnaire.*]

ROYA: I hate California. At least in Chicago they let you pollute yourself any way you want. I've been smoking since I was fifteen! It's the longest relationship I've been able to maintain. Gimme your stupid questionnaire—and an extra pack. "Are you a (1) high school graduate (2) college graduate (3) graduate student?"

YOUNGSTOWN: [*Writing.*] None . . . of . . . the . . . above.

ROYA: I can't fill this out: they don't have a box for "college reject."

CARLOS scores a triumph at the pool table.

LOUIS: Check him *out!* Check this dude out! He cleared the table on one run. I cremated! How about I pay you in Luckies?

CARLOS: I'll take the money.

DEWEY enters.

YOUNGSTOWN: Hey!

ALL: Dewey!

DEWEY: Yo, peoples. Hey. Gimme an O.J., Youngstown, had a delivery at Maritime Plaza and the po-pos started to sweat me so I was ghost. Seen Neville? [*They haven't.*]

ROYA: I've been meaning to ask you, Dewey, you got dibs on him, or is he—

DEWEY: No, man. Neville's like my brother. We were the only two misfits in the projects. If I didn't get my cousins to back him up he could've got got. And he showed me there's more to life than drugs and gettin' over on people. For real, he didn't come in yet?

YOUNGSTOWN: Neville might not ever come in. I told him nothing more on his tab.

DEWEY: Yeah, well, after today, Neville won't be needing no stinking tab. And maybe we won't even be up in this hole in the wall—cuz my homeboy's about to get paid.

LOUIS: Straight shootin'—Neville took a temp job?

DEWEY: Not *even* close. My man got a publisher!

CARLOS: *Coño!*

DEWEY: Subatomic Comix.

YOUNGSTOWN: That is groovy. I mean, that is cool. I mean, that is, that's, hey.

ROYA: A publisher for *Revenger Rat?*

DEWEY: He was always thinkin' it would never happen. But I'm always, "Have faith, homes, have faith!" Now this dude Slumburger at Subatomic, he saw Neville's genius, man. At two o'clock today they signed the contract.

NEVILLE enters.

ROYA: He's here!

DEWEY: My man.

YOUNGSTOWN: Revenger lives!

NEVILLE heads straight for the bar.

LOUIS: Revenger's gonna be bigger than *Spawn!*

ALL: Yeah!

CARLOS: Bigger than los X-men.

ALL: Yeah!

LOUIS: Bigger than *Gargoyles.* I can see we're gonna need some T-shirts and stickers, baby. I can get this sweet deal down at the swap meet. We gotta put this on the Web. Beautiful, baby: I see green!

NEVILLE: Stoli straight—put it on my tab.

YOUNGSTOWN: [*Takes this as a joke.*] On the house, ol' buddy. [*Pours.*] When's the first issue come out? I wanna autograph copy.

ROYA: Neville, you are the example I need in my life right now, to hold onto my dream. I'mna get that Ph.D.! This calls for a cigarette.

NEVILLE: Save it.

DEWEY: Whassup, homes? [*NEVILLE shakes his head.*] They try to gaffle you? Try to make you sign a chump contract?

NEVILLE: They weren't there.

DEWEY: You got to the office and they weren't even there?

NEVILLE: Office wasn't there. The building burned down last night. [*Gasps and groans greet this news.*]

YOUNGSTOWN: Now that, really, I mean, wow, that sucks.

NEVILLE: Slumburger either burned, or he booked—cops can't find him. Video store owner next door? Lost half his stock. He thinks it was an arson-for-insurance fire.

YOUNGSTOWN: [*Pours NEVILLE another one.*] On the house.

DEWEY: That's foul.

CARLOS: *La Chupacabra, esto!*

ROYA: I need a cigarette.

DEWEY: Yeah, but Neville, blood, this ain't nothin' about you, though. So what, you almost had a contract. You're still an artist, you still got your art!

NEVILLE: Uh-uh. *He* had it. [*Only DEWEY understands.*]

DEWEY: You give that sleazebag your originals? Four years of drawings?

NEVILLE: I didn't have a hundred dollars to make copies. I guess it's just my kharma, right? It's all good. Hey, ain't nothing major been lost—it's just my trip, just what keeps me sane, that's all, just the only reason for my existence! You try to educate and entertain. Try to enrich fantasy with a few facts, try to project some positive direction to the lost youth of postprosperity America—might as well be just blowing smoke.

DEWEY: Neville—

NEVILLE: In that smoldering rubble, I read my sentence: "Temp for life!"

DEWEY: It don't have to be like that!

NEVILLE: Right, I could make something out of myself. I could study mortuary science like my mama wants! [*Opens his drawing pad.*] But first, I'm gonna dead Revenger.

DEWEY: Kick back, Neville! [*To OTHERS.*] He's not himself.

CARLOS: Should consult to the orishas, 'mano.

NEVILLE: [*Brandishing his pencil.*] I'm gonna have to put him out of his misery.

DEWEY: There's other publishers!

LYDIA [*Enters in disguise. Aside.*] I've scoured slums from coast to coast
and still come up empty. But this neighborhood—begins to smell right: a
pungent blend of poverty, raw young energy, and drugged-out despair.
Mm—they look alienated! Bartender, can I get a place to sit?
[*YOUNGSTOWN obliges.*]

NEVILLE: Lemme see. How should His Rodenthood leave the planet?

ROYA: On opium.

YOUNGSTOWN: No, on a Harley. Draw him flying off a cliff, man, goin'
ninety down Highway 1.

LOUIS: No, sippin' on a martini in a velvet room fulla beautiful buck-naked
babies bathing him!

ROYA: Jesus Christ.

LOUIS: Draw him doin' the last do!

DEWEY: Don't draw, it's murder!

NEVILLE: Does a Harley have dual pipes?

YOUNGSTOWN: [*Indicating on the drawing.*] Like this.

LYDIA: May I see? [*NEVILLE complies.*] Looks like curtains for a very cool character.

ROYA: An icon for the post-Reagan generation. Revenger had what we've
given up searching for: a way to put awareness into action.

LYDIA: Only one thing missing from this picture—why don't you draw him
smoking a last cigarette?

NEVILLE: Nah! Revenger only smokes weed.

ROYA: Right now, believe me, he needs a cigarette.

CARLOS: Or a cohiba cigar.

ROYA: No! A cigarette!

YOUNGSTOWN: No—Bogart-style.

NEVILLE shrugs and obeys.

LOUIS: Nihilistic and cool as hell, baby.

DEWEY: He don't look right with that! Come on, Neville, you need some grub:
let's hit the falafel spot. You'll feel better.

LYDIA: Just a moment, Miss.

DEWEY: *Miss?*

LYDIA: I see your friend's a very talented artist. I'd like him to tell me about this rat. [*Others exchange significant glances and fade to background.*]

NEVILLE: He's a metarodent.

LYDIA: I see, a super rat. What's his special power?

NEVILLE: He eats misleaders.

LYDIA: Excuse me?

NEVILLE: Lying politicians, corporation heads, media hypers, like that. He gets huge, and he eats them.

NEVILLE and CHORUS sing "Rat Rap."

NEVILLE:	Rodney Rat was born in a storm drain in the Bayview
	The year a toxic-waste dump started to spew
CHORUS:	Rodney
NEVILLE:	First there was an earthquake, and then there was a flood
	So little Rodney Rat got born in radiated mud.
CHORUS:	Rodney
NEVILLE:	Rodney was normal for a rat his age
	But he'd turn into a monster when he flew into a rage.
CHORUS:	He's a mutant rodent, a real rad rat
	Little Rodney really got zapped! [*Repeat*]
NEVILLE:	Rodney loved learning, he thought it was cool
	So his mama moved the family to the walls of a school
	Peepin' from his rathole, he studied every day
	He only took a year to pass the first five grades.
	Readin' was easy, writin' was a breeze,
	He learned English, and Spanish, and Cantonese.
	One day he hopped a ride to the local library
	And those books turned that rat into a revolutionary!
CHORUS:	He's a megarodent, he's a real bad rat
	Rodney went through school in nothing flat.
NEVILLE:	The principal was talkin' on Columbus Day
	Rodney was trippin' when he heard her say
	"America was discovered in 1492!"
	But there was already people here: he knew it wasn't true.
	Some say there was a thunderbolt, a blinding flash of light
	And a giant rat came through the wall, standin' upright

People were screaming in their fear and their fright
And Rodney ate the principal in one big bite!

CHORUS: He's a megarodent, a real rad rat:
Big Rodney, eatin' up the fat cats.

NEVILLE: That liar was gone when Rodney was done
And that is the end of Book Number 1.

LYDIA: Then what?

NEVILLE: Then it goes on like that. Went.

DEWEY: See, at first Rodney doesn't know he's Revenger. Rodney goes around lookin' for knowledge and truth, but wherever he goes, Revenger ends up having to eat somebody.

LOIS: Then comes to, feeling . . . [*YOUNGSTOWN belches.*]

ALL: "Must be something I ate."

LYDIA: [*Aside.*] Across-the-spectrum appeal! An inner-city animal with an attitude . . . and antiauthoritarian action! [*To NEVILLE.*] Tell you what: Revenger's too good to die. I'd like to save his life. Could we talk one on one?

DEWEY: I'm his manager. [*LYDIA hands her a card, she passes it to NEVILLE.*]

NEVILLE: [*Reads.*] "Lydia Gutsharp, senior partner, Gutsharp, Mudworthy, and Gelding—*Advertising*"? Who you think you talking to, Bob Dylan? "The times they are a-changin"—to Nike?

DEWEY: Now don't go off—

NEVILLE: Aretha Franklin? "R-E-S-P-E-C-T, Tell you what it means to me"—buy life insurance?

LYDIA: Was I talking television? This character lives on the page. Strictly print.

NEVILLE: Revenger does *no* kind of advertising. That's the difference between the sixties' generation and ours, lady—they cashed in. We may starve but we keep it real, we do *our* stories.

DEWEY: It don't hurt to listen.

NEVILLE: I'll kill Revenger before I'll sell him out!

LYDIA: Did I offer to buy him? I want to publish your book. I want to distribute it, quarterly, to comics stores all over the country. I see an initial press run of, say, 100,000 copies.

DEWEY: [*To NEVILLE.*] Slumburger was only gonna do 1,500!

LYDIA: You'll get the standard royalty, 10 percent of the cover price, but I can offer an advance of, say, $50,000.

DEWEY: Blood, don't blow this.

NEVILLE: What's the catch?

LYDIA: I will promise you, in the contract, complete artistic freedom to tell the stories you want to tell exactly as you want to tell them, in the pictures you want to draw. Of course, we've gotta find a sucker to pay for it. Now, I've got a client who, frankly, is not too bright; if you can just work his product into your background some way, he'd think that was advertising!

DEWEY: So he'd write the check! Check it out!

NEVILLE: What are we selling here? Rainforest beef? Ozone-eating cars? Animal-tested deodorant?

LYDIA: All you'd have to do is what you did in that sketch. [*Indicates the new drawing.*] Show Revenger always smoking a cigarette.

DEWEY: Oh, hey, I dunno.

LYDIA: And, once in every book, let us know his brand: Dukes.

DEWEY: Neville, you don't wanna do this—

NEVILLE: Hey, do kids turn into superheroes because they read comic books?

DEWEY: Course not, but—

NEVILLE: So why would they turn into smokers? Rappers sign with major labels so they can get airtime, right? Skaters skate for board companies so they can get into tournaments.

DEWEY: Right, and you're always clownin' 'em for it.

NEVILLE: But now I understand! It's just a means to an end, Dewey. This would mean I get my message out! And what I put out's a whole lot more powerful than any little picture of a smoke. By the time Mr. Big Tobacco sees it's not working, kids all over the country will be down with Revenger Rat, hooked on his adventures, wanting more of his wisdom—I'll be ready to go independent! [*To LYDIA.*] I need it in black and white: complete artistic freedom.

LYDIA: Except for the cigarette. [*Music. They shake hands.*] Drinks on me. [*Stumbles.*] Excuse me—I don't know what's wrong with this foot. [*More music.*]

Sign crosses: MONTHS PASS

ACT TWO

Scene 1: Outside a high school. CARINA, JUN, HERB, DAVID, SNAPPY, ALEXANDRA, MARISSA, VICE PRINCIPAL, LYDIA.

CARINA: [*Enters and sings.*]

> Tell me
> Will I be the one?
> Tell me
> My heart's on the run
> Tell me
> Baby, what's your trip?
> I gotta know right now
> What's goin' down
> Are we gonna get together?
> Will you love me forever?

JUN: [*Enters.*] Carina, what're you doing, girl? [*Grabs the pack.*] These cancer sticks will kill you.

CARINA: Why you haten on me, Jun? Anyways, where are your Newports at? Yo jankiness.

JUN: [*Lights one from her pack.*] Naw, that ain't me anymore, if it ain't Dukes, it ain't me. [*She grabs for the pack, but he blocks her.*] Girls shouldn't smoke, it makes you unattractive—you're puttin' salt in yer own game. You wouldn't find these on the lips of that little hottie friend of yours, Marissa.

CARINA: Why you all of a sudden jocking my girl? And now you're really trippin', you're not my daddy and you can't tell me what to do. [*Grabs for the pack.*] Give me my pack, you buster.

JUN: [*Playing keep-away.*] Thought you knew, once she sees me in this Lex I rented, it's going to be on.

CARINA: Fool, you swear anybody is trippin' off that tiny grip you got, but she wouldn't pay attention to your nickel-and-dime ass if you really had shit on lock.

JUN: You better recognize, girl, how could she resist the shot calling of this big baller. She could be having thangs. I seen her peeping out my ride earlier today, so I know it is all good.

CARINA: She was probably wondering why you're so sheisty, with your trifling ass rental.

HERB: [*Enters in Revenger Rat T-shirt, having a nicotine fit.*] Hey Jun, dude, can I bum one? I'm gonna ask this girl to the prom but I don't know if it's cool for me and—I need a smoke. [*Jun starts to pull out a sack from his pocket.*] No, bro'—I mean Dukes, please.

JUN: Oh, f'sho, you're my favorite custie. Oo, that Revenger Rat T-shirt is off the hook! Look, we're both smoking Dukes, like a couple of pimps.

CARINA: [*Aside.*] Couple o' simps.

HERB: Killer, but this issue is the bomb. [*Acts out what follows.*] Remember last book, Rodney finds out he's Revenger cuz a *Chronicle* photographer caught him chewing on the mayor? So now Rodney's trying t' chill but next door this kid Peewee can't read, gets in the gangs: gats a child in the dome by mistake. The governor shows up and— [*Acts out Rodney's transformation and meal. Meanwhile, DAVID and SNAPPY enter.*]

JUN: Herb, you're a fool.

DAVID: He is a straight foolio. See, the capitaliscious nature of the man gots Herb blind to the truth. The governor is saying, "The way to stop crime is to cut back on schools, build bigger prisons." Revenger Rat is no average Mickey Mouse *ratón.* He's like Che, crushing the lying oppressors.

HERB: Hey relax, David, it's just a comic book.

DAVID: It's Daa-veed, my gavachoistical friend. And I am relaxed, I'm trying to let you know what's really going on and you're just stuck on some kind of opiumation of the masses.

SNAPPY: Kick back, home skillet, I need to chop it up with you.

HERB: Yeah chill, "homeboy."

DAVID: Don't *patrónize* me, *ese.*

SNAPPY: Hey, don't lose your cool over Herb, I gotta tell you something.

DAVID: *Tienes un* Duke?

SNAPPY: [*Shakes his head, DAVID remembers SNAPPY doesn't smoke.*] Guess who got a prom date.

JUN: A'right, Snappy, I thought I saw you pushin' up on that freak Pilar, she's poppin' like corn.

DAVID: *Orale,* you asked that Mayan queen Leticia, right? You asked that Morenita, *como se llama?*

SNAPPY: No, none of them. You know that girl that sits in front of me in first period?

JUN: Oh, Snap, that blonde mama.

HERB: She's killer, a real beauty!

DAVID: What? Let me conversatiate with my *carnal* for a minute. *Que onda?* Have you been sniffin' chemo? You're gonna take some *guera* to the prom? It's not true. Are you selling out *La Causa* for this anglomonious Saxonite pilgrim? We're the indigenous peoples of Aztlan, *ese,* you're falling prey to the European traps of white flesh.

SNAPPY: Aw, see, you're the one not recognizing—she's not white, she's Russian.

DAVID: Fool, where do you think the Caucasian Mountains are? I'd understand more if you kept it underground, for a late night booty call, but—

SNAPPY: I didn't plan on asking her. We were just talking, and she's got game, she got this accent. You're my homey, you're supposed to have my back. [*ALEXANDRA enters.*] It's her!

DAVID: *Malinchiste,* I'll talk to you later.

ALEX: Hi Snappy.

SNAPPY: Uh, hi Alexandra.

ALEXANDRA: I am happy for prom.

SNAPPY: Should be off the hook.

ALEXANDRA: Um—

SNAPPY: Uh. [*ALEXANDRA takes out pack of cigarettes, lighter.*] Here, let me hook you up. [*Lights her cigarette.*] So, you smoke Dukes?

ALEXANDRA: Yes, everybody say they are the coolest. [*Offers him pack.*] You smoke?

SNAPPY: No, well, yeah, sometimes.

ALEXANDRA: Let me hook. [*Lights his cigarette.*]

SNAPPY: [*Puffing tentatively.*] You know, it's kinda tight just parleying and just puffing on a cigarette.

ALEXANDRA: So relaxing. [*Both take deep drags.*]

SNAPPY: [*Coughs.*] Let's get our stroll on. [*Exeunt SNAPPY and ALEXANDRA.*]

JUN: [*Calls off.*] Russian women desire romance!

Enter MARISSA.

JUN/HERB/DAVID/CARINA: Hi, Marissa!

[*In chorus.*] Tell me, tell me, tell me

Got to chill so I don't choke

All I wanna do is have a smoke.

Help me, magic cigarette,

To make a play.

JUN: I'm your dream date, dime piece

Rolling in style

It's a Cinderella story for you, girl-child.

It's a first-class trip

Just say that you wanna

Versace, Armani, or Dolce Gabana.

MARISSA: You need to come out of the closet with your dresses, man, with yer ol' Market Street fake Versaucy, Arphony, and Sike.

JUN: Why are you throwing shade at me? I could be your ticket out of the ghetto, baby.

MARISSA: A ticket to where? Jail? It's not going to happen.

J/H/D/C: [*Repeat chorus.*]

HERB: I feel you, David: it's the information

You say I'm a fool: watch my transformation.

Don't need no limos, candies, or flowers

I got chick-gettin' Rodney Rat super-powers.

Uh, Marissa, uh— [*Does a nervous dance.*] Dude, well, uh—want the new Revenger?

MARISSA: Sure. [*Takes it.*]

HERB: Uh, want a smoke?

MARISSA: I'll have to pass.

HERB: Go with me to the prom, dude. Please.

MARISSA: Herbert, I will . . . have to pass!

J/H/D/C: [*Repeat chorus*]

DAVID: Check it out

I ain't wired, ain't even upset.

I look cool with my cigarette.

Watch and learn, I'll school you all

It's like a How to Get a Prom Date study hall.

This little dance they speak of is nothing more than capitaliscious promdeganda. We as people of color must look beyond the Anglo man's institutions and come together in unity.

MARISSA: Are you asking me to the prom?

DAVID: I am asking you to unite with me in defiance of the prom—at the prom.

MARISSA: I'll have to pass.

CARINA: So, you gonna tell us who you *are* going to the prom with?

D/H/J: Yeah!/Hey?/Who?

MARISSA: [*Takes a deep drag of CARINA's cigarette before answering.*] My girlfriend, Carina.

D/J/H: *Chale!*/ No way!/They're perverts!

HERB: Gimme back my book, you damn thesbian! [*Grabs it.*]

MARISSA: That's lesbian, and what's it to you?

JUN: There's AIDS germs on that! [*HERB drops it and both exit.*]

DAVID: See, this is the white man's work.

CARINA & MARISSA: *What?*

DAVID: The paleface invader brought this perversion to our continent, because he don't want us to procreatiate!

CARINA: Shows how much history *you* know—there's always been gay people!

DAVID: You're dooming generations not to be born! You are cooperating with genocide!

MARISSA: This is us, got it?

VICE PRINCIPAL: [*Enters.*] Okay, break it up! Proceed to home room. Disperse!

DAVID: You dykes are gonna rot in hell!

CARINA: You better step off, you ignorant retard!

VICE PRINCIPAL: No hate speech at this school! [*The three fall silent and drag on their cigarettes. LYDIA enters.*] You are all in violation of the no smoking rule. There go your prom tickets.

M/D/C: Aw, Miss Fabiani!/That's bunk!/You can't do that!

VICE PRINCIPAL: You heard me—disperse! [*Exeunt KIDS, muttering. VICE PRIN-CIPAL picks up comic book.*]

LYDIA: [*Approaches.*] Excuse me, Ma'am: I'm a concerned citizen and I think it's terrible how many young people smoke these days!

VICE PRINCIPAL: Pretty bad. [*Takes out a pack, lights one.*]

LYDIA: Out of curiosity—do they prefer any special brand?

VICE PRINCIPAL: Dukes. [*LYDIA exults.*] They all think they're Revenger Rat. Will you look at this garbage? Can you believe the way kids will copy some stupid image?

LYDIA: What do you smoke?

VICE PRINCIPAL: Virginia Slims.

LYDIA: You've come a long way, baby. [*Exeunt, in different directions.*]

Scene 2: Headquarters of Beauregard Tobacco in New York. L.B., COMPANY SCIENTIST, LYDIA.

SCIENTIST: [*Brandishing a report.*] R & D's done the balance sheet on the Brazil project.

L.B.: Shoot.

SCIENTIST: On one hand, clearing rainforest to plant tobacco will deplete soil, destroy wildlife habitat, pollute rivers with chemicals, and displace indigenous tribes. Curing fires burning around the clock will create a permanent smog belt, accelerating destruction of the ozone layer. Within ten years, soil will be completely exhausted and more forest will have to be cleared.

L.B.: Lotta negatives.

SCIENTIST: On the plus side, you'll save five billion a year. [*Lights a cigarette.*]

L.B.: Very enlightening. [*Grabs the cigarette and puts it out in scientist's hand.*] Never smoke in my office. Good work, Fensterman. [*Exit scientist.*]

LYDIA: [*Enters, using a cane, with one foot bandaged.*] How's it feel, being number one?

L.B.: You saw the headlines!

LYDIA: Must be very strange for you.

L.B.: Like standing on top of Everest—no one else up here! Biggest increase in smoking since the invention of ready-made cigarettes—nearly all in the under-seventeen age group—a quarter of it in the under-twelves—and they're smoking Dukes! Incredible when you think of it—we're selling death, and they're buying! We did it, Lydia!

LYDIA: We? Oh, no, L.B., you did it. I'm stale, I stink of yesterday. [*Lights up and blows smoke in his face. He doesn't protest.*]

L.B.: Lydia, Lydia. I knew you needed a kick in the butt, so I said those nasty things to challenge you. You have fabulous radar. You could sense a microtrend starting on Mars.

LYDIA: Noticed the new Joe Camel ad? Old Joe with big shoes, big teeth, and a baseball cap—trying to look like Revenger Rat?

L.B.: This Rat, now, I'm concerned, I finally *read* one of these things. He eats rich people!

LYDIA: Fantasy revenge, that's what sells the books. Don't worry. The politics? That's just style. The pitch *works*. Do your peace of mind a favor, don't read the stuff.

L.B.: God, you're good. Your raw energy works like a transfusion on my pale blue blood!

LYDIA: Where were you all weekend?

L.B.: Family stuff I had to take care of.

LYDIA: You haven't asked me, "What's with the cane?"

L.B.: What is?

LYDIA: You haven't asked what's wrong with my foot.

L.B.: What's wrong with it?

LYDIA: Tobacco-induced cardiovascular syndrome. Clogged arteries, from smoking! My veins are constricted, blood doesn't flow, if the condition gets anywhere near my heart, I'm dead. For starters, they cut off my toes. If that doesn't work, they'll cut off my foot. Then my leg. Could you cut my check, please? [*She starts off.*]

L.B.: [*Following, under music.*] How many times did I tell you, "Quit smoking!"

Scene 3: NEVILLE's loft, late one night. NEVILLE, DEWEY.

Phone rings.

NEVILLE: [*Enters on phone, carrying brand-new 14" x 17" drawing pad, handful of sharpened pencils.*] Hello, Lydia? I'm sorry, I forgot it's 3 A.M. in New York. But listen, hey, I got a *sick* new idea working for number 5: *Revenger Goes to Washington!* Working his way up the food chain. *Revenger 3*, a third printing? All right! Listen, Lydia, I think it's time to talk about my percentage. New place? It's dope. Yeah, Mama's happy with her new house, but look here, didn't either of us know *Revenger* was gonna be this hot. Okay, right. Yeah, tomorrow. Okay, bye. [*Hangs up, opens the pad, sketches intently.*] Inside a storm drain, looking up—water here, man-hole grate here, Rodney huddled up in this corner here.

DEWEY: [*Enters with takeout food.*] Whassup? You s'posed to be sleeping!

NEVILLE: [*Reaches for a container.*] An idea hit me.

DEWEY: That's breakfast! [*NEVILLE eats and draws.*] You shoulda seen Youngstown. Blown away.

NEVILLE: Good.

DEWEY: He jus' stood there and stared at that Electraglide! Say he wish you'd
come in, though.

NEVILLE: Maybe next week, when I'm a few pages into this.

DEWEY: And, you got a letter from Roya. [*Shows it.*] Says she don't know how
to thank you for paying her tuition. She loves all her classes at Yale.

NEVILLE: Cool, I guess.

DEWEY: Homes, you remember my baby cousin Kelvin?

NEVILLE: One that loves Revenger.

DEWEY: He started smoking.

NEVILLE: Damn.

DEWEY: Dukes.

NEVILLE: Damn!

DEWEY: He's nine.

NEVILLE: Bring him over, I'll talk to him. I'll tell him that's not what Revenger's
about, man. I'll straighten him out.

DEWEY: All his friends smoke Dukes.

NEVILLE: Bring 'em *all* over.

DEWEY: You gonna talk to all the kids in the country? Remember you said,
once Revenger got known, you'd take him independent? I think it's time,
blood. Say hell wit Dukes, start our own company.

NEVILLE: Yeah, well, first lemme get through this series. I got books poppin'
out of my head; I would be dissin' my muses if I interrupted the flow. I
mean, publishing ain't simple, Dewey. There's a lot to it. Copyrights,
lawyers, printing, distribution. I'm just an artist, man.

DEWEY: I'm your manager—I'll take care of the business side.

NEVILLE: Right. That'd be cool if we were just starting out, man, but Revenger's
up there. See, we're dealing on a pretty high level. I dunno if you're
coldass enough for the business world, Dews. It's fulla people like Lydia.

DEWEY: It wasn't me who believed her when she said this wouldn't really be
advertising. Look, homes, I understand the money's good, and you ain't
never had no money. I understand you deserve to get paid.

NEVILLE: You don't understand jack, cuz it ain't even about the money.

DEWEY: You don't need them people. You the man, Neville, you got it going
on. Thoughts other people just start to think about, you already saw the
whole ins and outs of. You lay 'em right out on the page.

NEVILLE: Yeah, well, I would like to be doing that. But you gotta come talk to me when I'm working.

DEWEY: You're always working. You didn't think this thing through. You didn't realize you'd be juking cigarettes.

NEVILLE: Know what's gonna happen in *Revenger 5*? [*Dewey doesn't.*] Rodney stumbles into a secret, CIA-installed storm drain, gets swept all the way to Washington, D.C. Meanwhile, Clinton's sold out to the Right, blaming the bad economy on immigrants. Gets votes, but he knows it's all a lie. He's in the Oval Office agonizing over whether to sign this bill putting troops on the border, when Guess Who comes out of the heater?

DEWEY: Your books are always an education, man.

NEVILLE: You've seen my reviews! Is it my fault some people are so dumb, they pick up on the wrong part of the message? [*Silence.*] Besides, tell the truth, I like Revenger with a cigarette. Looks cool, it's part of the image.

DEWEY: You taught me everything, Neville.

NEVILLE: [*Drawing.*] That's right.

DEWEY: Nigga, you were my idol.

NEVILLE: Back when three people knew about my books.

DEWEY: I was proud you let me run with you.

NEVILLE: [*Drawing.*] I love you too, blood. It's just, I'm getting into this story, I don't wanna let go of the thread. I mean, you're raising some good points, but now's just the wrong time for me to be distracted. So whyn't you go on home, catch some z's, come back around noon with a sandwich for me. I got a feeling I'm gonna be working straight through.

DEWEY: You gotta get your own sandwich. I ain't coming back.

NEVILLE: Huh?

DEWEY: I can't be with what you're doing, homes. I'm gettin' a messenger job again.

NEVILLE: Dewey?

DEWEY: Later for you, homes. I can't hang. [*Exit.*]

Scene 4: The same, immediately following. NEVILLE, REVENGER RAT.

NEVILLE: Dewey! [*Pause.*] She can't understand, she's not an artist. She never experienced the rush of inspiration—she don't know what it's like when an idea's got its hooks in you and you live inside of it, gotta stay inside your vision till it's all on the page. She's got no concept what a high it is, when a million people out there are waiting for what you create! [*Letters furiously. Offstage, we hear coughing, but NEVILLE doesn't notice.*] "Deep in the flood flushed sewers of San Francisco, Rodney Rat hides from the horror of his double life."

REVENGER: [*Enters behind him, leaning on a cane.*] Don't forget the cigarette.

NEVILLE: [*Resignedly.*] Oh yeah. [*Draws, stops. Still not seeing.*] Who?

REVENGER: [*Belches.*] Musta been something I ate.

NEVILLE: You! Whoa. This is incredible. My own creation, standing in front of me.

REVENGER: *Your creation?* Think we're next thing to God now. I'm your alter ego, dude, I was *born* with you! I was always inside of you.

NEVILLE: This is deep.

REVENGER: For some funny reason, right about now, I wanted to look you in the face.

NEVILLE: A cane? I never gave you a cane. [*REVENGER is seized by a coughing fit.*] Hey, you okay?

REVENGER: "Okay"? *Okay?* You ask if I'm okay? You pimped me to the death dealers! You made me chain-smoke!

NEVILLE: What—

REVENGER: You gave me lung cancer!

NEVILLE: Lung cancer?

REVENGER: You know what this disease is? [*Rips open his chest to display his charred lungs.*] Slow death by drowning. Every day the muck in my lungs rises closer to my throat. Every day I get less and less air. One day soon—

NEVILLE: You didn't have to inhale!

REVENGER: [*Lunges for him.*] Clown!

NEVILLE: I didn't know! I never meant to make you sick! Don't eat me!

REVENGER: I'm a dead rat.

NEVILLE: I'll draw you quitting! I'll think of something. Wait, the radiation that made you Revenger gave you an extra super power that makes you immune to tobacco. [*REVENGER scoffs.*] It could work!

REVENGER: Yeah—for me. What about the twenty, forty, fifty thousand children, doomed because they followed my example? Dewey told you, but did you listen? No, all you could hear was the roar of your own fame, all you thought about was what you could create!

NEVILLE: I've perverted my talent! I've disgraced the name of artist! I'll never draw again!

REVENGER: You don't get off that easy. You're gonna draw my death.

NEVILLE: No!

REVENGER: In all its disgusting details.

NEVILLE: I can't!

REVENGER: [*Pointing to the sketch.*] Start right here. Stretch it out over two books. Make it sad, so they'll cry for me, but funny enough to keep 'em reading to the final panel. And most of all, make it so real that no kid who sees *Revenger 6, End of the Story* will ever light another cigarette.
Music. REVENGER disappears. NEVILLE exits.

Sign crosses: MORE MONTHS PASS

Scene 5: Beauregard Tobacco. L.B., LYDIA, WOMAN WARRIOR.

There is a crowd outside yelling. This continues through scene.

L.B.: [*Enters with suitcase, talking on cellular phone, frantic.*] "Take it easy?" That's easy for you to say—there's a mob of delinquents downstairs howling for my blood! Listen! [*Holds phone to catch chanting, then barks into phone.*] What do you mean a limo? They'll tear me apart. Get me a helicopter. [*Punches in another number.*] Hello, Fensterman, I gotta make this quick. Cut the whole tract—
LYDIA enters on crutches, one leg missing, carrying comic books.

LYDIA: Nasty mood down there.

L.B.: Lydia! [*Into phone.*] Hold on. [*To Lydia.*] You here! Christ on a crutch! How'd you get through? [*She shrugs.*] To see you here, when all of New York's turned its back on me—and you just out of the hospital! Words fail me. I always meant to pop in on you, but I was in and out of town, and then this—How's the leg?

LYDIA: The remaining one's fine, thanks.

L.B.: [*Hasn't noticed till now.*] Jesus! Uh, gee, that's tough. I, well, otherwise you look terrific. Nice shoe.

LYDIA: You're toxic, L.B. You kill everything you touch.

L.B.: Excuse me. [*Into phone.*] I want that chopper on the roof!

LYDIA: Smart. Know what those kids are yelling? "Crush Dukes!" Kids don't like you L.B. Seen this? [*Displays comic.*]

L.B.: *Revenger Rat?* You told me not to read it.

LYDIA: The decline and death of Rodney, from lung cancer. [*Flipping pages.*] The doomed rodent decides to spend his last months in research—on the history of Beauregard Tobacco. Look: your glorious beginning in World War I. L..B. the First has the brilliant idea of putting cigarettes in our boys' rations, so a whole generation comes home addicted to nicotine!

L.B: It's not addictive, it's not a drug.

LYDIA: See? Rodney can barely get out of bed. But Revenger's got to carry out one final mission—he comes here, to this office, and devours you! So, L.B., I look "terrific"? [*He shrugs.*] I'm a dead woman. But I am going to die satisfied. You're number 35 now, and falling! Kids are swearing off tobacco!

L.B.: But they're such a small market. American teenagers—against the entire female population of Asia?

LYDIA: Excuse me?

L.B.: Asia, where all the men smoke—but so far, only the men. Now, Asian women—billions of them—are breaking loose, speaking out, moving up, demanding all the freedoms men have—and Beauregard Tobacco will be right there for them. Suey Lin, could you come in, please?
[*Enter a gorgeous Asian woman in clothes every girl would die for.*]

L.B.: Meet the Woman Warrior: a character drawn from tradition, future role model for little girls all over Asia. [*SUEY LIN lights a cigarette.*] And the name of our new export brand. Suey Lin lives in Hong Kong—she's a marketing consultant as well as a model. She's created Woman Warrior fashions, Woman Warrior cosmetics lines—launched, of course, with giant cigarette giveaways. Woman Warrior will sponsor the Chinese women's skating team, the Korean women's cross-country team, and the first beauty pageant in Vietnam.

LYDIA: Don't do this—it's murder and environmental disaster—it's eco-geno-femicide! [*SUEY LIN shrugs. LYDIA turns on L.B. and, snarling, swings at him with her crutch.*]

L.B.: [*Snatches it, throws it.*] Fetch! [*Back on the phone.*] Hello, Fensterman, are you still there? Yes, clear cut the whole tract, plow it with nitrates, and plant it: all 49,000 acres.

LYDIA: No!

L.B.: No, don't sell the logs downriver, keep 'em for the curing barns—to cure one single pound of tobacco, you gotta burn twenty-five pounds of wood. I'll call you from Beijing.

LYDIA: My paradise—so that's your "long-term investment"?

L.B.: Yeah, and I'm gonna make it pay.

SUEY LIN: Mr. Beauregard? The helicopter is waiting on the roof.

L.B.: Sorry, Lydia—we gotta fly. Be good to yourself.

LYDIA: You smug, smirking strangler!

L.B.: Gee, I guess I won't be seeing you.

LYDIA: You serial killer!

L.B.: [Pushes her over.] Too bad you couldn't kick the habit. [Exit with WOMAN WARRIOR.]

LYDIA: [Lights a cigarette.] Forgive me. [Dies.]

THE END

Adolescence and Activism:

Theatre for Survival

Lucy Winner

Theatre has been recognized as a transformative force for centuries, from rituals and celebrations marking peaceful transitions within people's personal and communal lives, to performances of political resistance and calls for radical change. Recent Western history suggests that activist theatre, theatre that makes an overt attempt to create social or political change, flourishes in times of social upheaval. For example, the Federal Theatre Project during the Great Depression employed thousands of theatre artists working for social renewal all across the United States. Brecht's theatrical response to Nazi Germany urged the spectator to question the status quo. Many political theatre companies sprang up in the United States as integral parts of the civil rights and antiwar movements of the 1960s and 1970s. Each of these theatrical expressions developed during times of turmoil and civil unrest, when there was a sense of shifting identities and a great feeling of urgency.[1]

Adolescence, too, can be thought of as a time of transition, developmental rather than historical. Adolescents are between childhood and adulthood, swept in the tide of hormonal surges and vast bodily changes, searching for new identities. The urgency of this search expresses itself in extreme clothing styles, language, and music.

If we follow the historical pattern of socially responsive theatre flourishing in times of upheaval, we can see why adolescence is such fertile terrain for theatrical intervention. The instability created in times of developmental turmoil, as in times of social and political instability, creates both a need and a way in. People in a rapidly changing culture need to develop new identities. Like a society in transition, adolescence allows for experimentation and play; boundaries that are fluid allow new ideas to penetrate and take hold. A contemporary form of activist theatre responds to this adolescent culture in upheaval.

This study examines the work of Teatro Vida and the SPARK Peer Players, two of the many theatre groups that use "inter-activist" (interactive activist) performance to intervene in the chaos of New York City adolescence.[2] These companies address the interlocking issues that threaten the health and survival of inner-city adolescent communities: HIV/AIDS, drug abuse, racism, guns, and violence. Their intention is to reduce risk by providing information in a safe, creative, structured environment, and to create a feeling of community in which the audience can learn through experience, identification, and modeling. I have explored these companies through the Theatre for Adolescent Survival Project, which I founded in 1994. The project is dedicated to research, documentation and education in the field of theatre in education and public health for the adolescent.[3]

Audience at Risk

The liminal state of adolescence is a period of both vulnerability and power, during which the adolescent is both at risk and reachable. As overwhelming as the problems facing any adolescent may be, the external issues facing inner-city populations compound these to create a situation of life and death. For these teenagers, the outside world reflects and intensifies the chaos of developmental turmoil.

During adolescence a person becomes most vividly sexual and experimental—afraid of and enticed by emerging sexual feelings—and today an unprotected sexual encounter can kill. Despite a clearly developing knowledge of safer sex, a recent Centers for Disease Control and Prevention report found that often inner-city adolescent practice does not follow information. One reason is the complex relationship between the feelings of desperation and loss associated with violence and suicide, and the need to fill the vacuum with high-risk sexual behavior.

Barbara Staggers, a physician in a North Oakland, California, clinic, suggests, "Even though, in many ways, they don't want to get pregnant, they do it to replace some of the people they've lost" (quoted in Foster 1994). A young woman described by Douglas Foster as "striking and articulate" who "can rattle off safe-sex guidelines so expertly she could work for the CDC" is in for a pregnancy test and treatment for herpes. She "admits to having a hard time keeping a clear head" ever since the recent murder of her twenty-five-year-old cousin, a murder apparently set up by neighborhood people, including some of his friends. She describes her sense of betrayal, saying, "You learn not to trust anybody." Yet trust and connection are just what many young people crave. "Many of them don't think they have any control," says Staggers. "The boys tell [the girls] they don't like the feel of a condom. The boys say, 'Trust me,' and the girls desperately want to trust somebody" (Foster 1994:52).

Many of the things that define adolescents as susceptible to risk also make them susceptible to intervention. Boundaries and identities are fluid. Inter-activist theatre, which plays with these same boundaries and identities, can be a safe and powerful way to practice the skills necessary for survival. Theatre can provide a structure within which adolescents can experiment. The aim is to make it possible for them to take risks without real life consequences. The two theatre projects I have observed try to accomplish this by encouraging their adolescent audiences to consider, listen, discuss, model, and mirror.

Two Models of Inter-activist Theatre

Both the SPARK Peer Players and Teatro Vida weave the fabric of their performance out of the threads of urban adolescent culture, but they do so in significantly contrasting ways. The SPARK Peer Players, as the name suggests, are adolescents themselves. Trained as peer educators and actors, they are the "creative arm" of the New York City Board of Education's SPARK Program, which pioneered school-based drug-intervention and prevention programs in 1971. Their material is developed in workshops in which the company members, guided by adult staff, explore their lived experiences. The script and choreography is then loosely set, providing structure and predictability that protects the young actors from getting lost while working with material that is very close. SPARK generally performs in large urban high schools. The material elements of SPARK's production—the school setting with its metal detectors, echoing halls, and hard chairs— reflect the urban adolescent life. The onstage atmosphere evokes the cacophony of the audience, thick with sex, undulating, heavy beats, blasting miked sound, rap music, hip-hop dancing. The audience members invest in the play first with their bodies, dancing on their knees as they hang over the backs of plastic chairs, then begin to call out to the characters: "Uh-uh," "Smack her!" "You're dead, man."

Teatro Vida's actors are adult professionals who perform improvisationally. In a performance space defined by a circle of chairs, the air is saturated with words called out in a brainstorming session with the audience: *homosexual, death, condom, sex, drugs, fear.* Two performers careen into the space and suddenly freeze. Spectators call out character names and a situation suggested by the pose, creating a scenario for the actors to perform. As the scene plays out, the facilitator interrupts the narrative at key moments and allows the spectator to intervene in shaping the scene. The adult performers are sufficiently distanced from the imbalance and fears of their own adolescence to be able to negotiate the emotional terrain of this material while spontaneously creating characters and scenes in the moment of performance. Their obvious risk taking creates a bond of good will between the spectators and performers, inspiring spectators to invest in the performance.

Central to the work of both the SPARK Peer Players and Teatro Vida is the role of the facilitator, a figure combining some of the functions of director, stage manager, and actor with roles specific to the interactive nature of this theatre.[4] The facilitator creates and protects the liminal space between the real life of the adolescent spectator and the onstage lives of the characters, transporting audience members to a place where they can experiment with identities and actions. From what I have observed, most adolescents are readily transported. Psychodramatic experience tells us that the boundaries between direct experience and dramatic fiction can be vague, and the terrain in between, treacherous. The facilitator has the crucial role of controlling these boundaries.

The facilitator invites the spectators to make explicit what all theatre traffics in: the audience's projection onto the stage. In inter-activist theatre, however, the audience joins not only by projecting mental imagery but also by actively producing a story, characters, and text, sometimes to the point of becoming coprotagonists in the drama.

Facilitation, like any art, is imbued with the character of the artist. The artistic directors, founders, and facilitators of Teatro Vida—Ted Welch—and of the SPARK Peer Players—Rhonda Paganetti—employ quite different styles, but their approaches show similarities. They agree that successful facilitation demands considerable training and practice. Welch worries that not everyone who facilitates should be doing so. "Unreflective facilitating is dangerous," he notes. "If it's just another opportunity for an adult to simply foist their own opinion on a group of teens . . . that's really inappropriate. Facilitators are not there to place their own opinions."[5]

Welch thinks of the facilitator as a kind of priestly mediator whose role is immense: to keep the work progressing and to keep everybody safe. Welch studied for the priesthood and was a member of the Jesuit religious order for twenty years. The role of facilitator does seem akin to that of a shaman or priest in ritual healing, where the priest not only manages liminal activity but becomes the *limen* itself, the threshold or passageway. Indeed, Welch feels he goes into a kind of altered state when facilitating.

Paganetti's style is more down to earth. She draws on her background and training as a family therapist and stresses the need for counseling skills. She uses a prevention model, which suggests five strategies to develop: gaining knowledge, self-improvement, self-image, decision making, and positive peer pressure.

Both facilitators use the process as a bridge between the real lives of the adolescent spectators and the onstage lives of the characters. SPARK does so by means of a somewhat traditional Theatre in Education (TIE)[6] format, in which the bridging comes at the end. Teatro Vida uses facilitation throughout the performance as a method of play building. Both agree, however, that the facilitator must protect the audience to assure a space safe enough to be, momentarily, unsafe. "Even when you're interacting with a performer," says Welch, "you're scanning the audience. Is someone being agitated? Is someone moving back in their chair? Forward in their chair? Are their heads down? Are they kind of moving around? The facilitator can never check out."

Both companies perform largely for adolescent audiences, although Teatro Vida has expanded to other age groups. Both companies address primarily the needs of the African-American and Latino poor and working-class youth, the most at-risk and underserved adolescent population. For many in the audience, this is not only the first engagement with interactive theatre, but the first theatre experience of any kind. Performers in both companies are multiracial and the director and facilitator are white.[7] SPARK's performance style is specifically geared to its intended audience, while Teatro Vida's form is more malleable. SPARK generally performs for an audience of two hundred people or more, while TeatroVida performs for thirty or fewer.

The two companies' struggles with resources and funding are somewhat different because of their relationship to their sponsors. SPARK is housed within a larger institution, the New York City Board of Education, which provides both a certain stability and certain constraints. Teatro Vida is an independent project of the Bronx Council on the Arts. Although both reflect the culture of the audience, SPARK's aesthetic uses slick production values, while Teatro Vida's aesthetic is that of poor theatre.[8]

The SPARK Peer Players

I first saw the SPARK Peer Players performing at the 1992 Adolescent Theatre Festival at the Educational Alliance on New York City's Lower East Side. I couldn't take them in. The heavily amplified sound blasted into my head. The bold, sassy style crashed into me like a wave. I was overwhelmed. SPARK was polished, but I couldn't find myself in the brilliance.[9]

I came of age in the politically charged theatre of the late sixties, when poor theatre was valorized. I assumed that theatre for social change was, by definition, connected to the aesthetics of minimal material means, and associated spectacle primarily with Broadway-stage commercialism. Therefore, I was initially mistrustful of the glitzier production values of SPARK. Ultimately this conflict provided a way into this material. Something about my own reaction made me suspicious. What was it I couldn't hear? This was my first clue: SPARK's aesthetic mirrored the messy cacophony of the adolescent street life, and it made me uncomfortable.

Breaking Down the Walls

I skeptically rode the D train to Prospect Heights High School, in Brooklyn, to find out why. I was met at the door by six uniformed security guards. I successfully passed through a metal detector and then a female guard checked me out with the handheld scanner—rudely scanning two inches above my entire body—down each leg and up the inseams. It was June; the school halls were hot, empty, and cavernous. There was crumbling plaster, holes in the walls, and, near the ceiling, paint was peeling in large sheets. I was directed to a crowded classroom with fixed rows of uncomfortable wood and metal seats, many of which were broken. The room was already steamy. Though several windows were open it felt airless and heavy in the summer heat. The SPARK "techies," clad in jeans and black, fluorescent SPARK T-shirts, were busy setting up an elaborate sound system: two synthesizers, a PA, mixing board, monitors, several stage mikes. Students were still ambling through the door, shouting greetings, shuffling, snapping fingers, cracking gum. Kids sprawled in their seats or leaned against the wall, ready to be entertained.

"*Calm down.* Don't you hate when people say 'calm down'?" Paganetti takes the floor, shouts into the mike. Her "costume" radiates show biz pizazz and sexuality. Her earrings and vest glitter above a short tight skirt and impossible heels. Underneath very short black hair her huge brown eyes dart and invite. She's out there, with a look calculated to bypass the habitual adolescent response to figures of authority. She prepares the audience: "Now, the subject matter is pretty serious, and for that reason I will be back again and you will get a chance to talk about what you think about a lot of the topics that were brought up. The actors are going to go back into their characters so you can talk to the character and the character will answer you."

The music blasts, jazzy and cool. The cast enters—some bursting, some ambling, all *very* cool—an ethnic mix but mostly African-American and Latino, costumed in street eclectic: baggy pants with no belt, sweat pants with one pant leg pushed up, black T-shirts with neon graffiti reading *The SPARK Peer Players,* baseball caps (some backwards), ponytails, dreads, long curls, vests, huge $100 sneakers. They strike sassy, angry, dejected poses, silent, isolated in ones, twos, and threes in what stage director Cheryl Paley calls "the wall of pain," but otherwise a typical inner-city street populated by neighborhood kids, idealized by their absolute cool and a greater than usual percentage of physical beauty. As they break the freeze—a slow glance into another's eyes, a flare of temper, a face-off, a secret told, a shove, a little joke—the beat picks up. They explode into upbeat hip-hop to the lyrics:

> Standing strong together, catching those who fall
> Wiping out the fear and pain, breaking down the wall.

Performers butterfly and undulate, the drum always pulsing underneath; eyes glitter; the air is thick with sex, tension, and cool. The audience is in full swing now, clapping and waving arms, bouncing and swaying. "That's cool." "All right, girlfriend!" " Take it!" "Uh-huh!" "I have a feeling this is going to be bad. I really do."

I find myself rocking and bobbing with them. Three girls are up on their seats, dancing on their knees. Yet I also see more troubling reactions. Directly in front of me a boy sits with his head in his hands, his face completely covered with a white baseball cap. The performers turn to face and challenge the audience:

> We must take the power, before we take a fall
> Our responsibility, breaking down the wall
> Change, the answer is in our hands
> Change, it's time to take a stand.

And the stories begin. *Breaking Down the Walls* (*BDW*) is a collage of scenes—Paley calls them "modules, short playlets with a theme"—of urban youth street life. There is no through line, simply what Paganetti calls a "smorgasbord of issues, just what's important to us," which is, after all, the enactment of a chaotic life.

The first playlet presents one of SPARK's recurring themes, HIV prevention. The opening rap introduces a character named Cool Joey with a "guys like me don't get AIDS" attitude.

> Woo, Yeah, Woo, Yeah. You, you heard about Joey?
> Yeah, I heard he got AIDS.
> [*Chorus, in harmony*] Cool Joey, no glove, no love,

Cool Joey, no glove, no love.

C-O-O-L. That's his name, C-O-O-L. Women are his game. Cool Joey didn't wrap it up tight: *Y salio buscando chicas,* every single night. He thought he was "the Man." He said, "It can't be ME!" But *salio, examen positive,* HIV!

[*Chorus*] Cool Joey, no glove, no love,

Cool Joey, no glove, no love.

He said, "It takes away the feel, the feeling won't be real. We should be together in the heat of love and pleasure. Not stopped by some plastic, elastic—what do you call them?"

Prophylactic!

"How can I be a lover if I have to wear a rubber?"

[*Chorus*] Cool Joey, no glove, no love.

Cool Joey, no glove, no love.

Later Joey's character, a combination of cool, sexy, and self-destructive, will prove an exemplary foil in the facilitation sessions.

The other major theme in *BDW* is self-destruction: gun violence, drugs, and suicide. In a mosaic of monologues a young woman says, "I carry a knife in my bag. I see the way her and her friends look and whisper when I walk by them. I'm scared they might jump me, I need to protect myself."

"You need a *piece*," says a voice behind me. I turn around, catch half a face, eyes behind a black baseball cap. His friend beside him, all elbows, baggy clothes, and huge sneakers, echoes, "You need *protection,* man," like he was saying "You've got to eat." It is, in fact, a truism. These kids all need protection and the necessity translates into conflicting imperatives. Protect yourself—safer sex. Protect yourself—get a gun.

This time, the show blows me away. I've found my way in, through the students, the high school, the entire context in which the play lives. I am able to see how this performance engages the audience by mirroring their lives and matching their style.

End the Silence

The next show, *End the Silence* (*ETS*), developed in 1993, was performed over a two-year period. During that time I saw it in high school classrooms, libraries, and, most often, in huge auditoriums. The company was shaken by a series of shootings at Jefferson High School, in East New York, the first time in ten years that students were killed inside a New York City public school.[10] As a result, they decided to focus the show on kids destroying each other. Finding themselves with some extraordinarily talented kids and intense feelings about the rising violence, the Peer Players developed a highly theatrical tragedy.

The stage is covered from floor to ceiling with five tall panels, each with one letter in the name SPARK. Painted to look like grey building brick, the panels are boldly graffitied: *SPARK Peer Players, Stop the Violence, End the Silence, Respect Yourself. No Glove, No Love* is scrawled inside a heart; *Respect* is slathered across the front in bright yellow paint, and *Rage* is splashed in thick red. Three musicians are on stage: musical director Reggie Woods on keyboards, flute, clarinet, and tenor saxophone, the other two on guitar and bass. Paganetti introduces the performance: "Today's show is all about survival: protecting yourself, safe sex, nonviolence." The show begins with an offstage voice, singing a mournful tune a cappella:

> A bullet cries out and then there is silence,
> living in the rage in the age of violence.
> It's time to teach our children to cope and not to kill.
> Let's show them how to live in peace and maybe someday—

Before he gets a chance to finish we hear shouting and fighting in the audience. A moment of confusion, but it quickly becomes clear that this disruption is part of the piece. The cast takes the stage, hostile and tense, some fighting and screaming, but still cool and sexy. Suddenly, random gunshots explode and performers drop, scatter, cover their faces, and freeze. All is silent and still, except for nervous laughter from the audience. Two girls who have been dancing over the backs of their chairs sit back and laugh it off; a few others look away. A drum beat begins a funeral march, and we are at the grave side of "one who died too young." Another song begins, "Listen! Listen! Listen to me. Listen to my voice." Its complex and beautiful harmonies, its African rhythm, and its call-and-response style accompany a preacher's eulogy. The characters say their goodbyes one by one, and the character J.R. closes his brother's invisible casket to the sireny wail.

In a later scene called "No Glove, No Love," the focus shifts to another problem of adolescent survival: safe sex. Here Jessie needs some advice:[11]

JESSIE: I don't know what to do. He wants to have sex and I'm not ready. My mind is saying no, but my body's saying yes, and—

QUEENIE: [interrupts, hands flying in a "valley girl" imitation] Girl, go with your body, go with your body. Look, I don't know what your problem is, but I'm sure this story from the expert will help. Now—guess who took me out this weekend! Joey!!

KENDRA: You go, girl! Joey looks fly!

JESSIE: Please tell me we are not talking about the same Joey.

QUEENIE: The Joey that look good?

JESSIE: He's been with every girl in school!

Queenie dismisses her and describes an elaborate seduction, ending on a leather couch listening to Luther Vandross.

QUEENIE: So we start kissin' and huggin' and it's getting kinda hot. So I look at him and I say [breathing this line directly into the mike], "Baby, you gonna wear a—condom."

KENDRA: Oh, Queen, that was smooth!

Jessie interrupts, saying that just because he bought her burgers doesn't mean Queenie owed him sex.

JESSIE: This is the 90s and we have the right to say yes or no.

KENDRA: That's right, and she was just exercising her right to say—Yes!

JESSIE: That's not funny. There are a lot of diseases out there, you could get pregnant. Queenie, what about abstinence?

QUEENIE: Abstinence? I wasn't *in* class yesterday! Anyhow, can I finish my story??? He was *not* going to wear a condom. Oh my *goodness!!* He tried to *dis* the *queen!!!* Let me tell you what I did. I got off that leather couch and I slipped back into my red dress. I looked him in the eye and said, "Boyfriend! You may look good, and you do, but—no glove, no love!"

The girls in the audience cheer, "All right, girl!"

Later, Cool Joey, who was held over from the previous show as a major AIDS-prevention element, appears with Mark and Nick, bringing us the male version of the above scene. Joey is bragging about his sexual exploits; Nick admits to spending a whole night in bed just talking to Jessie; and Mark recounts his night with Tasha.

MARK: And she says, "Hey, baby! I'm ready, are you ready, cuz I'm ready."

So I go and get my wallet, ya know, cuz skins is in.

JOEY: Yo! Chill! Chill! What's up with the *wallet?*

MARK: Oh, she said she wanted to see some *ID,* make sure I was old enough. [*Joey doesn't laugh. Mark continues to try to tell his story. Nick is with him, Joey incredulous.*] All right, my last condom was in my wallet, okay?

JOEY: You used a condom?

MARK: [*trying to get on with it*] Yeah.

JOEY: And she still *did* it with you?

MARK: Yeah.

JOEY: And it felt *good?*

MARK: *Good?* [*singing*] Somebody rockin' knocking the boots, baby!

JOEY: [*disgusted*] No man, *no! No!*

NICK: Joey! How can you say that? It's not only pregnancy, it's diseases, too.

MARK: [*singing*] Protect yourself!

JOEY: Yo! First it's not the right time, then it's diseases. Get it together!

NICK: What about Doreen?

JOEY: What about Doreen! She's like *Bam! Bam! Bam!* [*His hands describe her body as he bumps and grinds.*]

NICK: Doreen *has AIDS!*

After establishing that Joey has slept with Doreen without a condom, Nick suggests that he talk to someone.

JOEY: What are you sayin'? You sayin' I *got* somethin'? Just step! *Be out! Step!* [*alone with Mark*] I thought we were boys, man. We look out for each other. Look, I don't need to talk to nobody cuz *guys like me don't get AIDS!!!!*

In the next scenes *ETS* moves back to another kind of danger and peer pressure: kids killing kids and the issue of revenge as a way to maintain respect. J.R., whose brother, a gang leader, has been gunned down, is struggling with whether or not to join his friends and avenge the death.

J.R.: About that thing you and your boys have planned.

MARK: Don't worry about it. We're gonna handle it.

J.R.: But I don't think I'm gonna make it.

MARK: Don't worry, kid. We'll pick you up tonight.

Imani's death in *End the Silence*. Kelly Danticat (in background), Learie Corbin (J.R.), Jeannette Torruella (Imani). Photo by Penny Coleman.

Later, J.R.'s girlfriend, Imani, confronts him:

> J.R.: Look, Imani, what we were talking about is between me and Mark.
>
> IMANI: No, J.R. It's not just between you and Mark. This concerns me and everyone else in this neighborhood. I know you're planning on getting the guy that killed your brother. Well, let me tell you something, J.R. It's not the right answer. You have other choices!
>
> J.R.: Well, why don't you tell that to the guy who killed my brother?
>
> IMANI: It's too late for him. I don't think it's too late for you, J.R., and I'm scared.
>
> J.R.: Imani, please! I'll see you later!

In the end Imani is the one who is gunned down, by a bullet meant for someone else. As J.R. crumples in grief, the company begins to sing about finding a way "to make it to another day." During the song, the cast streams into the audience, many of whom are in tears, covering their faces.

> We are the children of a shattered past,
> Turning pain into power, proud at last.
> I've got the power, I know you got it too,
> If we stand together, there's nothing we can't do.

Educate ourselves so we can be free,

You've got to stop and turn it around,

Turn that pain into—power.

This celebration of the transformative power of pain is interrupted when one of the Peer Players, Eilene, breaks out of character, motions for the music to stop and declares that this is "not the right ending, preaching positivity with dead bodies on stage." Carlton mocks her sarcastically, "Oh, it doesn't *feel* right." Others, breaking out of character, argue, tease. "I am *so* embarrassed about this," vamps Queenie. Imani, though, gets up from the floor and agrees that the ending doesn't work because, "It's the same thing we see in the newspapers, on TV. I'm tired of seeing young brothers and sisters killing each other. We've got to find another way of communicating with each other than picking up a gun. And brothers and sisters who feel like respect is worth dyin' for. How you gonna get that respect if you dead?" Queenie steps forward and grabs the microphone, "All right, all right," beginning a call and response with the audience:

QUEENIE: What we need to do is we need to End the Silence!

AUDIENCE: *End the Silence!*

QUEENIE: Our people are dyin', and what we need to do is to Stop the Violence!

AUDIENCE: *Stop the Violence!*

QUEENIE: And there's one more thing we have to do after that, and you all know what it is.

AUDIENCE: Uh-huh!

QUEENIE: What we need to do is Stand up! Stand up! Stand up for your life!

The whole audience is up, clapping, singing, dancing in their seats and down the aisles: "End the Silence! Stop the Violence! Oh, Oh, Ohhhh, Ohhh!" This is followed by a reprise of the opening song: "It's time to teach our children to cope and not to kill."

SPARK Facilitation

When the play ends the players introduce themselves by their real names, the high school they graduated from, and the college they now attend, and the audience simultaneously applauds and cheers both the performance and

Rhonda Paganetti facilitating with SPARK Peer Players at a Bronx high school.
Photo by Penny Coleman.

these symbols of individual success. Then the facilitation begins. Usually, the kids in the audience talk to the actors in character. Time permitting, Paganetti may break the audience into groups or production companies that devise alternative endings to the different playlets. Sometimes students actually come out of the audience to perform. Paganetti announces, "We're going to create magic," inviting the spectators to talk to the characters, to come up on stage and persuade Cool Joey that he needs a condom or to tell J.R. not to avenge his gang-leader brother's violent death. She suggests, "Let's pool our resources and everybody in this room try to think of one thing that would convince this person to change, because you care about him. Pretend he's your brother." Responses range from "Kick him in the butt" to urging Cool Joey to "respect himself and his women."

Respect is a major theme in all the SPARK plays I saw and a major topic in facilitation sessions. In one case, Cool Joey responds to an audience member, "I'll tell you what respect is. Respect is trust; you trust each other. I trust my women, right? I know they're clean. They trust me." Paganetti interrupts, "Wait, wait. You trust him?" she asks the audience. "No way, man." "Anybody here trust him?" "No!" "We know a whole lot about him, right? He's a pretty stubborn guy, but he's headed for a lot of trouble if he isn't in trouble already." In one brave moment a young woman from the audience climbs on stage in front of hundreds of her peers to play a potential partner and try her hand at convincing him. She brazenly pulls a condom from her pocket and offers to show him how to put it on. The audience hoots and cheers. Paganetti—who is, after all, an employee of the New York City Board of Education—quickly stops the action.

Although facilitating workshops around issues of HIV prevention is often painful and difficult, the solution is rather clear cut: use a condom if you have sex. But the work confronting peer-to-peer violence is more complex; there is no clear answer. Paley—who occasionally facilitates if Paganetti is absent—describes a workshop in the South Bronx where a young woman "popped up and started giving it to me: How could I possibly know what it is like not to even be able to go to the bathroom because you're afraid somebody's going to slash your throat?" The message, which the company heard over and over, was, "You can't tell us not to protect ourselves when we have someone at our back." Paganetti and Paley finally decided to turn the issue back to the audience. "Okay, what can we do? Let's work together to find an answer, because if we don't, it will be your sister, your mother."

Certainly these young people have problems that extend way beyond the possibilities of even the most brilliant interventions. Sometimes these facilitations evoke startling testimony. At one performance in the South Bronx, a hand shoots up in the back and a boy addresses J.R.: "You gotta play it, right? My mother and my brother got shot, right? You can do mad, bad stuff like sell drugs and whatever, but, bottom line is not to go out and avenge it, cuz I could avenge my brother's death with his friends, but instead you got to, like, live the dream for them cuz they died. What comes to me is shining on them cuz you are a reflection of your people." The room erupts with applause and cheers.

The fear is that this may be a drop in the bucket. Or worse, that the Peer Players may land in a school, stir things up, and then leave the mess. In addition, the Peer Players themselves, though somewhat trained in peer counseling, are young and sometimes find themselves in over their heads. Paganetti tries to end the sessions by urging the students who are overwhelmed to see a counselor. She urges them all to keep talking about these issues, and to "Give yourselves a hand, and protect yourselves. Please, you're wonderful." Facilitations do not always end so neatly. Time is short;

typically a school allows two forty-minute periods for the entire performance/workshop process. There are sometimes hundreds of kids in the audience, and the piece deals with a multitude of extremely difficult issues.

That is why another aspect of the SPARK program is so critical. Two SPARK counselors, adults trained in drug-prevention and intervention counseling, are in the aisles, scanning the audience. Their purpose is to identify kids who might be at risk, based on what they say or, equally importantly, express nonverbally. Indeed, the audience reactions are strong, sometimes fierce. A boy sits with his baseball cap over his eyes; a girl presses her jacket firmly against her cheek. Several students turn away, hide, or laugh loudly at inappropriate moments. A girl runs from the auditorium in tears. A SPARK counselor follows her and learns that the girl's father has just died of AIDS. The counselor comforts her while she cries and invites her to join a grief group. The performance becomes an access point for other kinds of interventions: comfort, counseling, sometimes referrals to outside social services.[12]

Paganetti recalls a facilitation when several kids from the audience talked about their own suicide attempts. This was the first time they had disclosed these attempts, and several of them were still "in the middle of it. There was a whole team—thank God!—of counselors there, writing down names. We thanked the kids a lot for sharing the information with us. We talked about how you survive that kind of thing, because everyone feels overwhelmed *sometime* in their lives. I ask other kids in the audience who have already gone through that, 'What do you do now when that happens to you? What can you suggest to people who are feeling that way now?' But they *have* to go to a counselor."

Although SPARK typically uses the identification between Peer Players and audience to advantage, occasionally it poses problems. Since the material has increasingly addressed violence, facilitations have become more emotionally intense. Sometimes the boundaries between players and audience blur. Audience members seek advice from the players whose fictional stories they identify with, and Peer Players are confronted with a situation they are not equipped to handle. For example, once a boy spent the entire workshop interrupting with inappropriate jokes. After the workshop was over, he went directly to one of the Peer Players, telling him that his younger brother was using crack and carrying a gun. "He was frantic!"

recalls Paganetti. "My kids were of course trying to give him advice, and it was a nightmare." The room was packed and in motion, the SPARK counselors were busy organizing the flow of students. One Peer Player—who was later fired—was telling him to beat his brother up. Finally, Paganetti succeeded in getting the attention of a SPARK counselor.

The Peer Players were upset and scared. Paganetti met with them to process their feelings about this experience and to come up with a model for handling this kind of situation in the future: to listen, to empathize, to establish that these things happened to the *character,* not the performer, and, most importantly, to identify a SPARK counselor and refer the student. "Sometimes," she says, "they need to bodily bring him over."

This experience illuminated three critical issues. First, the Peer Players themselves needed tools to deal with what might come up in workshops. Both their characters and their positions as role models gave them power to ignite an emotional response from the audience. Outside the structure of performance and facilitated discussion, they were unequipped to handle this. Second, the SPARK counselors needed more preparation for the performance. They had to be ready for explosions of feeling and troubling personal disclosures. Third, there needed to be many more counselors. Paganetti remembers feeling as though the company had finally opened a door they had been working to open for years, "and we hit against a brick wall, because nobody was there to back us. That's where the program is supposed to have its strength, in SPARK counseling. We leave, and they're still there."

In the last two years the company has initiated two ways in which the Peer Players' work can more successfully extend beyond the immediate experience of the performance. First, they have begun SPARK counselor trainings at the beginning of each school year. In addition, this year the Peer Players have begun doing their own follow-up workshops, in which Paley and Jeannette Torruella, one of the older Peer Players, work with smaller groups of kids who were in the audience the previous week. Typically there is also a SPARK counselor at each of these sessions, and he or she functions as another kind of bridge for kids to get involved in the SPARK program.

Casting and Play Development

Cast directly out of New York City high schools, Peer Players must be seniors planning to attend college. Generally they are "survivors" who were once at risk. Often they are already involved in the prevention and intervention aspects of the SPARK program, where they receive both counseling and training as peer leaders. Once cast, they will work twenty hours a week (at ten dollars per hour with full benefits) while attending college, usually part-time. Handling professional responsibilities while they still have one foot in inner-city adolescent life can be difficult. At every show I attended there was always at least one performer who simply didn't show, for a variety of reasons, ranging from "I had to take my grandmother to the clinic" to simply blowing the performance off. Paley often spends the preperformance minutes recasting and patching the show to cover for those who are missing; most players can and have performed many parts.

The Peer Player audition has two components: a choice of song, a monologue or a dance, and, most importantly, talking about "who they are" and the counseling aspect of the work. Paganetti, Paley, and Woods look for a combination of raw talent—of which there is plenty—a commitment to giving back to the community, and a hip, streetwise look. Paganetti will "never put a kid on that stage who will be laughed at." The actors must be role models the audience can not only relate to but also aspire to, or the shows will "come off preachy and the kids will turn off in a second," says Paley. The musicians also serve as role models. They are always placed onstage and are costumed in street attire. "We look just like the kids in the audience," says Woods. "I got my 'do rag' and my sneakers." And although Woods could perform the entire show with one instrument, he explains that he wants the kids to see him playing them all. "I run with my gut feeling, that maybe somebody might be motivated by it."

The plays are developed in workshops out of the Peer Players' experience and what Paganetti calls "passionate discussion of the issues." They begin with the group exploring and confronting some very difficult, highly personal material. In order to "insulate them in some way," Paganetti admits to being "very blunt" with them, "toughening them up. In other words, there's nothing I won't say to them, nothing we won't discuss, nothing is taboo. If we say it enough here, they won't be shocked by anything. They will feel free to talk on stage and won't be inhibited."

After the group is comfortable with each other and the material, they begin brainstorming, doing group exercises to trigger issues, making a wish list of what they'd like to give to other young people, improvising, writing monologues, doing research and training around particular issues. The Peer Players are responsible for having the information and resources to deal with the issues that the play addresses. Research involves everything from going to the library to interviewing gang members to sitting down with students and asking them "What are you dealin' with today?" Scenes and monologues coming out of "absolute, direct experience" are not used, particularly by the person whose experience it is, although sometimes these experiences can be disguised and given to another player. Everything must also go through the Peer Players' "corn meter": anything preachy is cut or reworked.

Finally, the piece is loosely set into scenarios and beats within which they improvise. The show may not be completely written down until the very end of the school year, if at all. However, some lines containing critical information are scripted. The music, too, is a collaboration. Woods runs songwriting workshops in which each player might write six to eight lines around a theme. "It doesn't have to have a rhythm. It doesn't have to rhyme. It doesn't have to do anything, just whatever comes off the top of their heads," says Woods. They then take the raw lyrics, edit them, and, with Woods's help, find a rhythm. Some melodies and rhythms come directly from the Peer Players. The workshops also serve as training in vocal technique, basic music theory and harmony (Woods 1995).

Woods, a professional musician who grew up in a rough neighborhood in Jamaica, Queens ("and believe me, I've been in trouble"), considers this his "payback" job. He feels he was hired to help bring in the "music of the children, the street music." He tries to write music the kids can relate to,

> and when I say "relate," I don't just mean relate, I mean tap their foot, clap their hands, move to feel, create some kind of emotions, some reaction that is *visible, because* of the music. All of the great jazz masters used to say, "It don't mean a thing if it don't have that swing," and one way of detecting whether or not the music is creating that vibe is, you look in the audience and see whether or not people are tapping their foot. If they're not moving their foot, then you ain't doing your job. It's just basic, you know, creating a rhythm people can feel.

Woods points out that most urban teenagers now listen to rap. "Kids cross-dress now: white kids wear $100 sneakers and baggy pants just like the black kids, and they also cross with the music, so it makes it easier to write music that everybody can relate to" (Woods 1995). Woods's eclectic musical style draws from jazz, R & B, Latin, and funk, sometimes with a bit of Broadway thrown in.

All developmental work is done as a team—up to thirty kids, Paganetti, Paley, and Woods—with some guidelines as to who is responsible for what. But Paganetti and Paley describe the process as being "all in there, hook, line, and sinker, swimming and kicking each other, body parts flying." Rehearsals and script-development sessions continue once a week after the show opens, as do meetings to process issues arising during performances. For example, during *End the Silence* actor Carlton Collier worried about playing Mark, who tries to persuade another character to avenge his brother's murder. There were guys in the audience "yelling things like 'Yeah! Yeah! Yo! Kill them!' and in my heart, you know, the real me is going, *not*, that is not what you want to do, but my character was like: 'Yeah! You see that?' and I was really, really scared at that character because he had so much power in those workshops to get all those people to want to be so violent" (Collier 1995).

Paganetti tries to convince the actors that there are good reasons to embody evil, in order to confront and conquer it. "First of all, I explain to them, the more you up the ante, the more they're gonna get involved and resist you. Also, if you don't let the kids who really *believe* that they should kill other kids hear *their* point of view, then you're not gonna hear from them about it. You need someone for them to agree with" (Paganetti 1995).

In fact, there can be a fine line between dramatizing a subject and modeling destructive behavior. For example, showing drug use may tempt a person who has quit to relapse. Or the actor playing Cool Joey might be *so* cool and charismatic that the audience is drawn to him and the AIDS-prevention work is undercut.

The mirror the Peer Players create is two-way. At South Bronx High a couple of kids told a teacher how much they liked the show. When asked what they liked about it, one struck his own chest: *"Porque es sobre nuestra vida—es sobre nosotros"* (Because it is about our lives—it is about us). The reverse is also true: "I look out into the audience and I see myself," explains Collier, who has been in the company for three years. He continues:

> I understand what it's like to get up every morning and go to school and
> walk past a bunch of people who are *not* going to school . . . . Who are

dressed to the nines—who got pockets full of money—riding in jeeps and all kinda different sports cars . . . and here you are, you know, trying to do right, maybe for your auntie, or for your grandmother. You're trying to live a straight and narrow life, and all around you, you see chaos. Everybody's got a gun. (Collier 1995)

Torruella adds, "I get up on stage to say, 'I did it, and so can you' " (Torruella 1995).

Teatro Vida

While Paganetti's style is tough, blunt, and in your face, Ted Welch— founder, artistic director, and primary facilitator of Teatro Vida—stands back, observes, and contains the experience. Whereas SPARK is elaborately produced, Teatro Vida's theatrical elements are the essential minimum: the actors, the facilitator, the audience, the space. While SPARK plays for up to two hundred people, Teatro Vida limits the audience to thirty. Where SPARK screams the chaos of adolescence, Teatro Vida's poor-theatre spirit provides something closer to a blank screen on which the audience can project their issues.[13]

A Teatro Vida performance is completely improvised in the moment. It begins with spectator participation; in fact, the audience actually creates the piece. The performance starts with Welch enlisting help from the kids in transforming the space, usually into an intimate semicircle with a large, open playing space in the middle. If he can, he makes some kind of verbal or physical contact with each person in the audience. "I'm Ted Welch. Welcome," he says, calmly offering his hand as each student ambles into the classroom. "It's a gentle way of connecting, and I also want to know what energy is there. Am I dealing with reticence? Fear? Openness? Hostility? So I'm trying to get my anchor, too."

Ray and Raven

Each performance is framed by a specific theme. At a performance at the East Harlem Tutorial Program, Welch introduces the subject for that day: substance abuse. "But that's kind of the overall theme," he continues. "It's really not even about abuse; it's about substance *use* and all the dynamics

Ted Welch facilitating with Teatro Vida actor Dennis Pressey at East Harlem Tutorial.
Photo by Penny Coleman.

when people get caught in that kind of pattern of life. We're not here to make a judgment or condemn anybody." Next he elicits what the audience knows about the theme.

After some time spent gathering information, Welch moves on. "I'm going to call out two actors, Thea and Peter, and ask them to just move around in the space." Thea Martinez darts, winds, curls. Peter Mentrie, more contained, follows. "Freeze!" says Welch to the actors. "I'm going to ask you to give them each a name." He proceeds to elicit the elements of the scene from the audience: the characters, the setting, the relationship and "what's going on between them right now?" Raven, thirty; Ray, forty-seven; they're married; they're in a park; they're fighting.

The scene begins. Raven, we discover, has just dropped out of a drug recovery program. In the playground, their child has just taken a fall and Ray blames Raven, implying that she can't take care of her child because of her drug problem.

RAVEN: Look, I'm not going to play, like the victim. I'm going to *tell* you something, and you need to promise me that you're not going to, like, go wild.

RAY: [*with a palpable edge*] I won't go wild, just tell me. I bet you I know
    already, let me see, let me see if I can figure it out. You're getting high. Let
    me see if I can guess what you're getting high *on,* or maybe I'll leave that
    to you.

"Shit," murmurs Raven under her breath, twisting herself into impossible
shapes, thrusting her fist into her stomach. "I knew it," says a boy in the front
row, snapping his fingers. Welch leans against the wall, behind the audience,
arms folded. His eyes dart between the two characters and the audience.

RAVEN: That's not it. That's not, what, like—you're so *perceptive,* but what you
    don't know is that I can't do this, I can't do this program, I can't do this
    recovery, I can't do it. [*Her voice modulates quickly back and forth between
    a high pitch of desperation and a quiet determination. Her Latina accent
    gets stronger as the tension mounts.*] I can't *do* this program. I can't do it.
    This is what it is. This is *me* now. *I take pills!* This is what it is, okay? And
    we're going to stay there and either you accept that or you don't. So I—
RAY: What are you talking—?
RAVEN: *No!*
RAY: What are you—?
RAVEN: No, I'm *saying* I think I can manage with what I do and the right
    kind of support, and you need to step off and stop putting me down, *All
    the time, all the time all the time. This is where I am. This is all I can do!*
RAY: I don't know what's going on!
RAVEN: Then you don't want to hear it, that's all.

At this point Welch intervenes: "We're going to stop this scene right there.
We're going to ask the husband to walk away and we're going to talk to our
friend Raven. What's happening, Raven?" he asks soothingly. "A lot of
things are happening all at once" she confides in a blur of stories: her
daughter, the pills, the recovery program she flunked out of.

"There are a lot of neighbors here, and we are out in the park, and I guess
everybody kind of heard what was going on," Welch observes. "Would you
be willing to talk to some of these neighbors?" Welch opens it up to the audience, inviting them to ask a question, get more information, or maybe even
offer some direction or advice. The questions come. A boy asks, "Why are
you taking pills?" He looks a bit embarrassed. Welch validates the question

with a raise of his eyebrows, turns to Raven, passing it to her with his glance. To get off coke. Pills are the lesser of two evils, she explains. "I'm 50 percent better than where I was, but this is not a problem that is going to go away in two weeks," she adds.

"Did she answer your question about *why* she's taking pills?" asks Welch. He repeats audience questions, summarizes her responses. "Yes?" He gestures to a boy in the back, who asks Raven, "Is there something you're doing to make him put you down?" She flares: "Is there something that I'm doing to make him put me down?" "Yeah, well, yeah," he wavers. "It's a good question," Welch moves to protect the boy. "Is she—?"

> RAVEN: [*interrupting*] No, let me tell you, could I speak to that, please? I don't
> mean to jump on you but sometimes it's easier to front because, when you
> admit that you have a problem, then that's when people call you weak,
> you see. When you act like you don't have a problem and you try to front
> like nothing is wrong, they'll talk about you behind your back, but you
> know, they won't come up and disrespect you. When I admit that I don't
> have all of this together, that's when I get disrespect, not just by my hus-
> band, but a lot of other people "Oh, I thought she *knew* better. Oh, what *is*
> her problem? Doesn't she know she has a kid?" All of that, all of that.

"I think you're strong by admitting you have a problem," ventures a girl, maybe thirteen. Another boy leans forward. "You sound like, probably, before, you never spoke up for yourself. If you had spoke up from the get go, you might not be feeling like that right now." "Wow, wow, that's deep," Raven's tone softens. "Because, I tell you, one of the things, when I tried to get sober, I started noticing things I never noticed before and I didn't like them. One of the things I *did* notice, he was always arguing. If I say it's green, he'll say it's blue—*blue, blue, blue,* what's wrong with your eyes? I always got it wrong. And I didn't notice that until I got sober." One girl, brow wrinkled, very quiet and serious, just watches and nods.

"How do you feel about yourself?" asks Welch gently. "You had one of your neighbors here saying you're strong. You're acknowledging your problems, and you're working on them. You have someone else here saying that maybe if you spoke out about yourself and took care of yourself and were forceful about yourself, your husband would back off. How are you feeling about yourself?"

"Well, life is not a therapeutic community, you know. When you're in recovery it's like you're in a bubble, and in there everyone keeps tellin' you, you can do it, you can do it, and then you get out here, and it's just real hard to remember that. And I'm not saying I can't do it, but I don't think it's going to happen this week."

"I want to know, what did you see in your husband when you first met him?" a girl asks. Raven lets out a deep sigh. "Well, he may not be *your* type, but at the time he had more hair." The first ripple of laughter breaks up the seriousness of this endeavor. "And all of the stories he can tell me about his experience, it's fascinating, like he was in the army, and—"

"Why are you putting your child in danger?" asks another boy. The tone changes. Welch nods and turns to Raven, hands clasped behind his back.

"Let me ask you a question?" returns Raven. "Do kids have accidents normally, even parents who don't get high, their kids have problems, they slip, they fall? Look, the bottom line is, for me right now, I have to learn to not beat myself up, to not blame myself all the time—"

"How old is your daughter?" asks Welch.

"Four."

"Your daughter's four? She had an accident, she fell down and hurt herself?"

"She fell *down,* you know, she—"

"And your husband went wild "

"He went *wild,* and so did everyone else, they started staring at me like I was—"

Welch calls a halt. "Okay, we're going to give you a chance to rest a bit. Give her a hand for talking to us" (*applause*). "And we're going to bring the husband out for a minute."

Ray's questioning begins.

"Why are you putting your wife down?" a boy asks.

"I didn't know I was putting her down," Ray explains, "I thought I was just trying to straighten her out."

"Straighten her out?" interrupts Welch.

"Yeah, you know, I don't understand where she's coming from half the time, I get mad."

"Ray," Welch cautions, "I just want to lay a few ground rules here. Your wife has been really straight with us, so we don't want to walk around like you don't understand, because we know you do understand and so we'd like you to get right to the issues here. We don't need the preliminary stuff, you know what I'm saying?"

"All right. Okay."

"All right, so the question was why are you putting your wife down? We do know what's going on, and I think you know what's going on too, so why are you using that method?"

The audience asks questions about how long Ray has known about his wife's drug problem. "You may be tired of this stuff, but you're mentally abusing your wife, and that's not right," says one boy. "You're supposed to support her. You're putting her down all the time. That's mentally abusing her."

"Think about it for a minute," suggests Welch.

"What do I do when she shuts me out?" Ray asks.

"Did you ever have a problem?" asks a young girl, maybe fourteen.

"I got lots of problems," laughs Ray.

"I mean, did you ever hit a woman, because that's a problem, so I want to know, did you ever hit her and have a problem?"

There has not been any indication of domestic violence in the scene. The girl is projecting what she needs to talk about. Mentrie follows her lead:

RAY: Did I ever hit her? I sort of—

GIRL: *Sort of?*

RAY: I sort of slapped her.

GIRL: So, in your point of view, did you accomplish anything?

RAY: No, I don't think it did, because she's still doing what she was doing.

GIRL: So, apparently, the method that you used to try and straighten her out didn't work?

RAY: No, it didn't. You know, I'm trying to figure it out, because you're saying that my put-downs don't work and the other stuff don't work. What do I do?

GIRL: When you see that she's trying to improve like going to programs, you should say, "Very good, I'm proud of you, I'm glad, let me take you out to dinner, let me treat you somewhere, you're doing a good job with our daughter." Just little things that she do, just encourage her. She says you're shutting her out. *Tell* her, "I want to be part of your life again," that you want to help her.

The entire audience is quiet, leaning forward, mobilized in the effort to coach Ray.

"But I don't have the problem, *she's* the one with the problem. *I* handle my life, I control my life." Ray insists.

"You *hit* her, you got a *problem*," another girl, maybe twelve, says quietly.

After a bit, Welch wraps it up: "There's a lot of things to think about. You've given good advice to both, because we're really not going to know how they resolve this. They have a lot of thinking to do, a lot of work together in their family. Let's see in this last moment we're going to be with them just what their conversation's going to be."

Ray and Raven resume the scene. Maybe, Raven comes back to say, she needs to put her recovery first. Maybe that's all she can do. In any case, they need to talk. They want to stop this cycle but don't know how. Teatro Vida characters don't accomplish a miraculous change. They remain suspended.

Martinez finds the substance-abuse work tricky, and the least rewarding of Teatro Vida's themes, because it tends to become a moralizing, right-or-wrong exercise. "AIDS is a relational issue, whereas in our society junkies still bear the ultimate moral responsibility for their problem," she explains. "It's such a dangerous line. I don't want to see the audience go into justifications for taking drugs or selling them, but on the other hand, we need to have some analysis of why people who are marginalized take drugs so that the kids can be more forgiving of themselves. They need a language for understanding" (Martinez 1995).

She feels that the complexity of Raven's character might help the kids to accept "their torn and conflicted feelings about their own family members who are drugging and abusing. Perhaps this might begin to help them to be able to look at the hidden-away parts, the compulsions that can make us do what we most hate and fear and condemn in others, so these don't become hidden, powerful demons that can attack by surprise, taking the form of high-risk behavior like dropping out of school, risking HIV or pregnancy, getting involved in abusive relationships" (Martinez 1995).

The theme built into each Teatro Vida performance is flexibile and responds to the company's read of the audience. For example, the company was once hired to do a series on bias in the public schools. Before the group was to perform, students were asked by their teachers to identify what bias issues were most important to them. At Central Park East High School, in East Harlem, the students chose homophobia, and the company had prepared to address the issue. But, as it happened, the performance took place the day after the L.A. riots and when Welch wrote the word *bias* on the blackboard and asked the students to say whatever came to their minds, what they expressed was terror and rage about racial violence. The company followed their lead.

Evolution of Teatro Vida

Many people in the Adolescent Theatre Network, including Rhonda Paganetti of SPARK, locate influential origins of their work in training they did with Welch in the 1970s. Welch traces his own theatrical roots to childhood dramas he created and absorbed. "We'd play for hours after school, with battles and princes and castles and every kind of story you could imagine. Then there were movie serials every Saturday. *Sheena, Queen of the Jungle* always ended with her falling through a trap into the alligator's mouth and you had to come back next week and there was a secret other door and she got shunted off down the river and was safe." Entranced by the play, the magic, and by finding that secret door that makes safety amidst great danger, Welch took this childhood fascination into his life's work. After college, while still in the Jesuit order, Welch went to Brazil to do community work that included teaching kids to draw, sculpt, and put on theatre. There he became immersed in community and social issues and the radical pedagogical theory of Paolo Freire. Welch was also influenced by his studies of psychodrama with Zerka Moreno and Jonathan Fox.[14]

In 1973 Welch was invited by Maria Boria to create the Family Life Theatre (FLT) within the Department of Obstetrics and Gynecology at New York Metropolitan Hospital. Boria, who had been inspired by theatre she saw in villages during ten years in India, was looking for a way to help young people in East Harlem to connect to their own healthcare and to health providers. FLT's performers were teenagers who created their own pieces. They developed a model that had enough structure to create what Welch calls a "security reference" but left room to play and take risks. This model influenced groups like SPARK as well as numerous other groups across the country. Welch directed FLT for ten years, ultimately handing it over to comembers Irene Daimant and Wilfredo Medina.

In 1988 Welch founded Teatro Vida to respond to the HIV/AIDS epidemic and the danger it posed to adolescents. In order to create a "theatre-in-the-moment"[15] he decided to work with adult professional actors, who would have both the improvisational skills and the necessary distance from adolescence to tackle the intense, frightening issues raised by HIV/AIDS. The company loosely followed the FLT model at first, creating characters whose stories they could mix and match. Eventually they began to feel that they were no longer telling a fresh story, that even in the mix and match they had played out all the possibilities.

"I needed to move us to another level," explains Welch. "We were always watching the young people in the audience take the risk of asking the first question, opening themselves to respect or disrespect from everybody else." Welch continues, "So I thought, *we* ought to take a similar kind of risk and just walk out there without any more than *they* have" (Welch 1995).

In fact, Teatro Vida actors still do have more of a safety net than the audience. They have their training, age, and experience, as well as a finely developed sense of trust and responsibility for one another. Even so, the actors never know what's going to be thrown at them. Welch explains:

> The agreement is that the actors will sustain the scene until the facilitator feels they're at a point for intervention. But *they* don't worry about that . . . so that's the first safety the facilitator provides, watching the curve of the scene, and intervening where there's *enough* information about the two characters . . . enough of the emotional core of conflict for the audience to have something to grapple with. But, if the facilitator waits too long, the scene begins to unravel, the characters go off on tangents. It's just like any acting, they have to completely let go and trust the facilitator, who is their partner.

"The facilitator watches for a peak," Welch continues, "a moment of high interest; you intervene, you isolate, bring out the character" (Welch 1995).

When the actors are frozen and listening to the audience inscribe a life onto their bodies, "it's a parachute moment," says Martinez. "They must be right there, taking in all the information, quickly embodying the character they've been given" (Martinez 1995). Sometimes the choices are far-fetched and difficult to play. Contrary to what one might expect, the audience often casts against type and with great imagination. Irene Diamant, a fifty-five-year-old actor, is seen as a nine-year-old. During an early HIV/AIDS performance, Martinez is cast as a body trying to protect herself from the urgent desires of Williams, who is cast as a virus.

This element of surprise is an important aspect of Teatro Vida's work. When an actor suddenly takes a scene in an unexpected direction, when an audience member asks an unexpected question, Welch believes the opening that is created allows space for new solutions to familiar problems. No matter how outrageous the suggestion, Welch believes in trying it out, trusting the actors and the audience to find their way.

Butter and Jelly

Last year I attended a performance at a day program, an alternative to incarceration for juvenile offenders between the ages of eleven and sixteen. The performance takes place in a tiny room filled with tables and chairs. The boys are accompanied by two female guards. The company does several scenes, and there is time for just one more. The audience is engaged and loose. Welch calls out two women, Thea and Ebony. The boys name them Jelly and Peanut Butter. "They're lesbians." I sneak a look at one of the guards, who pulls herself up straight. "Relationship?" "Lovers." "What's going on right now?" "They're planning on having sex." "All right, what else is happening between them? Are they a couple?" "Yeah. Jelly's trying to push her into having sex." Hooting, squirming. I am uncomfortable, concerned for the actors. Welch doesn't flinch. "All right. So Jelly and—we'll call her Butter, that's easier. Butter and Jelly. Okay? Let's see what's going on here."

Jelly opens the scene: "Not now, I'm tired." Soon she reveals that she is confused, this is a new experience for her, she saw her ex-boyfriend and "feelings were stirred up." The scene moves quickly to a relationship on the brink of collapse. "Just leave me alone. You're killing my life! Just playing with me!" Jelly says. Butter answers, "Why do you have such a hard time just walking out and saying good-bye, then? You tell me!" When Jelly threatens, "Okay, fine! I'll leave. Just give me my shit. I'm outta here!" Welch intervenes.

"Almost every time we bring up same-sex actors we get a gay scene," remarks Welch on the train ride home. "What does that mean? This audience wants to *talk* about it." In this case, the audience jumped on these two women. "They dissed them," explains Welch. "What do we do? We let it roll. That is our task. By the end we have these same guys managing the relationship. 'Don't you hear how she cares about you?' How *quickly* they become a working, problem-solving group of people."

"In a safe environment," says Welch, "you can discuss anything. You can have varying opinions, but you want to honor the different opinions and say, 'We're not going to necessarily find agreement here tonight, that's not why we're here.'"

The actors help to make all opinions safe by embodying "bad" characters. They let the characters speak, no matter how misguided. "The audience often will really fight for characters who are on the brink," says Martinez. "The parts that are the most renegade are the best accepted and cared for by the audience, and that's very healing."

But it is the facilitator who has primary responsibility for making it safe for all of the diverse members of the audience to participate. "You want to open it up, ask open-ended questions, as invitations to participate. The potential for 'dissing' or putting somebody down is enormous, especially when you have very volatile and emotion-filled issues." The facilitator must "acknowledge the audience, affirm them, thank them for their comments. I'll say, 'Look at the way we're thinking. Look at the diversity of opinion we have here.' As facilitator, I cannot stand before the group as a judge."

When I ask Welch what would happen if someone in the audience said something racist, he replies, "I depend on the community to answer that, because if I step in to take one position or other, then I lose my credibility as facilitator." When I press him, Welch acknowledges that this does not always work. There may be a moment when he needs to remind people to respect each other's differences. But on the whole, he trusts the community. This is, in fact, one of the keys to Welch's work. He does not believe that Teatro Vida performances provide the education, but that the community is activated. The experience affirms the audience's ability to process and think and help the characters. The audience gives advice, prods, argues, discovers together. "It's a calling forth from the people, honoring their knowledge and their ability to think, very much along Freire's line and kind of a Jesuit tradition also," Welch explains (Welch 1995).

Trusting the audience, however, in no way absolves Teatro Vida from responsibility. Its members must have the information to deal with issues they confront. The company is thoroughly trained before tackling a new issue. They have received training from the Department of Health HIV/AIDS, from the New York State Office of Domestic Violence, and from experts in the field of substance abuse. During the HIV/AIDS work, when funding allowed, they traveled with Gloria Jenkins, a nurse practitioner/health educator from Bronx Lebanon Hospital, and each performance began with a review of basic AIDS prevention. Welch would then tell the audience, "We are all people with health information. All of us, as a collective, have what we need."

But Welch believes that knowledge alone is not enough. From its inception in 1989 the troupe wanted to address the emotional life of young people, "because that's the place where the barrier is—it's not so much in information and the how-to and the techniques—it's what is going to *inhibit* or *prohibit* someone from moving in that direction. For example, in an AIDS scenario, we would want to look at two characters standing up to one another, demanding and expecting things of each other, because that's where the problem comes" (Welch 1995).

Pursuing the emotional life of the participants beyond the performance itself is usually impossible for Teatro Vida. Unlike SPARK, Teatro Vida does not currently have the funding to support follow-up. Often, the company is hired within the context of a prevention or intervention program, where follow-up discussions are led by teachers or counselors. However, since Teatro Vida is not present at these sessions, they do not have the opportunity to measure their impact beyond the performances.

Theatre for Survival

Political Context

Politics and money play a major role in what the companies can and cannot do. In today's conservative political climate, each group is experiencing difficulties. SPARK, part of a city agency, was practically decimated in the spring of 1995 by a series of buyout offers from the administration of New York City Republican Mayor Rudolph Giuliani. These attempts to reduce the municipal workforce enticed over half of the company to leave. In addition, each year the New York City Board of Education issues guidelines for HIV/AIDS curriculum that are quite restrictive. For example, they require that a certain percentage of each lesson be devoted to abstinence. In such a climate, companies may have to make a virtue out of necessity by choosing their battles.

The SPARK Peer Players have been criticized at Adolescent Theatre Festivals for rarely addressing sexual preference in their performances. One of the main reasons for this, says Paganetti, has been the board of education's restrictions. Although SPARK generally does what they feel is necessary to comply with the board, Paganetti chooses to not address homosexuality in the context of HIV/AIDS for several reasons. She wants to break the connection between sexual orientation and the virus in the minds of her audience. After all, she says, HIV/AIDS is not just a gay issue. The company, she feels, has to make choices between the many pervasive and life-threatening problems that affect the adolescent population. They do so based on what's "up" for the Peer Players, what this particular company can do best, and what they can get away with without jeopardizing the survival of the theatre itself. SPARK, mandated by the board of education to promote drug prevention, must justify everything they do in this context. So their choices—gang violence, AIDS, peer pressure, suicide—all have clear connections to drugs.

SPARK's latest show, in fact, has pulled away from even addressing HIV/AIDS in a sexual context, instead telling the story of a young woman's grief and consequent alcohol abuse at losing her mother to AIDS. This choice was made not because they think it is no longer necessary to address safer sex, but because they could thus completely avoid the restrictions. Moreover, the company wanted to address the growing number of AIDS orphans in the audience.

Teatro Vida, too, is affected by political and economic realities. For example, their HIV/AIDS funding was not continued by the Department of Health. One reason, says Geri Hayes, director of public programs for the Bronx Council on the Arts, is that the conservative trend "is moving away from the whole notion of prevention, of examining and exploring something before it becomes an irreversible issue. Instead of funding conflict resolution, funding goes to jails, after the fact" (Hayes 1995). Fortunately, Teatro Vida's material is quite malleable from one performance to the next, so no matter what theme they are contracted to address, the company can still find ways of responding to the immediate needs of the community. They have, however, been scrambling from contract to contract. Their rehearsals, particularly necessary for the actors as a way of grounding and reconnecting, are infrequent because of their limited funds. They now perform at most twice a week, so that the actors must have other jobs while remaining available for bookings. Their sponsors at the Bronx Council are constantly seeking new avenues for funding, the most creative recent one being working with the youth summer workers at the Bronx Zoo.

Questions and Conclusions

Many questions emerge from this study. What are the results of using inter-activist theatre to intervene in adolescent lives? What remains of the momentary feeling of community, and of the spectators' experience of the moment of "aha"? Is inter-activist theatre a catalyst for change? To phrase it in the most reductive terms, does it work? The answer to—in fact the meaning of—these questions depends on one's frame of reference. A public health practitioner would want to know if this kind of theatre slows the rate of HIV infection. A school social worker might ask whether more conflicts are mediated without violence and whether kids who have been involved in this type of experience are more likely to seek help from a counselor, clinic, or conflict mediator. Yet it is difficult to evaluate this material quantitatively or clinically. For example, since adolescents are not routinely tested for HIV, it is hard to judge the impact of an intervention designed to reduce infection. For this reason there is skepticism among some public health workers about the effectiveness of theatre as a tool in health education. It is often seen as an expensive way to use limited resources that has no readily identifiable immediate results (Ball 1993:235).

Ted Welch suggests that the value of interactive theatre is that it can "touch the whole." The process, he says, affects people's lives beyond the forty-five-minute session. "One student thinking differently is the opening. When you *begin* something here, the change happens" (Welch 1995). He cautions against grandiose ambitions, however. Clearly these interventions are but one element in what needs to be a constellation of efforts that includes collaborations among artists, health educators, the medical community, social workers, and others. Teatro Vida rarely has used audience questionnaires—although they were required to do so by the Department of Health during the HIV/AIDS work—because, according to Hayes, one of the theatre's goals is to break down hierarchies between spectators and the company. She reminds me that their goal is not necessarily to demonstrate or dictate behavior, but to suggest that, "there is another choice and we want to explore it with you."

The SPARK Peer Players, says director Rhonda Paganetti, have done some informal evaluations of their program at the request of the board of education. These consisted of questionnaires in fourteen schools, handed out after performances, specifically focusing on the relationship of the performances to students' further involvement in SPARK programs within the school. The most significant finding, she feels, is that 98 out of 264 students voluntarily identified themselves by name and checked "Please contact me." Also significant was that 242 said they learned that SPARK could help them to help a friend.

This kind of theatre responds to a multitude of needs and functions on many levels. On the most literal level, these companies identify participants' needs and facilitate referral for prevention and treatment, or give participants an opportunity to seek help themselves. They also disseminate specific prevention information.

Beyond this first level, the experience of inter-activist theatre gives participants an opportunity to practice survival in a safe environment without real-life consequences. For example, having said, "You need a condom" to Cool Joey in *End the Silence,* or having participated in trying to heal Ray and Raven's family, the participant is more prepared to respond the next time similar issues arise. The "next times" are likely to occur in heightened emotional states at moments of great stress. The learning experience of inter-activist theatre occurs in parallel conditions of risk, excitement, and the heightened emotions that come with dramatic enactment. However, in this theatre, there are controls. Entering and interacting with the drama, adolescents venture out into an in-between world, experiment with the behaviors and feelings of defeat, illness, violence, and death. They can then retreat, bringing back with them—in their bodies and voices—the memory, which they may be able to access in their daily life. This time, though, they leave behind the sometimes devastating consequences of real-life choices.

The performances of Teatro Vida and the SPARK Peer Players function as a means of recording and validating the struggles of these adolescent lives. No longer secret or singular, their struggles become less frightening, less potent. These performances may also build community recognition of shared experience; the experience of participating together as experts and problem solvers creates, at least temporarily, an empowered community that is respected for having the tools to heal itself. Further, identifying with role models, seeing them make art, and making art themselves may inspire these young people to get involved in other artistic endeavors. These experiences may in turn help them feel less alienated and more apt to care for themselves and others.

The final level is the most mysterious and subtle. This kind of theatre functions to create order out of chaos. These adolescents are in an internal and external state of upheaval and unrest mirrored by this kind of theatre. Some public health practitioners question the appropriateness of programs that seem to encourage aggressive and noisy behavior (Ball 1993:235). In fact, as SPARK performances show, noisy, aggressive behavior is the heart of this work. The conflict and chaos of inner-city adolescence allows theatre to step into this situation and, ironically, to create more conflict and chaos. Underneath the superficial layer of disorder is a new, structured core that allows the participants to do something with the madness rather than become lost in it.

Theatre groups like Teatro Vida and SPARK propose a place to put the chaotic experiences and feelings of adolescence and then draw a boundary around it. Providing a larger, stronger structure around these experiences gives participants permission to let go momentarily of their own boundaries and find a new structure.

The ability to structure and make order out of chaotic experience, independent of any particular content or message, gives participants a feeling of control and allows the space and distance for reflection. These adolescents learn something they could not possibly learn in a lecture or discussion. Perhaps it is not conscious, perhaps it is a memory lodged in the body, of dancing to "Stand Up for Your Life," or of their own voice fighting with Cool Joey or of quietly thinking through the lives of Ray and Raven in the circle of chairs. What they learn may help them survive their own transformation from childhood to adulthood.

Notes

I am deeply grateful to the members of Teatro Vida and the SPARK Peer Players for the work they do and generously opening it to me. Thanks are due to Buz Alexander, Jessie Allen, Todd London, Leslie Satin, and Diedre Sklar for helpful comments on earlier drafts, and to Tim Connor for insightful midnight edits.

1. I am indebted to my colleague, Jan Cohen-Cruz, for illuminating the relationship of activist theatre and social upheaval, for our many discussions about theatre and social change, and for her invaluable contribution as a sounding board throughout this project

2. I observed a number of performances of these two companies between May 1993 and June 1995. All performance descriptions in this essay, unless otherwise attributed, are drawn from these observations.

3. The initial research and development of the Theatre for Adolescent Survival Project (TASP) was supported by a grant from Arthur Imperatore and the Empire State College Foundation. In the fall of 1994 the project convened a community forum, "Theatre for Adolescent Survival: The Use of Theatre in Adolescent AIDS Education," to reflect on the work of theatre in adolescent AIDS prevention. The forum brought together the diverse players interacting in this field: artists, social workers, health educators, physicians, counselors, teachers, and students. Many participants had formerly worked with the Adolescent Theatre Network, founded in 1988. The forum was a committee of the AIDS and Adolescents Network of New York and was run by Cydelle Berlin, of STAR Theatre (Sinai Teen Arts Resources). Forum participants included directors, performers, and teachers from STAR, the Irondale Ensemble, the Greater Brownsville Youth Council, the SPARK Peer Players, Teatro El Puente AIDS Drama Project, THINK International, YAI Raymond Jacobs Educational Theatre, Creative Arts Team, AIDS Theatre Project, Elders Share the Arts, and the New York University Drama Department. Other forum planners and members of TASP include: Katt Lissard, playwright; Thea Martinez, performer, arts educator, and member of Teatro Vida; Jaqui O'Shaughnessy, health educator; and Ted Welch, founder and artistic director of Teatro Vida, Bronx Council on the Arts.

4. Similar figures can be found in other interactive performance, for example, what Augusto Boal calls the Joker, and in psychodrama what Jacob Moreno calls the director and Jonathan Fox calls the conductor.

5. All quotations from Ted Welch, Rhonda Paganetti, and Cheryl Paley come from a series of personal interviews between May 1993 and July 1995, or from my recordings of facilitator/performer/spectator discussions during performances within the same time period

6. For more on TIE structure, see Jackson 1993 and Redington 1983.

7. Both facilitators are aware of the significant issues of power that arise from this situation and try different strategies to address them Because of the structure of Teatro Vida, Welch sees himself as a conduit for the concerns of the audience; in Welch's view, this position helps to blur the racial boundaries somewhat. Paganetti, though somewhat more directive in her facilitation, tries to divest herself of some of her power by "being a bit kookier than the kids expect," by investing the Peer Players with more power during facilitation and depending on them to "catch and respond to" whatever she misses. According to one Peer Player, Paganetti sometimes misses things that come from the audience, which she might have understood better had she shared the audience's cultural background. Paganetti acknowledges that this is a big problem and continues to look for solutions. (For example, she recently suggested that Reggie Woods, the only adult of color in the SPARK Peer Players, cofacilitate; at the time of this writing, this had not yet happened.)

8. *Poor theatre* is a term coined by Polish director Jerzy Grotowski. Although covering an array of styles, poor theatres eliminate any nonessential elements of production, focusing on the actor and the spectator.

9. This first experience with the SPARK Peer Players was, admittedly, somewhat compromised. It was in the context of a festival, each group doing its best twenty minutes. They were performing under pressure and there was some feeling of competition.

10. In December 1991 a fourteen-year-old killed a classmate and wounded a teacher inside Brooklyn's Jefferson High School. In February 1992 two students, both seventeen years old, were shot and killed (Del Barco 1992).

11. All excerpts from SPARK's performances are derived from the company's recording of their scripts and my own performance observations, including stage directions and other descriptive detail. In recorded scripts the spelling reflects the written choices of the company, for example, "kissin' and huggin'." In my own transcriptions of performer/spectator interactions and interviews, I have chosen to use standard English spellings, although I perceived significant divergences and variations from that base.

12. I do not mean to suggest that kids who react emotionally are more likely to be at risk but that SPARK counselors look for behavior that seems somehow incongruous.

13. Initially formed as a bilingual company to address HIV/AIDS and adolescents, Teatro Vida lost its funding from the Department of Health and the Department of Youth Services in 1992. They have since performed through special contracts and have focused on a range of issues—violence, bias, substance abuse, domestic violence—each of which is separately funded by organizations concerned with particular issues.

14. Zerka Moreno is one of the foremost practitioners of psychodrama. Her late husband, Jacob Moreno, was the founder of psychodrama and sociodrama. Jonathan Fox is the founder and director of the Playback Theatre, an interactive company in upstate New York.

15. Welch uses the term *theatre-in-the-moment* to describe any time when theatre is created on the spot. We used this term in the Theatre for Adolescent Survival Project community forum to define the spontaneous theatre projects emerging from conference workshops.

Works Cited

Ball, Steve, D. 1993. "Theatre in Health Education." *In Learning through Theatre: New Perspectives on Theatre in Education.* Ed. T. Jackson. New York: Routledge.

Boal, Augusto. 1985. *Theatre of the Oppressed.* Trans. Charles A. McBride and Maria-Odilio L. McBride. New York: Theatre Communications Group.

Del Barco, Mandelit. 1992. "Teen Held in Brooklyn School Shootings."
    Morning Edition, National Public Radio, WNYC. New York, 27 Feb.
Foster, Douglas. 1994. The Disease Is Adolescence . . . and the Symptoms
    are Violence, Suicide, Drugs, Alcohol, Car Wrecks, and Poverty."
    Utne Reader (July-Aug.): 50–54.
Fox, Jonathan. 1994. *Acts of Service: Spontaneity, Commitment, Tradition
    in the Non-Scripted Theatre.* New Paltz, N.Y.: Tusitala Publishing.
Freire, Paolo. 1968. *Pedagogy of the Oppressed.* Trans. Myra Bergman
    Ramos. New York: Seabury Press.
Grotowski, Jerzy. 1969. *Towards a Poor Theatre.* London: Methuen.
Jackson, Tony, ed. 1993. *Learning through Theatre.* New York: Routledge.
Redington, Christine. 1983. *Can Theatre Teach?* London: Pergamon.

Personal Interviews

Collier, Carlton	A SPARK Peer player, 1995
Hayes, Geraldine	Bronx Council on the Arts, 1995
Martinez, Thea	A Teatro Vida actor, 1994, 1995
Mentrie, Peter	A Teatro Vida actor, 1995
Paganetti, Rhonda	SPARK Peer Players director and facilitator, 1993, 1994, 1995
Paley, Cheryl	Peer Players stage director, 1993, 1994, 1995
Torruella, Jeannette	SPARK Peer player, 1995
Welch, Ted	Teatro Vida director and facilitator, 1993, 1994, 1995
Woods, Reggie	SPARK Peer Players music director, 1995

Straight Talk about Sex

and AIDS in Zambia:

The *Nshilakamona* Radio Drama

P. Stanley Yoder and Kwaleleya Ikafa

Reports from Kitwe say a group of women stormed the ZNBC studios last week to protest against the explicit language used in the weekly Sunday night drama. According to the women, the explicit depiction of "highly sensitive social issues" is not what they expect from a socio-drama meant for the whole family.

Sunday Mail, Lusaka, Zambia, 10 May 1992

According to this excerpt from the Sunday edition of one of Lusaka's main newspapers, these Zambian women objected to the explicit language used in a weekly radio drama in the Bemba language that had been broadcast in Zambia for nine months. This program, called *Nshilakamona*, presented the lives and loves of two urban families and their friends as they went about their daily business of earning a living, raising children, and spending time with friends and neighbors. Combining a focus on dramatic situations (romance, domestic conflicts, teenage rivalries) resembling American soap operas with humorous dialogue similar to sitcoms, the drama showed characters interacting at home, in the street, in bars, at work, and in other public places. The program was broadcast Sunday evenings from August 1991 to June 1992 on the Home Service, the station that carries radio programs in Zambian languages.

This portrayal of contemporary life was produced to educate as well as to entertain. By showing characters as they grapple with issues of sex, money, friendship, loyalty, and the threat of AIDS, program planners working for an American development agency and the Zambian Ministry of Health hoped that listeners would improve their knowledge of HIV and AIDS, would begin discussing the problem among themselves, and would take measures to protect themselves against infection. Yet how can one persuade people of the reality of the risk of infection and, most importantly, that it applies to them specifically? Government officials, politicians, and the public in countries everywhere have reacted to talk about AIDS by first denying that the threat exists, then recognizing that certain groups (prostitutes, intravenous drug users, homosexual men) are at risk, and finally, that while everyone may be vulnerable, they themselves are not.

In addition, health education interventions discussing sex and condom use have provoked resistance by portions of the public everywhere. Reasons for this resistance in Zambia include not only an assertion that such talk would lead to increased sexual activity among the young, but that such talk is simply inappropriate for people who differ in age, gender, and kinship relations. With such concern among the public, how might a program on radio or television in Zambia promote more frank discussions of AIDS and associated issues without offending too many? That was the dilemma faced by those who planned and wrote *Nshilakamona*.

The script writers had three types of decisions to make about the type of language to use and the content of conversations. First, should the dialogue be always standard Bemba, with its rich repertoire of proverbs and allusions for making points indirectly, or "town Bemba," which tends more toward direct speech and slang expressions? About one-third of Zambians speak

Bemba as their first language, and they would all easily follow standard Bemba. But another third of the population speaks town Bemba, and they might miss the subtleties of indirect speech of standard Bemba. Second, how explicit should the program dialogue be about sexual activity in general? Most Zambian radio listeners gather in groups that include not only males and females, but also those of different ages and whose kinship relations demand great discretion in the style and subject of conversations considered appropriate. Nearly 90 percent of the population surveyed reported that they had listened to the radio drama with friends and family. Third, how much should the program talk about condom use? Very few people in Zambia use condoms either for family planning or for protection against HIV transmission.

In this essay we focus on the process of deciding on the kinds of episodes to be written, the incorporation of messages about HIV and AIDS, on the choice of language in the program dialogue, as well as complying with the objectives defined by the funding agency. We seek to show how these decisions were made as script writers drew on the messages to be communicated, on their own experiences with AIDS issues, and on their knowledge of what the public reaction might be. We present evidence from interviews with listeners to the drama showing that the writers opted mostly for town Bemba, that they were fairly direct in their discussions of sexual behavior, and that their suggestions to use condoms for protection against HIV transmission caused a great deal of controversy.

Relevant questions include the following. How does the nature of the language used affect what is heard? Are listeners stimulated to discuss the program, the characters, or the action with friends and neighbors? Do regular listeners to a radio drama acquire new knowledge that might correspond to "messages" that a communication expert would recognize? Do many listeners identify with key characters, and if so, do they then imitate their actions? What should we expect from dramas that entertain in order to educate? By examining the process of producing scripts for recording, the transformations that occurred as the writers worked from the AIDS messages in English to the final dialogue recorded in Bemba, and what listeners recalled about the program compared with the original messages, we hope to shed light on these questions.

Kwaleleya Ikafa served as production director and main script writer for most of the drama, and Stanley Yoder directed the surveys used to evaluate the program. The discussion draws on the experiences of developing and producing the scripts, on results of a survey of a randomly selected sample of adults in Copperbelt and Northern Provinces, and on open-ended interviews with listeners.

The Zambian Context

Zambia is a country of about eight million people just east of Angola and southeast of Zaire in south central Africa. Along with Malawi just next door, eastern Zaire to the north, and Rwanda, Tanzania, and Uganda further north, Zambia has very high rates of HIV infection. The AIDS virus in Zambia is transmitted mainly by heterosexual contact; a very small proportion of transmissions occur perinatally or from blood transfusions. The ratio of infection among men and women is about one to one.

The Zambian population is exceedingly diverse with respect to income, education, literacy, use of media, ethnic identity, and language. About 45 percent now live in towns and cities, most in the urban centers of the copper-mining area or along the railroad. The majority of the rural population earn their living through subsistence farming. The demographic and health survey (DHS) of 1992 found that 60 percent of the population had only some primary schooling, and 20 percent had not been to school at all (Gaisie et al. 1993). English is the language of instruction in schools and of government, but more than seventy languages are spoken in the country.

At the level of self-identification and of official discourse, Zambia is a very Christian nation. When asked about religion by the DHS, 97 percent of the population identified themselves as Christian. Prime-time television often shows pastors from Zambia, South Africa, and the U.S. preaching in an evangelical style similar to Pat Robertson or Jerry Falwell. President Frederick Chiluba even officially declared in 1994 that Zambia was a Christian nation. The newspaper, radio, and television contain programs each day related to religion. Thus public discourse about AIDS can easily take a moralizing tone, that is, beware, for AIDS is transmitted by prostitutes and womanizers.

Government concern about the spread of the AIDS virus in Zambia in the mid-1980s led to the establishment in 1988 of the National AIDS Prevention and Control Programme. With assistance from various donor countries, the Health Education Unit (HEU) of the Ministry of Health has directed or supervised a number of projects that have sought to educate the Zambian public about the threat of AIDS and about ways to avoid infection with the virus. One of those projects was the AIDSCOM project, a technical assistance project financed by the U.S. Agency for International Development, which assisted the ministry from December 1988 to September 1992 in educating health personnel and the public about AIDS. Project activities included developing educational materials, producing a counseling video and manual, conducting formative research about knowledge of AIDS and condom use, assisting in the development of AIDS drama with local theatre groups, and developing a radio drama that incorporated messages about the disease. We are concerned here only with the development of the radio drama.

The core group of individuals who instigated this radio drama included a family planning and communications specialist from Johns Hopkins University working with AIDSCOM, a communications consultant from Zimbabwe hired by AIDSCOM, and the director of the Zambian HEU, a specialist in health education. This group organized the formative research used to choose messages and outline the episodes, arranged for advertising the program, directed the script writers in their work, and arranged for financing all activities. The group also made the decisions about personnel and the timing of the production.

This planning group decided to use radio for health education because it reaches a wider audience than any other mass medium; about two-thirds of men and more than one-half of all women listen to the radio. Zambia has three radio stations for regular broadcasting: the Home Service, which broadcasts in seven Zambian languages; the General Service, which broadcasts largely in English; and Radio Mulungushi, which also broadcasts in English but plays mostly popular music. These stations are all managed by the Zambia National Broadcast Corporation (ZNBC), which also manages the single television station.

Bemba was chosen as the language for the radio drama in part because it is the language most widely spoken in Zambia. Although only about one-third speak Bemba as their first language, about 60 percent of Zambians speak some form of Bemba (Spitulnik 1994). English was not an option; since relatively few people speak English at home, a dialogue in English would not be natural or convincing. People who speak Bemba as their first language speak standard Bemba, which has a great repertory of proverbs and allegorical expressions to talk indirectly about sensitive issues. But many Bemba speakers converse in what is called "town Bemba," a dialect with a simplified grammar and many loan words from English and other languages. Using only standard or traditional Bemba would be less likely to offend anyone, but might not always be understood by those who speak Bemba as a second or third language.

Radio drama in Bemba was not entirely new to Zambians. Since 1978 the Bemba section of ZNBC has produced a weekly program, called *Ifyabukaya,* that presented dramatic episodes each week featuring the same main characters dealing with everyday problems. This program was extremely popular: the survey showed that more people listen to the radio on Wednesday, the day it is broadcast, than other days, and about 40 percent of the sample identified *Ifyabukaya* as their favorite radio program.

Although radio reaches a wider audience than any other medium, radio does not reach nearly everyone in the country. The 1992 survey of adults throughout Copperbelt Province and the three central districts of Northern Province showed that a little more than 40 percent of the sample reported owning a radio, and 60 percent reported listening to the radio (Yoder et al. 1993). About one-fourth of the sample claimed to listen six or seven days a week. Men listen to the radio more than women do, and urban residents listen more often than rural residents.[1]

Radio and television dramas have become increasingly popular as a means for educating the public about health issues in the developing world. Known as the entertainment-education approach, this means of communicating health messages was first used in 1969 to promote family planning in Peru with a television soap opera called *Simplemente Maria* (Nariman 1993). Six more such programs were produced for broadcast in Latin America from 1976 to 1983. In 1984 a television soap opera (*Hum Log*) about family planning was broadcast in India, and other soap operas have followed there. The series of dramatic episodes (*The Family House*) about family planning and other health issues broadcast on Egyptian television from 1987 to 1991 proved extremely popular (Elkamel 1995).

A group of researchers and communication specialists from the Center for Communication Programs at the Johns Hopkins School of Hygiene and

Public Health have used this approach widely for promoting family planning and AIDS messages in developing countries (Lettenmaier et al. 1993). The approach involves careful research into local knowledge of the subject before beginning the program in order to develop messages appropriate to the target audience. This approach assumes that characters in a drama can serve as models for behavior, and that if characters in an entertaining drama decide to change their behavior to avoid the risk of contracting HIV, this may persuade listeners to do the same. The AIDSCOM technical advisors followed this approach in planning the *Nshilakamona* program in Zambia.

Producing the Radio Drama

The process of producing the program included creating realistic characters, planning the dramatic narrative in a realistic fashion, framing the messages, writing the actual dialogue for actors to record, and taping the episodes for broadcast. Not only did the planners and writers have to deal with finding the right language for the public, they also had to reckon with differences in assumptions and experiences with AIDS among the planners, writers and actors, and the public. These differences were negotiated in the writing, producing, and recording of the drama.

Getting Started

The script writers chose the title *Nshilakamona,* in Bemba meaning "I have not yet seen it," in part to draw attention to the lack of public recognition of the presence and threat of the AIDS virus. In deciding what messages to concentrate on, the planners relied on what is current biomedical knowledge about AIDS, and on focus group discussions with Bemba speakers in three cities concerning local knowledge of AIDS and opinions about radio programs. The results of these discussions were used in determining which messages to emphasize and how the story lines should be developed for the drama. The following messages were formulated to guide the script writers:

- AIDS is an important health problem in Zambia.
- You can get AIDS (everyone is at risk).
- You can prevent AIDS.

- Women are no more to blame for the spread of the virus than are men.
- People should talk about AIDS with their spouses and their children.
- Care for people with AIDS, it will not make you sick.
- Condoms protect against infection from the virus.

The first four messages concern general knowledge about AIDS that the planning group wanted the public to acquire. The next two are specific suggestions for action to take as individuals have direct or indirect contact with the disease and people with AIDS. The final message suggests one way to protect oneself against HIV transmission.

The results of the group discussions were used to choose certain themes and characters for the drama. For instance, since some women described their efforts to influence the sexual behavior of their husbands in those groups, the drama included the example of a wife refusing unprotected sex with her husband. Four different story lines were also tested in group discussions for audience reaction. Since the truck driver character proved especially popular, his character was built into the narrative in ways typical of contemporary Zambia.

The scripts for the early episodes were developed from outlines describing the kinds of situations and actions familiar to urban Zambians. At the center of the drama were two Zambian couples, each with a teenage daughter in school, living in Lusaka and confronting everyday situations. The episodes portrayed these characters interacting with each other and with a truck driver and several other friends at home, at school, in bars, in the street, and elsewhere. The concept story lines were developed with these characters and then tested with an audience.

The script writers' task was to properly frame these messages within the narrative in ways faithful to daily experience of the population, to build a story that held listeners' attention in the long run, and at the same time to educate the audience about AIDS and ways to avoid HIV infection. They could draw on not only the results of the group discussions held with Bemba speakers, the AIDS messages mentioned above, and outlines of action prepared by the planning group, but also on their own experience and their knowledge of the public discourse about AIDS. They did not fully share the enthusiasm of the planning group for condom promotion, because they expected that the public would not easily accept them. The script writers and actors knew from their own experience that AIDS was a dangerous and mysterious disease, that people had trouble talking about it directly and were unsure about how to avoid HIV transmission. They were also unsure of how much explicit talk about sex the public would tolerate. The Zambian public knew that AIDS was a fatal disease transmitted through heterosexual sex, but for most AIDS remained associated with a marginal population linked to sexual promiscuity.

Writing the Script

Elijah Mabo, the journalist and radio producer from the Bemba section of ZNBC in Lusaka who produced the *Ifyabukaya* program for so many years, initially took on the role of writer, producer, and director. After he wrote the first four episodes, they were recorded and tested with an audience. Certain adjustments in the typical action were then made to ensure the audience would identify with the characters. With his wonderful sense of humor, Mabo molded the characters as set out in the objectives with remarkable ease and soon had a very interesting drama at hand. Content about AIDS was gradually introduced after the first ten episodes as topics of conversation among the characters.

Program planners first thought they would produce and tape the drama in Lusaka, the capital city, where the best recording studios are located. But it proved impossible to find a group of actors there able to take on the project. There are no salaried theatre companies in Zambia, and even experienced actors are rarely paid for their services. So it was decided to produce the program in Kitwe, a large city situated some two hundred miles to the north, in the heart of Copperbelt Province. Kitwe is home to the Kitwe Little Theatre, an association of clerks, secretaries, office managers, and other workers—amateur actors all—who performed plays in English. Kwaleleya Ikafa, an electrical engineer with the main mining company and also a playwright, theatre critic, and director, agreed to direct the production. Once the actors for the drama were selected, they called themselves the Kitwe Radio Drama Group (KRDG). All members except the director spoke Bemba fluently, though only one spoke Bemba as a first language. Ikafa's theatre experience had all been in English, and his first language, Lozi, bears little similarity to Bemba. He could understand Bemba quite well, but could speak it only a little, and did not write in Bemba at all.

The first cold reading of the scripts from Elijah Mabo was a revelation, for only two members of the cast could deliver lines in Bemba with ease and expression. The rest needed time to rehearse before sounding anything close to convincing. But they had to move quickly, for the advertising machinery was already in motion and the date for launching the broadcast had been set. Although fifteen scripts had been written before any recording took place, only four were completely ready, and they needed six episodes in the can before broadcasting could begin. But the cast soon came to grips with the scripts and began to sound polished, enabling the director to concentrate on the emotions and the mood of the text. Acutely aware of his linguistic constraints with Bemba, Ikafa concentrated more on the structure of the episodes as well as the pace and the rhythm of the action.

As director of the recording process, Ikafa set about cutting and changing scenes in order to dramatically enhance the story in preparation for taping. He found that while the earlier episodes were excellent, later the drama was stifled, the conflict became stale, and the subtlety had disappeared. The planning group had wanted Mabo to actively promote the use of condoms early on. Mabo followed their request and the next batch of scripts featured condoms prominently. Ikafa had the impression that in seeking to insert specific messages about AIDS and use of condoms, Elijah Mabo had sacrificed realistic drama and convincing dialogue.

After some weeks of rehearsing first at the Kitwe Little Theatre and then at someone's house, the KRDG was ready for their first recording session. The AIDSCOM consultant flew in from Zimbabwe for the occasion. This first taping session revealed how far they had come, for the actors were relaxed and very comfortable with their characters. The actors and the director thought everything went like a dream, but the consultant did not share their view. In making changes to the narrative in Kitwe, Ikafa was more concerned about dramatic impact than about messages, and he had not been party to the understandings about plot and messages between Elijah Mabo and the consultants in Lusaka. The consultant was hearing the KRDG version of Mabo's script; it was a far cry from the original script, with its flat and didactic messages.

The issue of final responsibility for the script needed to be resolved quickly to continue production. Ikafa thought he needed to take control of the plot lines in order to introduce the messages as unobtrusively as possible without impeding the dramatic flow. He was already reworking the entire plot of many episodes in order to generate sufficient strings to constitute the subplots through which they could introduce the prescribed messages. Meanwhile, the actors had warmed up to their roles and could ad-lib effortlessly, enhancing dialogue whenever it felt wanting.

Although Ikafa was developing a better understanding of the actors and their individual capabilities, and so felt he could utilize them more proficiently if he were responsible for the plot, he was unable to write in Bemba. So he approached a close friend and colleague, John Katebe, a writer with a reputation as an actor as well, to collaborate in writing the script. Ikafa would write the throughline for the entire series and then generate a detailed plot outline for each episode in English. Katebe would then transform these plot outlines into Bemba scripts.

The planning group accepted this formula, giving Ikafa control over the script, even though they were not sure he fully appreciated the importance of incorporating all the planned messages. Since he was already reworking the scripts with the cast, and the process was taking far too long, it made sense to let him take responsibility for finalizing the production. This arrangement also resolved the administrative problem of physically producing the scripts from Lusaka and then shipping them to Kitwe. Elijah Mabo was clearly overburdened with work and could not really be expected to churn out quality scripts with the level of sensitivity expected. In fact, Mabo was relieved to have the responsibility of writing the scripts lifted from him, for this was an extra assignment for him that had been made part of his normal duties.

Katebe was working as a management consultant trainer with a local company and did his writing with the KRDG in his spare time. He joined the rehearsal sessions and blended in easily, with his natural humor and his way with words. He studied how each actor spoke to enable him to shape dialogue in a way the cast would find most comfortable. The actors often brought experiences from their own lives and pitted them against the demands of the script, identifying what was realistic, what was offensive, and what was unacceptable.

At last they had a workable formula in place for completing the scripts after number 15. Ikafa would write the plot in English, sometimes including actual lines to be spoken. This ensured a balance of humor, substance, and steady progression of the plot. Katebe would then flesh out the script in Bemba to correspond to the twenty-seven-minute time slot of each episode. At first this was by trial and error, but soon he could predict fairly accurately the length of the dialogues. This arrangement freed Ikafa to concentrate fully on plot development.

Recording the Program

Since the recording studios at Kitwe were inadequate, the technical finishes had to be done in Lusaka. The only sound effect available at the Kitwe studio was a door that opened and closed. Furthermore, the studio staff in Kitwe was not familiar with radio drama techniques and had to go through a learning process together with the actors. A studio technician would be assigned to every recording session, but just as one got the hang of it, a different one would be assigned for the next session, and it would be back to square 1. On completion of a recording session the tape would be "piped" to Lusaka studios via a microwave channel. Elijah Mabo would then add other sound effects, signature tunes, and other trimmings before it was ready for broadcast.

The KRDG felt apprehensive about launching the program, for once they had begun there would be no turning back. They wondered if they could stay together as a cast for a year, and if they could hold the listeners every Sunday night for thirty-nine consecutive weeks. But with six recorded episodes ready, and scripts going up to episode 15, they were ready for the launch. The preparations had taken about four months.

The group of actors set a target of completing one script each week in order to have a sufficient number of recorded episodes in case of unexpected problems. But soon the insurance scripts had dwindled to almost nothing, and the group struggled from week to week getting episodes recorded for broadcast. A hastily prepared plot line would be frantically discussed over the phone with Katebe, who would scribble bits and pieces during his lunch break at work. Ikafa would pick up the handwritten script later in the afternoon in time for the recording session late that evening. The first hour of the three-hour recording session would be spent rehearsing that single handwritten script. Typing and photocopying had become a luxury they could not afford, and time had become precious. They had to have a recorded episode in the can or else there would be no broadcast that week.

Ikafa drove the cast hard and the recording sessions became very tense affairs, for they all felt under immense pressure. Perhaps their closest call came after some weeks of recording when they had no recorded episode in hand on a Wednesday for broadcast on the following Sunday evening. The actress playing the role of Peggy, daughter of the Shulas, had suddenly been fired from her regular job and had left town. In desperation, the actress who played the role of Mable offered to double in the role of Peggy. They quickly rearranged a scene in which the two characters had to talk to each other. After that experience the group managed to pick up the pace of recording episodes and they were able to maintain the broadcast without any interruptions over the nine month period.

Synopsis of *Nshilakamona*

The main plot of the drama centered on the homes of two families: the Shulas and the Bwalyas. Both the Shulas and the Bwalyas have a teenage daughter in high school. The Bwalyas have a new baby who is quite ill. The other characters are a local taxi driver, a long-distance truck driver, and a divorced man who is apparently unemployed. The main characters were:

Davies and Mable Bwalya, with daughter Grace
Chongo and Joyce Shula, with daughter Peggy
Peter Bulimbo, friend of Chongo Shula, divorced, unemployed
Mulenga Mawilo, taxi driver, who befriends both of the girls
Kangwa Mutale, truck driver, drinking companion of Shula and
    Bulimbo

The Bwalyas are a very close and communicative family consisting of Davies Bwalya, his wife, Mable, their teenage daughter, Grace, and a new baby. Bwalya's only blemish is a brief extramarital relationship he had with a girl who has long since died of what he now believes could have been AIDS. Although now a responsible husband and parent, he is constantly haunted by his past. It was intended that the listeners should identify with this man as a role model in society—he attends church, has a steady job, is well respected—and yet had succumbed, albeit only once in his life, to one small indiscretion that now threatens the entire fabric of his household.

Bwalya is not sick and has no symptoms of the virus. He chides his worldly male friends about their promiscuity and immorality, often quoting texts from the Bible. He need not divulge his one little dark secret. But his baby is sick and has been sickly since birth. Mable, the mother, is perplexed. What is "eating" the child? She has everything else a woman could wish for. A good home, good husband, a good Christian upbringing. What is wrong? Why is God punishing her? She is determined to get to the bottom of all this.

The mystery was planned to unravel in three distinct stages for the entire run of thirty-nine episodes, broken down as follows:

Stage 1: The Bwalya home is portrayed as happy and stable.
Stage 2: The mystery of the Bwalya's sick baby raises tension in the family. Bwalya becomes irrational and evasive.
Stage 3: The past catches up with Bwalya and he is forced to reveal his secret to his family.

The writers intended that listeners empathize with Davies Bwalya and get to love him to the point that when his little indiscretion is revealed, he is forgiven and listeners feel sorry for him. This was deliberately intended to counter the stigma associated with AIDS sufferers, who are shunned by society and looked down upon as having brought this upon themselves. The writers hoped to show that "model citizens" are also vulnerable to the AIDS virus.

In sharp contrast to the Bwalyas, the Shulas are a very unsettled family. Chongo Shula, the head of the family, is constantly broke and frequently drunk. His wife, Joyce, also known as Bana Peggy (mother of Peggy), is headstrong and outspoken. She fights with her husband when he is drunk and unreasonable. She refuses to feed him when he brings no money for food; and most daring of all, she demands that he use condoms after she suspects that he is seeing other women. She declares her rule: use a condom or have no sex with her.

Chongo Shula is astounded and is initially too embarrassed to tell even his friends. In his tradition it is unthinkable for a woman to behave in such a manner. That listeners accept this scenario as other than ludicrous was problematic. There was a danger that the drama might degenerate into a farce. Yet from the "message" point of view, Joyce's action was essential. After all, the tragedy of AIDS infection is that all too often the submissive and trusting wife gets it from the roving partner and might pass it to future offspring. It was essential for her own survival that she feel empowered to protect herself since she had reason to suspect that her husband was sleeping around. The script writers and actors were conscious of the danger of appearing to incite all women to become, in the traditional sense, disrespectful to their husbands. They were risking alienating the very people they wanted to reach and being branded "anticultural." How could they resolve this dilemma?

The writers found the solution in the identity of one of the actresses. The outstanding actress playing the role of Joyce Shula displayed a wide range of emotion and intensity in her speech. Her rough voice was a tonic and superb for heated arguments with her husband. Being originally from Zimbabwe, however, she spoke Bemba with a heavy accent, which identified her as a foreigner. Furthermore, Zimbabwean women are generally perceived in Zambia to be rather strongwilled and dominant compared to their Zambian counterparts. The writers turned this apparent handicap into an advantage, for as an outsider not in tune with Zambian traditions it was more acceptable for Joyce to be different.

The Shulas' teenage daughter, Peggy, goes to school with Grace, the Bwalyas' daughter. The turbulence in Peggy's home is reflected in her poor schoolwork. Being neglected and always short of money makes her vulnerable to Mawilo, a young, fun-loving taxi driver whose major aim in life seems to be to sleep with as many young girls as possible. They have to be schoolgirls, he argues, "because they are still young and therefore don't have AIDS."

Although best friends in the same class, Peggy and Grace are polar opposites. Grace is an excellent student, always at the top of her class. As a sensible and responsible daughter and a role model for young schoolgirls, she is swift to put off advances by the likes of Mawilo and does not hesitate to put him in his place. Most important of all, she communicates with her mother, even to the extent of confiding in her when she suspects that her friend Peggy is getting money from Mawilo for sexual favors.

Chongo Shula and Davies Bwalya are close friends at home and at work, but the two do not travel in the same social circles. Shula cultivates a circle of drinking mates: Peter Bulimbo, Mulenga Mawilo, and Kangwa Mutale. Bulimbo is an obnoxious man whose marriage ended in divorce. He encourages Shula to keep his wife under his thumb, to beat her if necessary. His unsavory habits include sleeping with other men's wives when their husbands are at work. Mawilo, the taxi driver, is an impressionable young man who idolizes the older rascals. He often assists Bulimbo with transport in his escapades. Kangwa Mutale is a truck driver who travels all over southern Africa and brings back stories of his many travels, bragging that he has women in the all the major cities. He even reveals the secret of his protection from the various venereal diseases floating around: use of condoms.

Mawilo eventually gets into trouble with Shula and Bwalya for pursuing their daughters. After hearing that both Davies Bwalya and his wife might have AIDS, Mawilo decides he must protect himself against HIV infection, but it remains unclear whether he will follow through. During the eighth month of the broadcast Shula, too, claims he has changed: he will be kind to his wife, take care of his daughter, and stop picking up women in bars. Knowing Shula, however, listeners were left with doubts about whether he would follow through on his declaration. At about the same time, Bwalya agrees to be tested for HIV, persuaded by his wife and by his fear that he might be getting AIDS.

Bulimbo is portrayed as a cynic. He laughs at Mutale for using a condom and ridicules its use to anyone who will listen, including his own bar cronies. It was these bar discussions about the condom that caused such an uproar among listeners and that led women to march on the Kitwe studio. The discussions about men picking up women were carried on in the sexually explicit language of a typical Lusaka bar. Unfortunately, this language is also demeaning to women who are frequent subjects of bawdy jokes, and is clearly unacceptable to a family-listening audience.

Shaping the Narrative

For each weekly episode Ikafa wrote from four to eight scenes in English for Katebe to translate into a dialogue in Bemba. Each scene consists of a descriptive paragraph of both speech and action. The level of detail and direction can be seen in the following examples.

This scene from episode 20 takes place at the Shulas' home, where their daughter, Peggy, has been in recent trouble with her parents. Mawilo the taxi driver had been trying to seduce Peggy.

> Shulas' home. Peggy arrives with the meat from Mawilo. She explains that she has won a competition at the Anti-AIDS Club and used the money to buy some meat as a way of apologizing for her bad behavior.

Joyce is very pleased with her daughter and praises her. Peggy takes advantage of the good will and asks if she can be allowed to stay up late the following day so she can watch a film that's being arranged by the Anti-AIDS Club.

In fact, Peggy lies about where she got the meat since she does not want her parents to know about Mawilo. She tries to pass as virtuous by claiming she has been participating in Anti-AIDS Club activities, clubs formed to help students discuss HIV/AIDS in some Zambian high schools.

In episode 26 Davies Bwalya and his wife, Mable, discuss their situation. Their baby has been hospitalized and diagnosed as having AIDS:

At the Bwalya home conversation now becomes more serious. Mable says she stopped by the hospital to see the baby and was told they should both consider being tested for HIV. Bwalya is dumbfounded.

Bwalya and Mable continue their intense discussion as the next episode opens. Mable insists on going to be tested, but Bwalya obstinately refuses.

In episode 34 Mable and Bwalya are again talking about their baby and their daughter, Grace:

Bwalya is sleeping. Mable wakes him up and says they have got to talk, their family is falling apart. He has refused to permit her to go mourn her sister's child and has refused her permission to continue working at the market. "Grace has started to get involved with men and now we can't even talk to her. The baby is dying and who knows, maybe we are also dying. We are sleeping in separate rooms, my husband, we have to do something about ourselves, we must be strong and pull ourselves through. The world is not over yet," Bwalya laments, "this world is cruel."

John Katebe followed such descriptions of specific scenes in writing the dialogue. Although the overall narrative progression was already set, Katebe had a great deal of latitude in both interpreting these directions and in setting the tone and language to be used. There was relatively little improvisation once the dialogue was written.

The writers made the scenarios more believable by inserting snippets of current events into the dialogue. Topical stories from the newspapers would be incorporated during the recording sessions while they were still reasonably fresh to add to the authenticity of the story. This heightened the interest of the listeners, for they enjoyed hearing their favorite characters talking about current events.

As mentioned earlier, the planning group had insisted that the drama dwell a great deal on the issue of condom use. In keeping with the idea of modeling behavior, the program needed a change agent, a character who would initially not use condoms but would later change his mind. Both Mawilo and Shula at least talked about reforming their behavior. The writers also had to introduce specific information on condom use. The drama was clearly functioning as a catalyst for discussing issues that were generally regarded as taboo. In responding to this concern, more explicit language was used in the dialogue, language that some people found embarrassing. As a result, some parents were finding it difficult to listen to the program with their children. A group of women felt obliged to publicly protest the use of explicit language by marching on the radio studios in Kitwe in May 1992, the ninth month of the broadcast. They felt the drama had gone too far. The studio director assured them they would not hear any more bar discussions, and they were mollified.

As the plot progressed the planning group asked that someone in the Bwalya family die of AIDS in order to underscore the possible consequences of even just one small indiscretion. Ikafa was very uncomfortable with this particular instruction, for he had grown to love these characters, and so had thousands of listeners. Who was he to condemn them to death? The baby was the obvious candidate, being already sick. Since everyone was expecting the baby to eventually die, this was a great opportunity for a twist to the story. The baby was kept alive right up to episode 38, and the planning group was not impressed. So Ikafa had to make up for it in the final episode, which has women wailing uncontrollably in the last scene. Perhaps the baby has died after all; perhaps not. Listeners were left with a cliffhanger for the next series, should there ever be one.

Responses of Listeners

The program launch was widely publicized by a firm contracted to generate newspaper advertisements as well as radio and television spots. Letters from the HEU had been written to church leaders asking them to announce the program to their parishioners. Three days before the launch an ad in the major newspapers displayed the following text next to the face of a young woman looking pensively at the reader:

Nshilakamona: An exciting new Zambian radio drama that portrays the ups and downs of an average Zambian family, on Radio 1 in Bemba every Sunday at 20:30 hours starting August 25. Don't miss it—radio entertainment at its best!

Survey Interviews with the Public

Yoder directed two surveys of the adult population of Copperbelt Province and three districts of Northern province, both areas where Bemba is the principal language spoken.[2] These surveys were designed to evaluate the impact of the radio drama on the Zambian public of these regions. The first survey interviewed 1,613 men and women, aged fifteen to forty-five years, just before the broadcasts began, and the second survey of 1,682 adults of the same age occurred just after the broadcasts ended. Men and women were asked about their knowledge of AIDS, their behavior, and their recent radio-listening habits. The second survey included the questions from the first survey plus questions about their having listened to the radio drama and what a person might have learned from the program. Comparison of responses to both surveys showed changes in both knowledge and behavior during the period between the two surveys, but it was not possible to attribute those changes to the radio broadcast alone (Yoder, Hornik, and Chirwa 1996).[3]

The second survey found that although slightly more than one-half of the sample population had heard of the *Nshilakamona* program, less than one-half of the sample reported having ever listened. Less than one-third were regular or recent listeners. Table 1 shows the responses of those who had ever heard of the program to four separate questions about listening to the program from the survey conducted just after the drama had ended. Those with better access to radio were more likely to listen than those with less access. Men had better access than women, and urban residents had better access than rural residents. However, if access to radio is

TABLE 1	Exposure to *Nshilakamona*	
	Percentage of entire sample	Percentage among those who had listened at all
Ever heard of *Nshilakamona*	53	—
Ever listened to *Nshilakamona*	45	—
Listened in the past two months	32	71
Listened two or more times in past month	29	63
Listened "very often" or all the time	12	25
	N=1682	N=759

equalized among men and women, women were more likely to listen than men. This suggests that the program may have appealed more to women than to men.

The persons who reported having listened to the radio drama at all (N=759, 45 percent) in the survey were asked if they had talked about the program to others or asked others to listen. Two-thirds of this group had discussed the program with others, and 55 percent of men and 62 percent of women said they had asked others to listen. As mentioned earlier, most people (88 percent) listened to the program in the company of family or friends; thus discussion was very common.

Listeners were also asked in a format that allowed for more than one answer to say what a person could have learned from the program. Table 2 shows the responses for the entire sample, as well as responses from men and from women. Considering the entire sample, the first five items were mentioned by from 20 percent to 40 percent of listeners: sleeping around is dangerous, ways that AIDS is transmitted, parents must be careful in raising their daughters, AIDS is a very bad disease, and AIDS is transmitted through having sex. Four of the five items mentioned most frequently relate to AIDS in some way.

However, separating male and female responses showed significant differences in what they reported as lessons learned from the program. From one-third to one-half of the women responded as follows: they mentioned

TABLE 2	Things a person could learn from the radio drama		
	All (percent)	Men (percent)	Women (percent)
Sleeping around is dangerous	37	39	35
Ways that AIDS is transmitted	36	24	54
Parents must be careful in raising daughters	28	20	40
AIDS is a very bad disease	25	29	16
AIDS is transmitted through having sex	22	12	33
You should have only one sexual partner	17	21	13
Drinking can have bad consequences	17	11	24
Condoms prevent AIDS transmission	17	19	16
	N=759	N=421	N=338

some way that AIDS is transmitted, said parents must be careful in raising their daughters, noted that sleeping around is dangerous, said AIDS is transmitted through having sex. Four items were mentioned more than twice as often by women than by men: citing a way AIDS is transmitted, parents being careful in raising daughters, AIDS is transmitted through sex, and drinking can have bad consequences. Two of these four items have nothing directly to do with AIDS, but rather concern the lack of male responsibility. Since women assume more caretaking responsibilities in the home than do men, and they sometimes suffer the consequences of their husband's drinking, it is not surprising that they should mention the issue of raising daughters and the effects of drinking as program lessons.

Thus women focused on somewhat different aspects of this radio drama than did men. They clearly were more concerned about how HIV is transmitted than were men, and in general named more items that could have been learned. The two most frequent male responses were that sleeping around is dangerous and that AIDS is a very bad disease. While the contrast in the responses of men and women may derive in part from differences in their lived experience, it may also reflect different ways of discussing the subjects of sex, AIDS, and individual responsibility.

While the large sample survey was under way, open-ended interviews were also conducted with seventy-nine individuals (forty-one men and thirty-eight women) who had followed the program regularly. These listeners were asked how they had heard about the program, who listened with them, what they thought about the language used and about the characters, whether they had ever used a condom, and what they had learned from the program.

More than half of those interviewed had heard about the program on the radio before it began, and many had heard about it from friends and neighbors. Almost everyone listened with their family or friends; only two persons said they listened alone. Listeners were attracted to the program because it was in Bemba, because they identified with the characters, they found them humorous, or they wanted to find out what happened next. A woman from Ndola stated, "I came to be interested in the program because of all the funny characters, like Mawilo and Bana Peggy, and normally the program depicted a real picture of what is going on in our society." A man from Ndola reported listening because "the program left me with a lot of expectations each time an episode ended, making me start wondering what happened in the next episode."

Listeners had no trouble whatsoever understanding the language used. This is significant because one-third of the large sample spoke a language other than Bemba at home, and because some speak standard Bemba while others speak town Bemba. Nearly everyone said the program used town Bemba rather than traditional Bemba, most likely because of the crude language used when men were conversing in bars. Several noted that if standard Bemba had been used, only adults could have understood the language. For that reason some suggested that traditional Bemba be used to talk about sex. One woman noted, "I didn't have difficulties with the language but tradition makes it offensive to talk about sex with people not in our peer group. It is sometimes easier to say sensitive issues in broken English or in a humorous way, it makes things lighter for the audience."

Because of the sensitive nature of talking about sex and condom use, listeners were asked if the program's language was too explicit. Most thought the language was appropriate. However, about one-fourth said they were sometimes embarrassed to be listening to the program with children or younger relatives when the program talked about sex and/or condoms. As one man remarked, "Discussions on sex were presented regardless of the age group. This made me walk away in embarrassment when my children asked certain questions which I could not answer." As another man put it, "The fact that the characters were so direct in their expression made some people uncomfortable and therefore they thought the program insulting, when in fact it was not."

Listeners' comments about the overall program and the characters demonstrated that they clearly understood the narrative and the contrasts in characters' behavior. They easily followed the difference between the two husbands (Shula and Bwalya), were all critical of the behavior of the taxi driver and his friend, and many noted the neglect of the two daughters by their parents. Listeners talked about the consequences of three types of harmful behavior: sexual promiscuity, excessive drinking, and failure to properly support one's daughters.

When asked if the program reflected life in Zambia, virtually everyone said that everything that took place on the program occurs in Zambia today. The characters seemed familiar to nearly everyone. The one unrealistic aspect of the program was having a wife ask her husband to use a condom with her. Listeners reported that this simply would not happen.

Several listeners thought that children and young people should not hear about condom use at all. About a dozen people objected to any talk about condoms on the radio, for they associate condoms with sexual promiscuity. A man who is a deacon in a church said, "Condoms are used by bachelors and prostitutes after drinking beers." These people said condoms would never be used by a husband with his wife, saying it is just not how things are done in Zambia. Five people, however, reported that they do use condoms for family planning.

The listeners did indeed understand the relationship between having lots of sexual partners and increased risk of contracting HIV, but this may have been well assumed before the program began. They distinguished between characters that acted responsibly and those that did not. Seven men said they had changed their behavior (no more girlfriends, only one sexual partner, no more drinking) after listening to the program. One woman said she had asked her husband to use a condom with her.

What can be concluded about how well listeners to this program understood the messages formulated at the outset about the dangers of AIDS? If we assume that asking listeners in a survey or in a more open-ended format provides credible evidence about this issue, we must conclude that what listeners gained from the program did not coincide perfectly with these original messages. Messages about how to prevent HIV transmission, when condoms should be used, that everyone is at risk for AIDS, that women are no more to blame than men, and that one can care for a person with AIDS without getting sick were not often mentioned. This does not necessarily imply that listeners did not understand those messages, for they may have been assimilated in a different form, or simply heard and judged not as important as the ones actually cited. The expectation that listeners should be able to repeat the messages formulated by program planners most likely stems from the way communication programs are often evaluated, programs that use jingles or songs as part of their presentation. Evaluations of such programs often rely on the ability of the public to repeat those jingles or songs to measure program reach. We should not expect that listeners to a program such as *Nshilakamona* would necessarily repeat specific messages as originally formulated since each listener interprets what was heard in terms of his or her own experience.

The issue of what ideas were retained is relevant because health educators and communication experts often talk about communicating specific "messages" to a target audience. They stress the importance of doing research to determine what messages will fit best with the audience, as well as what channels are most appropriate. This discourse implies that messages are discrete units of knowledge that are received and then may affect behavior. There is evidence in the literature to show that this can occur if the messages give information necessary to take action, such as when a project promoting the vaccination of children announces when and where to bring children. But when messages take the form of declarations about the world or about individuals, such as "everyone is at risk for AIDS," or "it is safe to care for people with AIDS," such a result seems improbable.

There are many reasons to consider such expectations as problematic. The process described of moving from short messages in English to the final recording in Bemba entails a series of transformations in concepts and language involving numerous linguistic and artistic judgments. The planning team and script writer agreed on a sequence of recommended actions involving the main characters that guided the narrative of this drama. But listeners interpreted what was heard in terms of their own experience and assumptions, as shown by the fact that the lessons learned by men and women differed. In addition, the assumptions about individual responsibility and the possibility of control over one's own life that underlay the original messages may not have been shared by the Zambian public.

Judging from listeners' comments, the script writers and actors seem to have included just enough references to sex and condoms to show the dangers of risky behavior and offend only a minority of their audience. It remains unclear whether the straight talk or more metaphorical speech proves most effective in communicating health messages. Might a proverb resonate longer with people than a direct declaration? Is getting people to think and talk more about AIDS evidence of program effectiveness, or should we expect more in terms of behavior change? Or are messages about AIDS so important that we should not be too concerned about evaluating effectiveness per se, since any intervention that produces a small change in risky behavior is worth the effort?

It is extremely difficult to judge the effects of such a program on the behavior of listeners in the long run, both because such programs are broadcast to populations that have many sources of information about AIDS and because the effects may take time to develop. The planning group and script writers together produced a program with wide appeal. It seems clear that the program provoked discussions about AIDS and condoms among listeners, since most people gathered in groups to follow the broadcasts, and more than half of those interviewed reported asking others to listen. That in itself is an important achievement. It is not known whether people have "modeled" their behavior after one or more of the characters, and hopefully one of the positive models. What is clear, however, is that the process of writing and producing such a radio drama involves a multitude of judgment calls about language, images, narrative forms, and character development that demand extraordinary skill and accurate understandings of the intended audience. These judgments made during production are particularly delicate with programs that seek to educate and entertain at the same time.

Kwaleleya Ikafa was the guiding spirit behind the activities of the Kitwe Little Theatre productions in Copperbelt Province for many years. He was a dear friend and artistic inspiration to many persons in Kitwe, Ndola, Lusaka, and Johannesburg. Ikafa died of AIDS in South Africa in 1996. We all deeply mourn his passing.

1. Radio listening varied sharply by gender and residence in the population. While 83 percent of urban men and 63 percent of rural men listened at all to the radio, only 64 percent of urban women and 41 percent of rural women listened. The contrasts in the percentage of those who listened often (six or seven days a week) are similar. While 38 percent of urban men and 26 percent of rural men listened often, only 28 percent of urban women and 12 percent of rural women listened often to the radio. The factors that affect ownership and exposure to radio also affect exposure to the radio drama.

2. Each of the nine provinces in Zambia is divided into Census Supervisory Areas (CSAs), which are divided into Standard Enumeration Areas (SEAs). A CSA has from three to five SEAs, and an SEA has from 50 to 140 households. The sample for both surveys was chosen in a three-stage process: random choice of the CSAs throughout Copperbelt Province and in the three central districts (Kasama, Chinsali, Mpika) of Northern Province; random choice of one SEA per CSA; random choice of households within the designated SEA. Usually ten men and ten women were interviewed within each SEA. For detailed information about the sampling and the surveys conducted see Yoder, Hornik and Chirwa 1993.

3. The population had numerous ways to learn about AIDS in the time between the surveys. Not only was there a television series about AIDS (*Talking AIDS*) broadcast, but AIDS-prevention clubs were active in many high schools, newspaper articles discussed the disease, brochures were distributed, discussions were held in businesses, and radio and television programs mentioned the problem frequently. The fact that the evaluation did not find evidence that positive changes were due to the radio drama alone does not imply that the program failed to have an impact. It suggests, rather, that we

should not expect a single source of AIDS messages operating in a context with multiple sources of information to be responsible for major changes.

Works Cited

Elkamel, Farag. 1995. "The Use of Television Series in Health Education." *Health Education Research* 10 (2):225–232.

Gaisie, Kwesi, Anne R. Cross, and Geoffrey Nsemukila. 1993. *Zambia Demographic and Health Survey.* Lusaka. University of Zambia; Columbia, Md: Macro International Inc.

Lettenmaier, C., S. Krenn, W. Morgan, A. Kols, and P. Piotrow. 1993. "Africa: Using Radio Soap Operas to Promote Family Planning." *Hygie* 12 (1):5–10.

Nariman, Heidi N. 1993. *Soap Operas for Social Change.* Westport, Conn.: Praeger.

Spitulnik, Debra A. 1994. "Radio Culture in Zambia: Audiences, Public Words, and the Nation-State." Ph.D. diss., University of Chicago.

Yoder, P. Stanley, Robert Hornik, and Ben C. Chirwa. 1993. *Impact of a Radio Drama about AIDS in Zambia: A Program Called Nshilakamona.* Philadelphia, Pa.: Center for International, Health, and Development Communication, Annenberg School for Communication, working paper 1013.

——.1996. "Evaluating the Program Effects of a Radio Drama about AIDS in Zambia." *Studies in Family Planning* 27 (4):1–16.

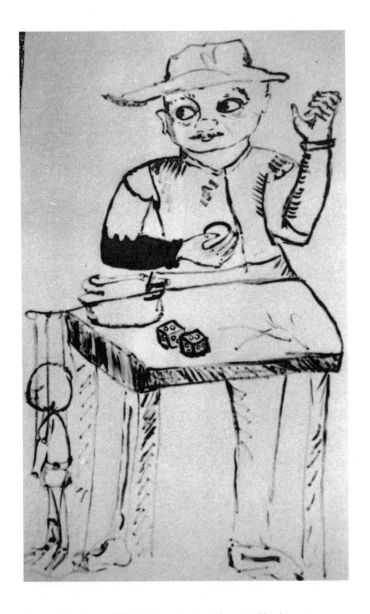

Set panel for *Piece of Wood*. From a tarot card, painted by the cast.

Piece of Wood:

Creating Pinocchio in

Community Mental Health

David Dan

PINOCCHIO: How can you be real if you let other people tell you what to do? These people—look around you [*gesturing to audience*]—they're not real. They're sheep, they do as they're told, working on someone else's schedule, missing all the wonder and passion of their lives, sacrificing themselves—for what? They're the wooden cogs, they're the puppets! (*Piece of Wood* 1992)

This text tells a story, a story of the process whereby a group of people—staff and clients of a community mental health center in the Philadelphia area where I had worked for some years—rewrote and performed the story of "Pinocchio." This story includes the initiation of the project, the dramaturgical challenges we faced, some of the clinical challenges that arose, and our discoveries about the meaning of the tale, including an exploration of Pinocchio's roots in commedia dell'arte, tarot, and Renaissance thought. Our story also talks about the joys and stresses of production, the creation of community through theatre, and reflects on the meaning of the process through its denouement. But perhaps we should return to the beginning: "Once upon a time there was a king . . . no, no, not a king, but a piece of wood." So begins the authentic Pinocchio, Collodi's Pinocchio. Not with a kindly Swiss clockmaker longing for a son, but with a freak of nature, a wood imp—but that's not how we'll begin today.

"Once upon a time there was a community mental health system"—no, not a system, but pieces, scattered, decomposing—no, that's not it.

"Once upon a time there was mental illness"—no, not madness, but a language, a state of mind, a contribution—no, that's too radical.

"Once upon a time there was a group of people who came together"— no, that too came later.

In the beginning was the discovery that the original tale of Pinocchio— written by Carlo Collodi in the early 1880s as a serial for a weekly children's magazine—was ribald and satirical, with obvious roots in commedia; it was like Shakespeare, all character and action. The tale had been debauched by Disney, planned and fitted to the clean-living suburban parents of the 1950s. I wanted to stage it, but in a style closer to Collodi's original narrative. I brought the idea to my friend and colleague in New York with whom I had worked off and on in community theatre over some years, thinking we could produce it together. But he demurred. Do it yourself, he said, do it with the people in your agency. That was an intriguing idea, more daring and ambitious than I had imagined.

Soon afterward a therapist told me she had confronted a client with the admonition to stop lying lest she become like Pinocchio. Another told me of a moving description of a patient longing to be "real." "I don't know what that means, I feel like Pinocchio," said the patient. The call of serendipity seemed clear, and I decided to take my friend's advice. So I broached the idea to my colleagues at the community mental health agency, and they were willing to explore the possibility of staging a play. At the very least, this would be an unusual therapeutic opportunity, an exploration in community mental health, discovering strengths, insights, and common themes among us through the exegesis and performance of a text.

I began by distributing a leaflet to all the therapists and clients associated with our agency advertising a meeting to discuss the tale. Much to my surprise, we drew a large crowd. We passed around copies of Collodi's original book in translation and read portions out loud. "This is Pinocchio?" they asked.

I was not aware of it then, but we were embarking on this project at the closing of an era, a time when community mental health had been able to combine social critique with relationship- and community-building among those labeled mentally ill. It was an era when the voices of the disenfranchised were striving for legitimacy, and community mental health provided a forum as a place to heal. But just as the glacial age is preceded by the unseen melting of the polar caps, so we were beginning to recognize the change in climate and context that would soon fall upon us. From the west came biopsychiatry and its assertions that pharmaceuticals mattered most in the treatment of mental illness. From the east came advocates, families of the mentally ill, who were skeptical of the self-serving nature of mental health professionals and the process of therapy itself in the treatment of serious mental illness. From the north came the managed-care tycoons anxious to make money through privatization, uninterested in social critique, and befuddled by the nature of therapy. If treatment effect could not be measured, how could it be financed? And from the south came the mean-spirited politicians who longed for limits on public spending: in welfare, education, healthcare, mental healthcare, and urban renewal. Anything that benefitted the poor had to be curtailed, including those poor who are over-represented in the diagnostic category known as schizophrenia.

Perhaps I was becoming frustrated that therapy as it was developing could not meet the challenges aggressively enough, or maybe the story of Pinocchio reminded me too much of the situation just described. In any case, it seemed an excellent opportunity for community mental health to loosen the tie and shed the pinstriped suit of Science, which was much too tight a fit, and put on instead the mothballed buffoonery and ridiculously big shoes of Art.

The Pinocchio of Collodi

In the original work, Gepetto carves a piece of wood to create a puppet that he hopes to exploit to make a fortune, but the character he carves turns out to be far more than he can handle. The entire story, in fact, is a combination of episodic plots serialized for weekly magazine reading: an endless rambling series of quixotic adventures designed, in the finest nineteenth-century tradition, to meet the economic needs of the author. All sorts of creatures as well as people become animated and participate in Pinocchio's misadventures. The episodes include disquieting representations of human nature, particularly as revealed in the ironically named institutions of Justice, Education, and Healing.

The narratives begin with the discovery of a piece of wood by a pauper named Antonio. However, when he discovers the wood talks, he is almost done in psychologically by the experience. His "colleague" and adversary Gepetto then arrives, always in search of easy money. After fierce arguments and fighting provoked by the talking wood, Gepetto takes the wood away. Each thinks he has outsmarted the other.

The next chapters deal with the relationship between Gepetto and this piece of wood, as the former discovers that, inveterate rascal though he might be, he is no match for this whining, manipulative, sociopathic piece of pine. Gepetto carves him and clothes him, gives him his only food, and sells the literal shirt off his back to get him money for schoolbooks, while the wood that has become Pinocchio focuses primarily on his own momentary gratification. Pinocchio takes round advantage of the old man, exposes him as a fool, and a sentimental one to boot. Nonetheless, as this part of the story ends, Gepetto has changed. He has gained something that Pinocchio cannot yet even imagine: the ability to love.

In the extended series of episodes that follows, it becomes clear that Pinocchio's guile is inadequate to handle the characters he meets; though he has bedeviled Gepetto, he is no match for the world outside the cottage. Fox and Cat are his special nemeses: they trick him out of money, hang him, and leave him for dead, then return and fleece him again. When Pinocchio finally realizes how he has been victimized, he protests to the authorities and finds, to his great surprise, that he himself is imprisoned.

Meanwhile, he has met the Blue Fairy, first in the guise of a sister, a peer, who is ghastly and morbid and obsessed with death. She is far from the kindly, angelic antiseptic blonde of the Disney movie. It is she who saves him from hanging, calling in doctors who are nothing but idiotic-sounding birds. She gives him medicine that saves his life, but he finds that when he lies to her, his nose grows. In gratitude to her he decides he will really go to school and make his father proud.

Then comes another series of misadventures, culminating in the boy's discovery that Gepetto, while searching for him, has been swallowed by the Dogfish. Pinocchio meets the Blue Fairy again, this time as an older woman, a mother figure, and he becomes an ideal pupil despite the cruel hazing a wooden puppet is bound to get. He is subsequently dissuaded from his studies by one Candlewick, who prevails upon Pinocchio to join him in Playland. Off they go on a midnight ride to a world of constant recreation, where there is school only on Thursdays, and it is never Thursday. Soon they are changed into donkeys, and treated brutally. While they are being dunked in the ocean in preparation for being made into a drum skin, Pinocchio escapes, only to be swallowed by the Dogfish. Thus he finds Gepetto.

In this situation Pinocchio is finally able to use his ingenuity, resourcefulness, and trickery to a productive purpose. He arranges their escape and pulls the faint old man a good way through the ocean. Once they reach the shore, with the help of the Tuna, Pinocchio is forced to work in the service of that infamous Cricket, who, unlike Jiminy, is aloof, pompous, and unfriendly. Pinocchio works hard to provide food and medicine for his father. All this is a far cry from the Disney version, which had so inverted the roles that Gepetto actually rescued Pinocchio from drowning. Perfect 1950s cant: how can a boy prove himself when the parent is already perfect? But in the original version the hard labor—and the love it represents— suffices, and one morning the piece of wood wakes up as a real boy.

Getting Started

Once we became familiar with the original story we began to improvise with a piece of wood. At first we were faithful to Collodi's script, reading the episodes together and improvising selected scenes, then writing out a script from our own improvisation. During the several months spent in this process of reading, improvisations, writing, and then acting with the script, the characters began to take shape. We used the dramatic encounters of the narrative to explore therapeutic issues such as dealing with frustration and accepting conflict as a necessary part of a relationship. We were seeking to do two things at once: to recapture the spirit of the original and to use the text as an opportunity to reflect on and express our own experiences. With their multitudes of adventures, rewards, and punishments, Collodi's episodes offer ample ammunition for personal reflection.

There was no shortage of participants from both staff and clients. The voice of the wood was performed by a young woman with a long history of abuse. Her coy and terrified reactions to Gepetto's efforts were chilling. Unfortunately, she did not last long in the project. Neither did the first Gepetto, who became so enraged at the wood's disrespect that he flung it into the crowd, injuring, fortunately not seriously, another client.

Several weeks into our improvising, a client spoke up, saying, "If I heard a piece of wood talk, I'd call my therapist." We improvised a scene and later revised it to include in the final version.

ANTONIO: Wood doesn't talk, does it?

THERAPIST: Is this Antonio?

ANTONIO: Who else? I pick up this piece of wood, it starts to complain—rude, you know?

THERAPIST: The wood was rude?

ANTONIO: Yeah, I mean, I wasn't trying to hurt it or anything.

THERAPIST: Of course. [*starts looking through papers*] Antonio, have you been taking your medication?

ANTONIO: Medication? I used to be a big shot around these parts. Everyone knew Antonio. Now the only person I can get on the phone is you.

THERAPIST: Are you thinking about the hospital?

ANTONIO: Put the piece of wood in the hospital!

When clients wrote and acted the part of a therapist, we were given a chance to see ourselves depicted as giving pat responses and meaningless interventions that were directed toward efforts at social control, such as medication or hospitalization. It also leapfrogged us into an understanding that was not yet clear, though it would soon crystallize: the wealth of creativity, talent, vision, and ability to take risks was not evenly distributed. It was, in fact, heavily weighted on the client side. This realization led us down the path of the blurring of roles toward what we hoped—and feared—might be role liberation.

To work as a therapist, especially in community mental health, is to manage a great deal of uncertainty. Many people do not make striking positive changes, so we measure our success in the hospitalizations they do not endure, the pain they do not suffer or inflict on others. We live in the negative space of what does not happen as much as in the reality of what does. Depending on the day, we can feel like acolytes of Zen or as confused as the patients we treat. As the world outside brought the triumphant chariots of objectivity and empiricism to our door, we struggled more and more with our subjective perspectives on what was real.

"Becoming real" became our organizing principle, and we experienced it in different ways. The theatrical challenge was, of course, paradoxical: to create "the illusion of the first time," to make ourselves real while acting. For most of us, this was new. People who had been in the mental health system a long time, some with many or long hospitalizations, equated real with "normal," and they longed for it. They yearned to be free of the symptoms that dogged them, of the voices, the fears, the moods, just as Pinocchio hated his wooden body and his nose with a mind of its own. Those of us identified with community mental health aspired to be recognized as a truly healing community, not simply a last resort for the chronic and the poor, a distant relation to "real" therapy, that is, to the private practitioners who made real money. We tried to bring this all together through Collodi's text, to *real-ize* it through our fidelity to his worldview and honesty about our own.

Among those suffering from and labeled with mental illness, becoming real equates rather quickly with being normal. The primary measure of normality is the ability to find gainful employment. During the course of the play several of the cast attempted transitions to the working world, some more successfully than others. In the case of one person who found work, his colleagues would sometimes talk him out of his lunch money, so occasionally he went hungry. It was the scenes with the fox and cat characters that inspired him to share what was a terribly embarrassing and demoralizing situation.

CAT: Well, if I had that money I certainly wouldn't go to school.
PINOCCHIO: You wouldn't?
FOX: I never went to school and can't you see what I've made of my life?

CAT: School never taught me anything I really needed to know.

FOX: I wouldn't spend money on school.

CAT: No way, Pup-pay.

PINOCCHIO: What would you spend the money on?

FOX AND CAT: [*coming up on each side and whispering in his ears*] I'd invest it!

These scenes gave us a chance not only to expose the situation but to discuss some alternative strategies for coping with it.

Pinocchio was the centerpiece, and our efforts to comprehend his behavior scene by scene led us to a startling realization: there were really two Pinocchios. The trickster wood sprite was a nasty, sociopathic fellow with huge appetites. The other was an innocent boy who longed for approval and was vulnerable to those who sought to exploit him. Disney had eliminated the first Pinocchio and projected all the evil in him onto his surroundings, the people who could not be trusted, a telling corollary to a cold war mentality. We defined the dilemma differently: Pinocchio's problem with becoming real was that he was not aware of how split he was. He acted as though he were two autonomous beings; neither took responsibility for the other, but each met the other in projected form. The whole story was, in a sense, an externalization of Pinocchio's inner fragmentation.

This was a profound realization for us, for it had direct application to our own struggles and to the level of trust and accountability we needed from each other. Pinocchio became the carrier of all of our hopes for integration, our struggles with our shadow, the ever shifting ground between therapist and patient, healer and healed, those who are stigmatized and those who set the standards. And it led us to a major dramaturgical decision: to cast two separate Pinocchios, to interject them into scenes where they belonged, to write the play so that they had the possibility of relationship as well as integration toward the end of the play. This also solved another problem. Since the part of Pinocchio was so demanding that each of us was intimidated by the prospect of acting it, the role could now be divided.

Creating Characters

By a process of improvisation and writing over a period of many months, the group produced a script in two acts and numerous scenes bound together by the role of the narrator. The first shift from one Pinocchio to the other occurs in the fourth scene of act 1, after Gepetto and Pinocchio are reconciled:

GEPETTO: You could have gotten me locked up for a year! Pinocchio, what happened to your feet?

PINOCCHIO: Oh, Papa, the cat must have eaten my feet. And I'm so hungry.

GEPETTO: Well, here, you can have this pear I was saving for my own breakfast.

PINOCCHIO: I don't like pears.

GEPETTO: You're pretty particular for a piece of pine.

PINOCCHIO: That's true, Papa, but I can't eat something I don't like [*gobbling it down*].

GEPETTO: Why should I make you new feet? So you can run away again?

PINOCCHIO: I promise you I won't run away. I'll stay here and learn to dance and make you a fortune.

GEPETTO: [*pauses*] No, Pinocchio, I want you to go to school, like a real boy.

PINOCCHIO 2: I will, Papa, I'll go to school and get a good job and earn money to care for you in your old age.

GEPETTO: Money, eh? Let's go, Son, I'll make you new feet, and clothing too.

PINOCCHIO 2: [*off stage*] I want jeans and Reeboks!

Gepetto reenters with second Pinocchio, Narrator holding the mirror up to him.

PINOCCHIO 2: I feel like a changed puppet. Thank you, Papa.

NARRATOR: I've heard of people changing, but this is ridiculous.

GEPETTO: Have you really changed, Pinocchio? Can you really be good?

This exchange is followed by Pinocchio playing and singing "I Can Change," an original song written by the actor. The scene also introduces us to the evolving character of Gepetto, critical to the play's development. As he emerged from Collodi, Gepetto was a much more complex character than we had first imagined. He begins the story as a lost soul, a street person living by his wits, who tries to hoodwink his friend Antonio into giving him this special piece of wood.

ANTONIO: I heard enough about a piece of wood.

GEPETTO: But you haven't heard my idea. I'm gonna make a puppet. Teach it to dance and sing and do tricks. People will pay money and I'm gonna invest in stocks. Foreign stocks, and retire to Florida.

ANTONIO: Why don't you just get a job! Some idea, a puppet, a puppet out of wood.

GEPETTO: Yeah, I could use a piece of wood if you have one lying around. [*aside to audience*] Like taking candy from a baby!

Nonetheless, the scheme proves harder to realize than he had thought. For one thing, the puppet has a mind of its own:

GEPETTO: What a piece of work, this puppet! There now, a name. Woody? Nah, Gepetto Jr.? Nah, not for a piece of wood, a piece of pine, pine, pine—Pinocchio, that's it!

PINOCCHIO: That's a dumb name.

GEPETTO: Dumb?

PINOCCHIO: It's been used.

GEPETTO: I don't care if it's all washed up. I made you. I give you your name—Pinocchio.

Pinocchio spits in Gepetto's eye, then jumps forward and falls.

Their first bond is created around the mutual desire to exploit the public, but this too goes awry. Pinocchio runs away, feigns abuse at the hands of his father, and thereby causes Gepetto to be imprisoned. It is only after he is released from prison that Gepetto discovers that he really cares for this puppet and wants to give him the opportunity to live like a boy rather than purely exploit him for monetary gain. But how does this transformation occur?

Here too we relied on the inspiration of the participants. The woman who played Gepetto saw the character developing in phases. Pinocchio's period of imprisonment strips away his antisocial phase, revealing a very immature capacity for caring. Though genuine of heart, this caring assumes the forms of codependency very quickly.

The rest of the play depicts not only Pinocchio's struggle for integration but Gepetto's attempts to accept responsibility for his own suffering, to move from codependency to real caring. One day the actor came to rehearsal with a poem she had written: Gepetto's lament from jail. We developed it into a scene, by including Pinocchio after his first confrontation with the cricket. They appear on stage simultaneously and recite these lines, alternating voices:

GEPETTO:	PINOCCHIO:
Water and bread	I'm on my own
Might as well be dead	Born full grown
Maybe I'm gonna prefer Hell	Ready to sail
To life in a cell	Old man's in jail
Gotta get out	That's his fault
It's my fault	It'll all work out
I lived alone	Hunger and thirst
Poor, no phone	Which is worse?
But I was free	Place is beat
Now look at me	Nothing to eat
Gotta get out	It's his fault
It's my fault	It'll all work out
Pinocchio	No school
Where will you go?	No work
You'll never survive	No growing up to be a jerk
They'll eat him alive	The Cricket's dead
I've gotta get out	That's his fault
It's my fault	It'll all work out
[together]	
I had a plan	He had a plan
Stupid, man.	Stupid man!
You can't control	You can't control
Another soul	Another soul
It's my fault	It's his fault
Gotta get out	It'll all work out

The actor who played the cricket developed the idea of a narrator through his personal vision of the play. He saw Pinocchio as a type of Hamlet, a puppet of fate haunted by paternal mandates and unable to act decisively on his own behalf. But this is a Hamlet devoid of nobility and intellect, who gives a contemptible comic flavor to these themes just as madness itself, awe-inspiring in Hamlet, has become medicalized and pitiable. This actor played Cricket in medieval armor and developed the character of the narrator as a version of the cricket. In this perhaps we were influenced by Disney. Narrator and Cricket both take a patronizing attitude toward Pinocchio, and, in the case of the narrator, toward the whole work. He developed a perspective toward the play that at first derides it for not being *Hamlet,* and then, despite his literary tastes, becomes involved with it. As Cricket, he plays with Pinocchio:

> PINOCCHIO: Talking cricket? [*fearfully*] Are you sure you're not a termite?
> CRICKET: My fine unweathered friend, I've lived in this room for more than one hundred years.
> PINOCCHIO: You must be bored stiff.
> CRICKET: Boredom is simply a question of insufficient imagination.
> PINOCCHIO: Get lost! There's only one trade that interests me. A trade of eating, sleeping, drinking, and partying. The life of a vagabond. I'll live by my wits.
> CRICKET: I feel sorry for you. Where most people have wits, you've got wood.
> *Pinocchio picks up bug spray. Cricket disappears.*

Later on, the actor who plays the cricket/narrator painted a mural for the set depicting Pinocchio holding a skull, eyeing a castle in front of which an armored figure stands, while below him a wooden puppet floats down a river pawed at by Fox and Cat. The creation of the set is a subject I will return to: its conceptualization and creation located Pinocchio in a tradition whose richness we could hardly have imagined.

The creation of the narrator moved the theatrical style from an attempt to be realistic in uncovering motivations of characters and meanings of actions to a style that created alienation and a critical attitude toward the issues raised by the play. We began our rehearsals attempting to be as realistic as possible in identifying underlying motives of characters and meanings of actions. In this we followed the Stanislavski (1977) line. Early on I stressed the parallels between the theatrical process and the therapeutic one. Two principles—noticing and caring—seemed fundamental to both. We further connected both of these skills to the very deficiencies in Pinocchio that contributed to his continual difficulties. In developing the play in a manner that allowed Pinocchio to develop these skills, we attended to our own process as well.

In the early scenes between Gepetto and Antonio, and Gepetto and Pinocchio, we explored the meaning of anger in the context of a relationship. Could such vicious expresssions of anger not result in the demise of a relationship? As a surprise to the group, two of the agency's secretaries joined a rehearsal and performed the fight scene between Gepetto and Antonio, which they had been rehearsing in secret. Their rendition illustrated dramatically that anger can actually be an expression of intimacy and spoke to the complexities of this and of other emotional states.

Throughout this process we walked a fine line, not wanting to challenge too directly the notion that persons with "serious and persistent mental illness" should be helped to cover, not uncover, the dark thoughts and strong affects that lurked close to the surface of consciousness. Defenses, particularly repression, are crucial to the survival of the ego; that is one of the purposes of strong medication. At the same time, however, some of these very patients were pushing us to consider issues that broadened the scope of the play, deepened the characters, made sense theatrically, and seemed in many instances to bring relief by the restoration of their confidence in their humanity, of psychological courage. Of course, there were limits, which we discovered along the way.

Eventually we moved our focus from motives and meaning à la Stanislavski to a more detached view of the play and the process. We sought not so much to be realistic but to use the play to raise social issues that were embedded within it. In this shift we relied on techniques first developed by Brecht, who promoted the concept of alienation as a way of disrupting emotional identification with the protagonist in favor of a more reasoned consideration of larger issues (Willett 1964). We critiqued Collodi's text and incorporated the critique into the play itself, allowing ourselves to recognize our anxieties and dilemmas in this work. For example, one of the actors was a very sweet man known to the group as being very gentle and nonaggressive. Because many other parts were taken before he volunteered, the group began looking to him to fill in some bit parts along the way, especially the periodic appearance of a policeman. He was not comfortable playing a cop, and could neither refuse outright nor play it with any heart. The group engaged him enthusiastically on this issue, trying to convince him that throwing himself into the role would help him to contact some of his own aggression in a positive way. It was only when we incorporated his reluctance to play such a role in direct asides to the audience that he was able to free himself to become quite effective and fearsome.

> POLICEMAN: [*to audience*] It's the story of my life. All the good parts are taken and I have to be a cop. [*to Gepetto*] What's the problem here?

And later in the play the policeman returns:

> WAITER: This is unthinkable! Police !!!
> POLICEMAN: What a ridiculous part. What is it this time?
> WAITER: This transient moron is unable to pay his bill.
> PINOCCHIO: But the Fox, the Cat—
> POLICEMAN: [*interrupting*] Tell it to the judge. [*He carries Pinocchio off.*]

We became very committed to this strategy of directly incorporating the actors' perspective as often as we could when the occasion presented itself. For instance, much later on, during a dress rehearsal, one of the local reporters quite familiar with the agency criticized the play for its chaos and timbre. "It's just too loud," he said. "You can't really make sense of it." We tried to convince him to join the cast as just what he was—a critical reporter, walking across the stage at certain moments to advise the audience of his opinions—but we were not successful in enlisting him.

With the introduction of Fox and Cat, the archetype of the trickster moved yet again; as it had passed from Gepetto to Pinocchio, so it darted from Pinocchio to the anthropomorphized rascals. Pinocchio comes to realize he is out of his league, that the fox and the cat combine skilled sociopathy with an apparent alliance with the judicial system. In other words, Pinocchio is jailed for their shenanigans, much as Gepetto had been jailed for Pinocchio's antics. The original story of Pinocchio contains elements of political satire, especially in regard to the arbitrary workings of the legal system. This was a theme that found deep resonance in the group, many of whom had suffered an incarceration for reasons they did not comprehend or accept. They were all too familiar with the rapid redefinition that transforms victim to perpetrator. In this we were able to recover what we felt were some of the original intentions of Collodi's text.

> JUDGE: Yes, yes, Pinocchio. You have been sorely, sorely wronged. I'm in fact quite moved by your story. Officer, take this young man to prison right away.

PINOCCHIO: To prison? Prison? But I'm innocent!

JUDGE: [*drying the tears from his eyes*] Exactly, my dear boy. Much too innocent.

For Pinocchio as well as Gepetto, it is the relinquishing of the trickster archetype that leads to the development of their humanity. Of course, the immediate result of such a relinquishing is suffering, as they go from con men to victims of con artistry. But in the long run, it is the first step on the path that Gepetto will travel toward fatherhood, and Pinocchio toward becoming a real boy.

A scene with the Blue Fairy ends the first act. Collodi's Blue Fairy is a morbid phantom obsessed with death who torments Pinocchio with her own fragility from the moment of the first encounter on through his escape from jail and subsequent wounding.

PINOCCHIO: You can't just leave me out here to die!

BLUE FAIRY: I told you, everyone in here is dead.

PINOCCHIO: Oh, wonderful fairy with the blue hair, take pity on a poor puppet.

BLUE FAIRY: All right, all right. Come around the side.

It is not the Blue Fairy's warm maternal love that impacts on him but her harsh judgment and her lack of tolerance for nonsense. Living so intimately with death allows her to cut through his pathetic attempts at self-justification that lead to the famous nose growing. It is in her house that the cricket reappears, himself resurrected from the dead:

CRICKET: . . . the wound may do him good, it may remind him of the pain he has brought to a kindly old man. This puppet is a rogue, a vagabond, a selfish good-for-nothing!

PINOCCHIO: [*sobbing*] You're right, I'm hopeless, a good-for-nothing piece of wood.

CRICKET: Exactly. A piece of wood, no more, no less.

BLUE FAIRY: I may as well get out the furniture polish in that case.

PINOCCHIO: No, no, I must become real, whatever it takes. Oh, Blue Fairy, you've saved my life, help me find my father so I can go to school and live the life of a real boy.

Attempting to play these scenes with some attention to the original text raised some thematic challenges. First, the growing nose in the presence of the Blue Fairy raised the issue of sexual stimulation, an association of which we were not unaware. Second, her preoccupation with death brought some difficult issues to the surface among a group of people who were familiar with death, in many cases the self-inflicted kind. It was clear that—although we were merely performing a play, and a fairytale at that—we could not keep the most pressing issues in our lives out of the work. We needed more time to process concerns, both inside and outside of rehearsals. As our work progressed, we looked with a far more savvy eye at the dynamics among the cast as subtexts that were being interpreted in more subtle ways, and the boundary issues that were being redefined. We needed to be particularly attentive to the dangers of decompensation as material was dealt with dramatically, and the possibilities that erotic energy, so helpful in forming coherence in any group, would not be misused or misrepresented in this one.

The other characters recede as the first act ends with the two Pinocchios on stage crying for Gepetto, each aware of the need to master his own personal flaw.

> PINOCCHIO 2: I've got to be careful who I trust. I can't be a dummy.
>
> PINOCCHIO 1: I've got to concentrate. I can't be lazy.
>
> TOGETHER: [*with whole cast*] Gepetto!

The realization that Pinocchio was much more than a children's story gave us a far wider berth in our development of the text. We discovered other treatments of the story that lent credence to our interpretations. Jerome Charyn's *Pinocchio's Nose* (1983) described a complicated relationship between the author and Pinocchio that he called "mythopsychosis," or identification with a mythical character. This was something to which we could relate. Charyn's Pinocchio was set in Italy during the 1930s, where, to spite Gepetto, a working-class socialist, Pinocchio becomes a brownshirt under Mussolini. Here we could see the nasty wooden imp we were portraying as well as his crusty, antisocial father.

Robert Coover's *Pinocchio in Venice* (1991) portrayed Pinocchio as an elderly professor who had become famous and was now returning home for an encounter with his mother, the Blue Fairy. Coover's book does an ingenious job of incorporating elements from Collodi's text into his vision, being both extremely faithful and extremely creative. This was what we aspired to: the combining of the erudite knowledge represented by more classical elements with the creation of our own experience and a new sense of freedom and inspiration about who we were becoming in this process. I was also beginning to make connections between the commedia dell'arte style of the Pinocchio characters and the humanism of the Renaissance.

It was Michel Foucault who gave us the link between the Renaissance as origin and the contemporary social problem of mental illness. In *Madness and Civilization* Foucault (1973) discusses how from the sixteenth century onward the ascension of the bourgeoisie had resulted in an obsession with classification, exclusion, medicalization, and marginalization of social groups that had once had legitimate voices in the culture. For Foucault the Renaissance represents the last time that madness was accorded respect, was recognized as having its own perspective and validity. Though it might be an affliction no one would seek or desire, it still had logic and credibility. Though it be madness, there was method in it. Shakespeare, of course, is full of it.

In the first act we attempted to be fairly faithful to Collodi, using some Brechtian techniques to call attention to some issues and injecting humor wherever we could. But the first act was primarily a re-presentation of Pinocchio, and this set a strong dramatic tone. In the second act we developed the relationships along the lines that we felt appropriate to our own needs. We had to take responsibility for what we were doing with this play, what we wanted to convey.

One strong theme that emerged was the repairability, and the transformation, of relationships. This obviously existed in the original, as Pinocchio is reconciled to Gepetto and the Blue Fairy. We extended this to other characters, for example, to Gepetto and Antonio, whose incessant combativeness led to a kind of intimacy. An exchange between them opens the second act:

ANTONIO: You're not really gonna travel in that thing, are you?

GEPETTO: What else can I do? I've got to find my son.

ANTONIO: But the ocean—you can't swim!

GEPETTO: Hopefully it won't come up.

ANTONIO: You must really love that piece of . . . wood.

GEPETTO: I must. [*Pause*] I'll miss you, my friend.

ANTONIO: Oh, I'm sure . . . I mean . . . [*They embrace*]

GEPETTO: [*gruffly*] Give me a hand with this, will you? I can't stand around talking all day.

ANTONIO: [*pushing the boat*] It never bothered you before.

At the same time, we began to realize that the focus of the fox and the cat on gain, avarice, and duplicity had ruined their own relationship. What mattered now was less who was victimized by whom than who was able to relate to others in a genuine way. Just as in Sartre's existential drama *No Exit*, they are eternally stuck with each other:

CAT: What do you mean, we're through? Have a heart!

FOX: Me, have a heart? You're the one who spent all our money on catnip.

CAT: Never again. I'm giving the stuff up.

FOX: Never again is right. From now on you're on your own.

CAT: Well, terrific then. You're impossible to work for anyway. You can't stand it if someone around you has some fun.

FOX: Fun? It's simply lack of self-control!

We changed the character of the Blue Fairy as well, though not along the lines Collodi suggested. In the original she changed from a morbid sister figure and a playmate to a mother, kind but disciplining. We gave her a new-age look:

BLUE FAIRY: You're a puppet. Puppets don't change.

PINOCCHIO 2: I can change, I can, I can. I'd do anything to be real, oh please, give me a chance.

BLUE FAIRY: Well, I can put you on a regimen that's designed to make you whole. Real is whole. Meditation, hatha yoga, affirmations, proper diet, abdominal breathing. We'll have to get your horoscope done, your palms read, assign you gems and mantras . . .

PINOCCHIO 2: Couldn't I just go to school?

BLUE FAIRY: School? Well, that's a much more traditional route.

Producing a Play

Once we had completed a text for the first act we sought feedback from the people at the Muse Theatre, a group of theatre professionals very interested in developing and supporting theatre projects by nonprofessional actors in community settings. In their own work they recognized the therapeutic value of drama but were committed to the actual production of a play before an audience. Because I was familiar with psychodrama and drama therapy I wanted both a realization of the text as well as a therapeutic experience for the participants. Yet my therapeutic colleagues and I were unsure just how far we could take this enterprise.

The night we gathered in a crowded group therapy room to do a staged reading of the first act—our temporarily final version—with members of Muse as invited guests was a great revelation for all. The text at that time ended with the judge's sentencing of Pinocchio, and when we heard it we knew it was meant for us as well. The people from Muse confirmed it: this process now had a life of its own, which would lead it inevitably toward performance. We had to take ourselves seriously; the play was on the road to becoming real.

That meant locating a rehearsal space, conceptualizing and building a set, dealing with costumes and stage props, creating folders with scripts, not to mention programs and stage design, and, most intimidating of all, finalizing the script. We were able to enlist the help of Muse to get us through this transition, to help transform us from a group of people in a community mental health center into a pseudo-company mounting a production.

The music had come first, and easiest, thanks to the creativity of the cast. The title song, "Piece of Wood," had a haunting edge, a punk rhythm, as it defined the ambivalences we were confronting.

> Piece of wood, piece of wood
> Was it bad or was it good?
> Was it good or was it bad,
> That piece of wood Gepetto had?

I played the guitar with the author of the song, partly for my own enjoyment but also because I thought that my guitar playing—rusty as it was—put me at a risk level comparable to how others felt about their acting. Acting did not unnerve me, but I was exposing significant musical limitations. We located a cafeteria belonging to another social service program that was available late afternoons, evenings, and weekends for rehearsal. It was far from ideal, not a theatre at all, without a stage and full of conspicuous and unusable props such as soda machines and countertops. It forced us to consider theatrical approaches that reinforced ideas we were already developing, such as doing the play in concert with the audience, among the audience.

By challenging the accepted division in bourgeois theatre between performer and spectator we were also calling attention to other divisions we were challenging, such as the clear separation of roles between therapist and patient, between mental illness and normality, or between being real and being a puppet. I saw how the physical setting, the resource issue, was tied to the thematics of the text and to the metatext as well: the social experiences of the patients and those of us who have chosen to work in community mental health. It gave me a richer understanding of a work I had encountered years ago, Grotowski's *Towards a Poor Theatre* (1969), which focuses on the actor and spectators while minimizing the elements of production.

How could we create a set that would impose the feeling of the play on an atmosphere so distinctively nontheatrical? The challenge here was to make a virtue of necessity, to view the extravagant productions of mainstream theatre as a deterrent to real audience engagement, and to understand and value the energy arising from the purity of a stage stripped bare of nonessentials. Our narrator, a visual artist, suggested we construct eight-by-sixteen-foot plywood boards connected with hinges, so that they would stand in accordion style and could be arranged behind the actors as a stylized backdrop. The artistic director of Muse suggested painting the panels as playing cards. This suggestion led us to a discovery that changed our understanding of the play: the rich tapestry of tarot.

Tarot cards are, of course, the predecessors of modern versions of playing cards. While there are legends of their existence in ancient Greece and Egypt, the modern versions seem to be traceable as far back as the Italian Renaissance. When we began to explore tarot as a group we were amazed at the echoes we found in Collodi's text. Pinocchio was a perfect Fool, even to the extent of having a dog snapping at his heels. Gepetto, the inventor, was a Magus, though we had spent much time on exposing his human contradictions. There was the Blue Fairy, the Wheel of Fortune, the Hanged Man, the fox and cat wailing at the Moon, Death, and the Hermit, whom we recognized as Antonio. The story of Pinocchio incorporated many of the archetypal icons of playing cards found also in tarot, even down to the designation of suits. What was a "club" but a "piece of wood"?

Once we began painting these huge pieces of plywood as tarot cards we began discovering other aspects of the Renaissance that seemed to contain elements of our story. For one thing, the work that the narrator was doing to incorporate themes from *Hamlet* into the play now made sense; it was more than a personal idiosyncrasy. Hamlet, as a kind of quintessential Renaissance man, was a Pinocchio: driven to please his father while feeling strong ambivalences about his mission; confused by the demands and treacheries of the world around him; daring and nasty but also stigmatized and ridiculed; and, most significantly, having a void, a feeling of despair and nonexistence, where a sense of self should rightfully be.

As participants in this play we were all discovering that our own voices had substantial merit; we were teachers and leaders and philosophers. We were struggling together with issues that had persistently plagued humanity, specifically: What does it mean to lead a "real" life as opposed to a life of puppetry? In these struggles the suffering, the distortions, the mental illnesses were not a disadvantage.

During the evolution of the play one of the cast put together an album of notes and comments about the work process. In interviewing cast members about their favorite lines, this speech by the "nasty" Pinocchio to his naive counterpart was the overwhelming favorite:

PINOCCHIO 1: How can you be real if you let other people tell you what to do? These people—look around you [*gesturing to audience*]—they're not real. They're sheep, they do as they're told, working on someone else's schedule, missing all the wonder and passion of their lives, sacrificing themselves—for what? They're the wooden cogs, they're the puppets!

Our own community was developing a cohesiveness that made some of us wonder, and worry, about what would happen when the project was finished. For every rehearsal, people brought food. It was never planned or requested. There were alway homemade brownies and plenty of chips; in the winter, Gepetto brought hot roast beef. We celebrated holidays together. On Halloween we wore what we had of our costumes. Thanksgiving we celebrated on our Wednesday night rehearsal. The extent to which this group could serve a surrogate function was wonderful and a little unnerving, for holidays can be a big source of stress for those who are alienated from or feel unwelcome by their families. But one thing we were learning from Pinocchio was the need to go forward, cognizant of the risk but not being dominated by it.

A sense of community is something that can be built out of shared social needs. In addition, we were developing a common purpose, an artistic mission, a sense of ourselves as a learning community. Together we reviewed other dramatized treatments of the Pinocchio story and found that the better-known adaptations disregarded much of the dramatic tensions of the text that had become so important to us. Disney was perhaps the farthest from the original: the shadows had been completely purged from Gepetto, the Blue Fairy, and Pinocchio, and were now totally projected onto Stromboli, a composite figure and a typical Disney villain. We could see how post–World War II America loved this version, with the kind burgher father longing for a son, the magical sweet mother and her kind tricks, the innocent little boy who needs to learn how to obey authority and avoid the evil others.

The Danny Kaye version was more substantial, though it too missed the political satire and the deep ambivalences in human nature while it redirected the story toward a father/daughter separation motif. The Pinocchio of Pee Wee Herman captured a little more of the lunacy but turned out to be all shtick with very little attempt to portray the complexity of the themes that Collodi presents. The only version we related to was a "fractured fairy tale" from Rocky and Bullwinkle, which, though only a snippet, conveyed a truer sense of the characters of Gepetto and Pinocchio as we had come to imagine them. This process of considering other renditions fortified us in our belief that what we were doing had an artistic coherence, that the play had value not so much as a result of who we were but of what we were creating.

We went too far when we viewed Peter Brooks's filmed production of *Marat/Sade* together. I thought Peter Weiss's play within a play, which depicts the Marquis de Sade staging Marat's assassination with patients interned in an asylum, might help us study the dramaturgical problem of dealing with diverse levels of narration and metanarration. Although I tried to select segments of Brooks's production that were less steamy and provocative, it was still too much for some members of the group. Perhaps it was that *Marat/Sade* demythologized and laid bare what we had been mythologizing and creating from: the phenomenon of mental illness. Brooks and Weiss indulge and embrace the aberrant while we had reached a point of questioning some of the distinctions between madness and normality. Showing that piece of film was something of a clinical setback, which we took time to address as a group.

Similarly, we had discussed for months how to represent Playland, where boys become donkeys, and how to present being swallowed by a whale (Collodi's dogfish). We decided to combine the two into one experience of seduction and engulfment. We discussed many metaphorical possibilities and landed on the idea of representing a decompensation, a psychiatric hospitalization, that would certainly honor the given circumstances of many of the cast. We experimented with psychotic breaks and drug overdoses, but soon realized that acting this scene was taking a toll on some of the actors and was becoming clinically problematic. It was a lesson for all of us in the value of defenses.

We finally settled on a political representation of this scene, bringing the fox back as a corporate executive who seduces Pinocchio with promises of power, of being able to control others. We created a slide show with glamorous advertising images and hoped to offer something of a cultural critique. Unfortunately, we did not find the right style and the scene hung there, discombobulated and fatuous, a dramaturgical problem we never successfully solved. But out of this scene came an important articulation of the central character's evolution, as the two Pinocchios unite to save Gepetto from the fox's manipulations. Once they find Gepetto, the old man's illness forces them into the fox's employ, for they must labor to provide for their father. This time, however, they are not deceived about what Fox is offering:

FOX: The illness of a loved one. There's nothing like it to break a boy's spirit and insure a sufficient labor pool.

We had reached a consensus about how to handle most of our themes a few months before the time we had set for public performance, but some of us were getting cold feet. The therapists among the cast began talking about what a great process this had been, how much everyone had learned, how valuable it had been even if we would not be able finally to manage a real production. The clients reacted with incredulity at these attempts at closure. "Are you crazy? We've got to perform, after all this," they insisted. This was one of the most dramatic illustrations of the permeability of roles, particularly emotional leadership, that we experienced.

Meanwhile, we had the problem of the ending to solve: how to dramatize a puppet becoming real? What did that mean, anyway? Gepetto and his old pal Antonio mused about it in the play:

GEPETTO: In my day, I worried about money. These kids, they're obsessed with being real.

ANTONIO: That's how it is these days; being real is what matters.

GEPETTO: What's a parent to do? We can't control what we create. That's what this play is about: the agony of a parent.

ANTONIO: I think this play is about time, how things change over time.

We had changed over time, too, and had long ago given up trying to control what we had created. Unlike a puppet, yet like Pinocchio, the play had taken on a life of its own, and we could not figure out a way to end it. Perhaps we no longer felt entitled to decide on an ending, despite our countless hours of discussion.

We decided instead to make the transformation from acting a part to being our own ordinary selves on stage before the audience. After Pinocchio's magic moment each actor shed part of his or her costume, stepped downstage, and addressed the audience individually, making a statement about what he or she considered being real. Some were rehearsed speeches, others were spontaneous, and not everyone did it. The impact was quite powerful. It seemed that we had found a dramatic structure that pushed the text beyond its limits.

We did three performances over a weekend and received excellent reviews from critics of the *Philadelphia Inquirer* and the *Main Line Times* who quoted actors' enthusiastic comments about the experience of the work process. In these performances we honored the convention of refusing to identify for the public who was client and who was staff. The program listed people only by first name. The middle performance, on Saturday night, turned out to be one of those special theatrical highs where the actors feel the audience's responsiveness and feed off of it, raising the play to a level of intensity and emotional verity that it had not achieved before. The cast was exhilarated. By the next day the magic had gone and we each performed as best we could. We went out to dinner to celebrate and began to deal with the moment that, a year ago, none of us could have imagined would come: the moment after.

Many people had become friends with others in the cast. Individuals who would never have been considered for the same psychotherapy group socialized and developed relationships. Many discovered mutual artistic and musical interests far beyond what the play required. We had all been deeply affected by the experience. While we were painting panels in the basement during the play's preparation, for instance, one member persuaded another to set severe limits with her son, who was abusing drugs. She spoke of Gepetto's enabling Pinocchio and how it had held the puppet back. She drew a picture of a grave modeled on the Blue Fairy's hoax on Pinocchio. The arguments were effective, and the son entered treatment some weeks later.

After the cast party there were discussions about continuing to perform. We had found a real theatre space, and I was encouraging the group to consider moving toward an even more professional production. The discussions around this were difficult, for very strong bonds had been formed, and some feared that they would be lost. Others were willing to keep going primarily because of these bonds, even though they had been exhausted by the process. Still others had just gotten a taste and wanted more. But we needed a solid consensus to continue, and that eluded us. It was time to deal with the reality of a closure that we could no longer avoid.

The cast members who were therapists remained in their therapeutic roles once the play ended. Likewise, most of the clients from the cast remained in treatment. One person felt ready to make the leap out of the mental health system entirely. Another decided to pursue the musical career that had gotten a boost from the process. Others made time for other writing or acting projects. Eventually the prominence of the unresolved personal issues returned, but they seemed transformed. The experience suggested that if only we could do this every year, we could redefine the role and the impact of a community mental health center.

However, the near future brought fewer rather than more opportunities for innovation. We received criticism from representatives of local august psychiatric institutions, one of whom expressed incredulity at the fact that we did not charge patients for this experience. How could it be therapy? We were moving into a fiscal year of rapidly shrinking funding and therefore rapidly increasing questions by some of our funders as to how wise an allocation of resources "this Pinocchio thing" really was. The mental health field was surging into an era of biochemical etiology and treatment. The understandings about mental illness we had developed through our process seemed as submerged as our understanding of the original Pinocchio, engulfed by a tide of Disney. We were ourselves smack in the belly of a whale.

And, it is safe to say, we remain here for the time being, living on the provisions of what we were able not only to accomplish but to undertake. The Blue Fairy represented for Pinocchio a kind of fate, the inevitability of his transformation. Likewise, the play was for us a fate, a possibility, a transformed understanding of therapy.

I no longer see what we therapists do as a process of curing, or healing, or even treating others so much as I experience it as a scene in a drama we are all caught up in—the struggle, the ambivalence, the desire to become real.

PINOCCHIO: Let me in, I'm hurt, I'm losing precious sap.
BLUE FAIRY: Everyone here is dead, including me.
PINOCCHIO: Then what are you doing at the window?
BLUE FAIRY: Looking at you, silly.

Works Cited

Charyn, Jerome. 1983. *Pinocchio's Nose*. New York: Arbor House.
Collodi, Carlo. 1883. *Le Avventure di Pinocchio: Storia di un Burattino*. Florence: Felice Paggia Libraio.
———.1986. *The Adventures of Pinocchio: Story of a Puppet*. Trans. Nicholas J. Perella. Berkeley: University of California Press.
Coover, Robert. 1991. *Pinocchio in Venice*. New York: Linden Press.
Foucault, Michel. 1973. *Madness and Civilization*. Trans. Richard Howard. New York: Vintage Books.
Grotowski, Jerzy. 1969. *Toward a Poor Theatre*. London: Methuen.
Stanislavski, Constantin. 1977. *Building a Character*. Trans. Elizabeth Reynolds. Hapgood, N.Y.: Theatre Arts Books.
Willett, John, ed. 1964. *Brecht on Theatre*. London: Methuen.

The Fictional Family Approach:

Dramatic Techniques

for Family Therapy Trainees

Muriel Gold

> Every family is a fictional family, constructed from the collusion (and often the collision) of two sets of stories, myths, parables and connecting links of the preceding generation.—Olga Silverstein (Gold 1991:ix)

I have always been intrigued by family relationships and the search for roots and individual identity. In my acting classes at McGill University, Montreal, I designed and developed an actor-training approach called the Fictional Family (Gold 1991). It is grounded in the recognition that the family forms a common basis of experience, a unit to which everyone can relate. The technique has been used mostly with university students, who, like everyone else, have had their perceptions, communication styles, and modes of interacting shaped within the processes of their own family dynamics.

Although the technique was developed for use in acting classes, it can be applied in a variety of disciplines. In 1994 I had the opportunity to apply the technique in the training of a group of graduate social workers and family therapists studying at McGill University. Therapists hope that change in awareness can lead to behavioral change. Therefore I hypothesized that this actor-training technique, which focuses on sustained character development within a family structure, would prove useful to family therapy trainees, helping them to understand themselves in relation to their own families of origin, to facilitate deeper understanding of the families with whom they were working, and to add to their repertoire of intervention techniques. After taking note of other ways drama has been used in family therapy and describing the development of the Fictional Family in actor training, this study explores an application of the method and the avenues it opens to family therapists.

The Use of Drama in Family Therapy

The use of dramatic techniques in family therapy is not new. Experiential techniques such as sculpting have been used extensively by such therapists as Papp, Silverstein, and Carter (1973). Virginia Satir (1972) is well known for her family reconstructions; Imber-Black, Roberts, and Whiting (1988) have incorporated ritual into their work with families. However, most family therapists have little or no theatre background and therefore feel ill-equipped to apply dramatic interventions. While most therapists undergo personal therapy as part of their training, their therapy generally does not reflect the creative, expressive nature of drama.

Nevertheless, it has been my experience that family therapists recognize the need for powerful techniques to effect change within the family system. The creative arts therapies have been effective in countering resistance and uncovering unconscious or latent thoughts (Johnson 1991). Drama therapy is a modality that has proven beneficial to a variety of populations. It allows people to explore their own psychic material within the safety of a nurturing environment and has been known to facilitate change in communication and relationships.

Robert Landy states, "In a broader sense, the family can be seen as a metaphor for any ongoing drama therapy group" (1986:36). Drama therapists often use role play to explore clients' family issues; sometimes they use dramatic techniques with real families. They are constantly shifting between the fictional and the actual. Clients come into therapy because they have a dysfunctional view of themselves in society. Through drama they recreate this image so that it can be examined, explored, and integrated, "allowing a more functional self to emerge" (47).

Dramatic interventions exist in a variety of domains, such as sociodrama, psychodrama, actor training, and creative/developmental drama. In her discussion of psychodrama, drama therapy, and creative drama, Jennings points out "the power of drama as a medium for change and understanding" but cautions that its use must be "properly harnessed" (1990:19). She also distinguishes psychodrama from drama therapy.

Psychodrama invites protagonists to enact past, present, or future events from their own lives using group members to play various roles in their story. A variety of techniques, such as empty chair, role reversal, role play, the aside, future projection, sculpting, and doubling, are incorporated. Drama therapy often uses themes from textual material drawn from dramatic plays and mythology. Even when calling on direct experience the emphasis is on the aesthetic, and clients are therefore distanced from the material. The technique of sociodrama was first initiated by Jacob Moreno. Unlike psychodrama, in which one person's issues are explored through enactment, sociodrama focuses on enactment of issues shared by the group that seeks solutions. Sternberg describes it as "a kinesthetic, intuitive, affective, and cognitive educational technique" (1990:4).

Actor training also stresses self-development and personal growth but its ultimate objective is the creation of a work of art. Sociodrama and psychodrama focus principally on process. Stanislavski, the father of twentieth-century naturalistic actor training, and Moreno, the originator of sociodrama and psychodrama, had different aims. However, as Sternberg suggests, "they both understood and respected the power of drama. Each of them worked throughout his life to help others discover that power and how to use it as a great equalizer for all people" (1990:12).

Just as many therapists use dramatic techniques, such as sculpting and role play, many acting teachers use psychotherapeutic techniques, such as imaging and kinetics. While the goals of therapists and acting teachers may differ, therapeutic benefits may result from both aesthetic and therapeutic approaches. Olga Silverstein, noted family therapist, recognizes the symbiotic relationship between the two fields. In her foreword to my book that describes the use of this technique in acting classes, she asks, "Is [Gold] a closet therapist, or am I really an acting teacher?" (Gold 1991:x).

Since family therapists emphasize the need to affect family relationships to permit individual change, the Fictional Family technique seems well suited to their work. Hoffman notes, "Family therapists are distinct as a group largely because of a common assumption: if the individual is to change, the context in which he lives must change. The unit of treatment is no longer the person, even if only a single person is interviewed; it is the set of relationships in which the person is imbedded" (Hoffman 1967: v).

Family therapy literature suggests that most approaches to treatment are conversational rather than dramatic. However, some family therapists use dramatic techniques such as sculpting, role play, magic, ritual, and storytelling. Papp, Silverstein, and Carter are known for their use of "family sculpting" in their preventive work with functional families at the Ackerman Institute (1973:202).

Janine Roberts uses a technique called Family Stories, which includes "reminiscences, jokes, family sayings, intergenerational myths and cautionary tales." She considers these stories to be "powerful resources for healing families undergoing major transitions like death, birth, a move, divorce and remarriage," and she uses techniques such as "story-go-rounds, unfinished fables, photo boards, and 'case histories' co-created by therapist and client" (Roberts 1991).

"Family rituals" are beginning to be used more often by family therapists who view this technique—with its emphasis on cotherapy, cocreation, and self-healing—as a powerful source of healing. In an article in *Family Therapy Network* Imber-Black states: "Rituals provide a safe context for the expression of intense emotion. They also connect a family with previous and future generations, conveying a sense of history and rootedness while encouraging visions of the future" (Imber-Black 1988:60).

Eva Leveton uses "doubling," a psychodramatic technique, to counter resistance in families. In psychodrama the double, or alter ego, speaks for the protagonist thereby articulating his or her unexpressed feelings and/or thoughts. In Leveton's technique the therapist/double speaks *for* the client rather than *to* the client. However, Leveton notes that many therapists, herself included, often hesitate to use "active" techniques because they may be afraid to impede the flow of the client's talk; on the other hand, she observes that "many clients talk and talk to avoid the issues they came to explore" (1991:242). In these instances she has found the use of drama, particularly doubling, to be most effective.

It is not surprising that drama therapists who work with families are the ones most comfortable working with experiential intervention techniques. Sue Jennings uses a variety of exercises to set the scene for the drama to be enacted. For example, her exercise called "Where, When, Who, What, Why" uses "family pictures" to act as springboards for dramatizations that she calls living drama (1990). Living drama differs from role play, a more familiar technique to psychodramatists and family therapists, in which roles are used to explore the specifics of the person's situation, for example, abuse. In drama therapy the therapist sustains the dramatic structure, directing the actors to remain in character for the climax and denouement of the scene. The themes are drawn from plays and myths, and the variety of props and costumes enhances communication between family members.

The Fictional Family Technique

The Fictional Family was devised as a transitional step in actor training occurring between stages three and four of Strasberg's methodology, that is, between physicalization exercises and scene work from written scripts (Strasberg 1987). Students create imaginary characters with whom they live and whom they enact for an extended period of time within a fictional family structure. The technique incorporates well-documented actor-training techniques from a variety of methodologies and performance theories. This character-development technique can be applied to both naturalistic and non-Stanislavskian styles and in rehearsal with scripted characters (Gold 1994).

In accordance with many other actor-training exercises, the Fictional Family begins with self-exploration. In the opening session I employ "ice-breakers" to heighten awareness of the body and its relationship to space: movement games to situate students within space and name games to acquaint them with one another. The games help students become more aware of their breathing patterns, reduce inhibitions, reduce tension, and build energy. As they become comfortable with themselves and each other they build self-confidence in an atmosphere of group trust and mutual support. The activities can promote personal development, communication, and social skills, as well as build awareness in participants of their own creative potential and unique inner resources.

Other early sessions involve exercises to help students connect verbal and sensory stimuli to their memory and imagination. For example, lying on the floor with eyes closed, they are asked to recall past events from their childhood that had special significance for them, taking note of as many details of time, space, and sensory perception as possible. They are then asked to imagine themselves as a participant in that event as it unfolded and to articulate who they are, what they want, and what they are actually doing. This introduces the idea of character objectives needed later in improvising within a fictional family. Such activities help students prepare for a role as a family member of their invention by stimulating sense memory and emotions from their own personal history.

Many sessions feature the use of visualization exercises to inspire creative writing of various kinds. These original texts then become vehicles for students' individual dramatic creations. Students imagine themselves in a particular physical setting or in the role of a certain character and write about that experience. They also write extensive descriptions of a fictional character they want to play in a familial setting. Once that character is chosen, they keep a journal of the thoughts and comments of that fictional character. These texts act as reference points and stimulation in character development.

In using this technique with acting students, the class is divided into groups of from four to six students who together invent a fictional family. They give their family a name, historical background, geographical location, and identify the various family members' ages and positions within the family. Participants develop a particular character by defining its birthplace, personal history, profession, income, religion, likes and dislikes, and personal relationships to and attitudes toward, the other family members. This structure was inspired by Robert Landy's model of extended dramatization with graduate drama therapy students (Landy 1986).

In identifying a character they wish to play, students are free to choose a position or age status that may or may not resemble their positions in their own families. Participants can choose to replay family conflicts and sibling

rivalry or invent new or previously imagined family situations and contro-
versies as they display family dynamics through improvisations. In fact, this
technique allows participants to establish a distance from their emotional
issues because they are enacting scenarios as fictional characters. Their issues
may be those that the actors share with the characters; or, in the case of
social workers, these may be issues related to their client families. Whatever
the basis, both origin of issues and personal insights gained from enactments remain private to the participants during sessions. The providing of
safe distance and privacy to explore remain an important aspect of the
Fictional Family methodology.

An exploration of subtext in both improvised and scripted roles can help
participants to understand how interpersonal relationships in families are
affected by incongruent messages. They can observe how facial expressions,
gestures, body posture, and tone of voice influence communication style,
often conveying meanings opposite to the verbal message. Within the context of an aesthetic form, personal conflicts, issues of relationships, cultural
identity, gender issues, and a variety of other social issues are introduced,
enacted, and evaluated. Since the acting pedagogy takes place within the
context of the family system, the relationship between these roles and
domestic interaction can be explored.

When conducted in the acting class, the course covers seventy-eight
hours. Throughout the year actors participate in a wide range of scenes
improvised from mental images and from written texts, each designed to
achieve particular character-development objectives. A range of exercises
has been designed to develop acting skills such as improvisation, scene
work, and introduction to performance style—elements that contribute to
characterization. However, in the pilot study with family therapists, the
time slot was condensed to twelve hours.

The Project with Family Therapy Trainees

This project took place at McGill University with graduate students who
were family therapy trainees of Diane Reichertz, professor of social work
and director of the McGill Family Therapy Clinic. Enthusiastic about the
idea of trying out my Fictional Family approach, Reichertz assigned eight
graduate students and two supervisors to participate. All ten participants

were working with families in their practice. Only one of the ten participants had any drama or theatre background.

Students met for two hours a week for six weeks; during the first session they were divided into two groups so each group could create a fictional family. All participants stated that they wished to create families unlike their own. In acting classes, students keep actors' notes or journals in which they record their experiences. If they wish, they can describe connections to their families of origin. However, in the present study, time limitations prohibited journal writing; writing was confined to character diaries.

The fictional families were named Van Buren and Ferris. The Van Burens were Baptists living in Montreal, Quebec; the Ferris family lived on a farm in Moose Jaw, Saskatchewan. The Ferrises were nonpracticing members of the United Church. The family members were the following:

Van Buren Family	Ferris Family
Alex, father, 45	Wilfred, father, 47
Martha, Alex's mother, 87	Gillian, mother, 45
Sara, daughter, 24	Erin, daughter, 22
Emily, daughter, 22	Susie, daughter, 19
Alexandra, daughter, 13	Mandy, daughter, 14

Both families were affluent and each had three daughters. Erin Ferris was the biological daughter of Wilfred Ferris and the stepdaughter of Gillian Ferris.

Work Process

The six workshops comprised a sequence of dramatic scenes, each designed to develop multidimensional characters and enhance interpersonal communication skills. Although I suggested the dramatic situations—conflict around a meal, conflict with one other fictional family member, a past incident—the participants themselves were entirely responsible for the content of the scenes they wished to play.

Each session began with physical warmups that involved moving individually in the space within the group to break the ice and make students more comfortable with one another in a performance context. The awareness of their own body postures and rhythms served as a starting point for the physicalization of their fictional families. A ritual of character preparation warmups included visualization and physicalization techniques (Gold 1991).

After creating their fictional families during the first session, students were asked individually to write their characters' autobiographies before the next session and design their "family trees." Toward the end of each session they were also asked to write inner monologues in their journals relating to the scenes they had performed. A student playing the role of Alexandra Van Buren, a thirteen-year-old, wrote:

> I had a big argument with Daddy today because Grandmama was com-
> ing to live with us; I couldn't handle it. We yelled and screamed at each
> other and finally I just left the room. I don't have anyone to talk to so that's
> why I'm writing in this diary. No one understands what it is to be a Van
> Buren. My sisters went to private schools and I go to the public school in
> town. People are only my friends because of what my Daddy has. They
> call me a snob and all sorts of names.

Dramatic Techniques

Participants were generally asked to center their scenes around a conflict issue designed to quickly provoke emotional interaction between family members. They were also asked to identify their characters' objectives. During enactments a variety of dramatic intervention/side-coaching techniques were used in response to the needs of the scenes from moment to moment. The challenge for me as facilitator, therefore, was spontaneously to intervene with the appropriate technique. For example, when actors appeared to lose focus, they were often directed to freeze. They were then asked to face their mother or sister and tell her directly what it was they wanted from her. This technique was used to assist actors, to define and reinforce their characters' objectives, to energize actors, and to facilitate articulation of objectives and expression of emotion. These elements served to increase the intensity of the scene.

Identifying and stating objectives in theatre parallels the use of assertiveness training in behavior therapy as developed by family therapists Bandler, Grinder, and Satir (1976). They state that family therapists should continually assist clients to identify their wants in an effort to initiate effective communication between family members.

Physical games were sometimes introduced to energize the students for the emotional conflict situation they were going to have with another fictional family member. Games were also used when required to refocus or energize the participants or as interventions during or after performance. Other types of interventions, such as altering stage positions and/or adding physical action, were suggested to heighten the intensity of scenes and change their dynamics. For instance, two of the daughters in the Ferris family enacted a scene in which Susie tells Erin that she is packing to leave. In order to generate action that would promote conflict, Susie was directed to pack throughout the dialogue. At the same time, Erin was coached to keep removing the clothes from the suitcase. This device helped the actor playing Susie to focus on her intention to leave and provoked the actor playing Erin to be equally determined to prevent her from going.

In a subsequent scene between the parents, Wilfred and Gillian, Wilfred discovers that his wife is lending Susie money to move out. He sees this as being disloyal to him and resents the relationship between mother and daughter. However, the actors seemed unable to externalize their emotions. In order to heighten dramatic conflict, to build anger and intensity, the actors were interrupted frequently and told that it was thirty minutes later and the argument was still on. This device helped them to express the frustration of a no-win argument where neither party is willing to concede to the other.

By delving into their fictional characters' past during training, actors develop multidimensional characters; in drama therapy, enactment of past events or autobiographical performance pieces are employed to assist clients to come to terms with personal issues. As drama therapist Robert Landy notes, these performance pieces or "psychodramas" are very powerful when the client achieves a distance between "self and other, and self and role" (1986:133).

Participants were asked to visualize a significant event in their character's past and then to write a few poetic lines describing the event. After reading their written pieces aloud they were each asked to join someone else whose piece may have contained a similar theme or related images. They then integrated the two pieces and presented them as one performance piece. The performances were symbolic representations of the fictional family relationships. For example, Gillian and Erin (mother and daughter) were seated back to back, touching in an attempt to connect, but were unable to do so. In another scene Alex and his daughter, Alexandra, were standing at the grave of his wife, Alexandra's mother. They were both sad but could not communicate because this family does not allow expression of emotion. The perceptions of the same process by the child and the adult were profoundly different.

During postperformance discussion the participants confessed that they deliberately chose to present nonconfrontational scenes that day because they needed to distance themselves from the emotional intensity of the previous sessions. It was subsequently noted that their social work training gave them no emotional preparation for handling the incredible intensity and emotional suction of client families.

In another scenario participants were asked to invent secrets for their characters, to record the secret in their diaries, withhold it from their fellow actors, and subsequently reveal it on stage to the person(s) in their fictional families from whom they expected confrontation. Through these new revelations story plots were advanced, allowing students to experience, both through enactment and observation, the myriad situational possibilities than can occur in families. Creating secrets for their characters was also designed to stimulate the actors to delve further into their characters' past lives so that unexpected aspects of their fictional families could emerge.

In family therapy the family secret can be a powerful theme. In her article about family secrets, Imber-Black (1993) describes their "systemic impact." The Fictional Family offers participants the opportunity to experience their power.

Alexandra Van Buren described her secret and the commotion it caused in a series of diary entries: "I took Mom's locket that she always wore. She said I could have it when I was grown up. Dad says Sarah will get it as she is the oldest but Mom promised me. I hid it in the little box that they brought me back from a trip to Europe." A second entry reads:

> The locket's gone! Daddy had one of the maids clean my room and the trinket box is gone. I can't believe it. . . . I'm going to have to tell Daddy about this—he will be so angry! What am I going to say? Daddy thinks that . . . one of the maids took it and he fired her. She was my favourite . . . she would listen to me and play with me and talk to me. . . . Daddy said he would kill whoever took the locket that now belonged to Sarah. Daddy said it was to be Sarah's. He didn't kill Carmella but he sent her away.

A third entry describes the scene that took place: "I have never seen Daddy so angry. I went to my room and cried and cried and cried. I want to run away but where can I go? I'm afraid if I run away no one will come to look for me. Daddy wouldn't care. . . . Sarah and Emily would be happy that they didn't have a little sister any more. . . . Grandma has already said she is tired of being here. . . . I don't know what to do. The locket is still missing!"

At the end of each scene characters were asked to deliver an "inner monologue," or spoken letter, to another family member. Subsequent to the two letters, characters were asked to face each other and make a statement. This technique was employed whenever it seemed appropriate immediately following, or as an intervention during, a particular scene.

Fictional Family Group Encounter

Modeled on a real-life therapy group, the encounter session I directed was designed to offer the fictional family characters an opportunity to listen to, and interact with, another fictional family who also had communication problems. This allowed the actors to develop new choices in communication style for their characters and gave them an opportunity to maintain their fictional family roles throughout an entire session.

Members of both families were seated in one large circle. The Ferris family was embroiled in an issue focusing on their mother, Gillian, who had disclosed as her secret the fact that she planned to go to Europe for a year to write a book. Feelings of rejection, abandonment, and anger were expressed by her family members, but they all had difficulty expressing their emotions directly to her. During the session her husband, Wilfred, expressed his anxiety that she would not return to the family and his need to know her plans. Gillian continued to be noncommittal. Wilfred was coaxed to ask her directly for a commitment.

Finally the discussion focused on Mandy, the youngest child, who needed her mother to remain with her. Mandy had considerable difficulty expressing her needs to her mother. Eventually, following considerable side coaching, Mandy went over to her mother to beg her to stay. Since Gillian was unable to give the commitment the family needed, Susie, Mandy's older sister, was asked to speak for her mother. She said that she (representing Gillian) was not planning to return to her family. Gillian concurred. Using a double in this way is a technique borrowed from psychodrama where the double speaks for the client. The technique has been used to effectively counter resistance to participation by both families and individuals.

The group was then asked to play a tug of war with an imaginary rope in which those who empathized with Gillian would pull the rope on her side, and those on the side of her daughter Mandy would pull on the opposite side. The rope was heavily weighted on Mandy's side. When the game ended the group observed that mothers in general have little support. However, Alexandra Van Buren expressed a lack of empathy for Mandy in her diary: "Today our family went for counselling. I didn't want to go but Daddy said I had to. There was another family there. It was strange. The lady thought I could talk to the 14-year-old because I knew what it was like to lose my mother. But they don't understand. The other girl's mother was just moving away for a while—she'd be back. Mine will never come back."

By incorporating competitive physical games in this fashion the energy generated by the physical activity can be transferred to their fictional family scenes. This provides the opportunity for participants to explore the relationship between inner tension and its physical representation. In a competitive physical game participants focus on winning the game. During an argument they should focus on winning the argument. In this encounter session the participants were asked to pull the rope as hard as possible in order to win. The activity was designed to parallel a family conflict situation in which each individual is trying to win the argument. Sometimes the argument may involve the whole family taking opposite sides. The technique is analogous to family sculpting, the physical representation of the family conflict.

Robert Cohen has pointed out that in a theatrical context, "the concentration on the game situation, and the intention of winning, lends a depth to the interaction and distracts the actor-player from contextual awareness, bringing out greater and greater personal energies. The combination of game-playing and situation-playing is, as a result, an intense theatrical mechanism" (Cohen 1978:27).

Ten Years into the Future

The sixth workshop was centered around a "future-projection" scene. Blatner (1973) describes the future-projection technique used with adolescents in psychodrama whereby they can enact their lives five years in the future. Through their enactments Blatner finds that the protagonists can gain more realistic approaches to their lives and discover that they can, in fact, achieve some successes based on their own work. In family therapy, instilling hope and the belief in the possibility of change is the major task.

Students were asked to write their characters' hopes and dreams for presentation to the group. Future scenes allow actors to expand the possibilities for change in their fictional families, to resolve their characters' personal and/or social issues, and to share an "ending" with the larger group. In the Fictional Family approach students constantly enact their past, present, and future lives in an attempt to fill in what Stanislavski refers to as the "missing pieces" of their characters' lives. In a scripted drama these are the pieces of the characters' lives that comprise the total person but are not written into the actual dialogue of the play.

Both fictional families clearly wished to resolve issues and have happy endings. The participants resisted any dramatic intervention technique that they perceived as leading to conflict. Recognizing this resistance, they were all allowed to end their interaction on positive notes. These happy endings included reconciliations between family members and the discovery of a means of coping with problems on an individual level.

Commentary

Following the final workshop all participants and their professor/observer discussed the experience to evaluate the project. The participants were also asked to create sculptures that represented the family dynamic. These "family portraits" were photographed and included in the videotape of the discussion. The discussion proved enlightening, not only in evaluating this experience but in imagining future applications of the Fictional Family.

The participants all found the course experience very intense. Although there were only six workshops spaced one week apart, they stated that they thought of their characters constantly throughout the week. The writing of character diaries contributed to the ongoing experience of incarnating a character. Some students found the dual family group encounter to be particularly intense because—unlike the other sessions, when they both performed their own scenes and observed other participants' presentations—in this scenario they remained in character throughout the entire session.

Several students stated that after they had presented conflict scenes with one other member of their fictional families in the second session, they sought to distance themselves from their characters so that they would not be exposed to the same emotional engagement in later sessions. Reichertz pointed out the parallel between their resistance and the resistance of clients during therapy. Other students claimed that the intensity of the experience grew in subsequent sessions. For example, the actor playing Mandy noted that during the group encounter scene she was in tears. This show of emotion surprised her, she said, because she is "not usually emotional." Her character did not want to attend the encounter group and was angry at the "therapist" for insisting she go over to her mother and ask her to stay at home with her. She said she maintained her character, but it was difficult.

I mentioned to the group that I constantly ask myself in my acting classes how confrontational I should be, to what extent I should spontaneously intervene, and to what extent I should allow actors to build emotion and intensity on their own. Reichertz said that the same questions apply to the therapist. She pointed out that when therapists generate or allow intensity to develop in therapy, they are engendering the kinds of emotional responses that the participants themselves were experiencing in this project. The clients are asked to expose themselves while the therapists remain fully clothed.

There was some disagreement on Reichertz's role in the project. A cosupervisor expressed the view that her presence as an observer may have impeded students' emotional involvement in their fictional family roles, because of the "hierarchy of Professor, cosupervisor, and students." For this reason she thought Reichertz should have taken on a role in one of the fictional families. Several other students suggested—without specifying why—that in future sessions their professor not be present. Others thought that her presence was unobtrusive or unnecessary.

One student mentioned that she thought Reichertz's observations and feedback were important. Another remarked that the presence of her supervisors and professor demonstrated to her that she could be relaxed with them and enjoy the class. She stated this feeling of relaxation had extended into her therapy work: "Now I don't feel as much pressure in the clinic. I feel more confident in expressing myself."

Still other students thought the professor could intervene more actively as a professional therapist. An alternative approach might be to give the professor the role of a fictional family member who happens to be a therapist. That way she could interact with both fictional families while still participating in the acting experience. However, that might complicate her role in making connections to client families. This idea might be more feasible with a professor who has some acting background and feels comfortable performing with her students.

A student remarked that after hearing some of his fictional family's secrets his character became "angry and drained," similar to the way he feels in actual therapy when the atmosphere becomes too intense. He stated that he constantly tried to parallel our workshops with his work in therapy. Other students said they talked among themselves and figured out as therapists what were the "real dynamics" of the fictional families. One student suggested that in the future the dramatic interventions might be followed by a therapeutic analysis of the dynamics by their professor.

Reichertz asked the participants if they had felt protected by their characters. Some said that they felt a degree of protection but that there was some commonality between them and their characters, so they were not sure how much they were disclosing about themselves when they were performing.

I explained that I had been deliberately using a Stanislavskian/naturalistic approach to acting in these workshops that calls for the actors to begin to develop their characters from their own experiences. However, my experience has shown that actors generally enact as much as they feel comfortable portraying. For example, in autobiographical performance pieces depiction of significant events range from falling off a bike to sexual assault. A cosupervisor stated that in therapy one also starts from oneself, and that clients go only as far as they wish.

Reichertz noted that sometimes students reacted with "giddiness" during emotional scenes. She defined this response as a protective mechanism when "things get hot." One participant stated that the emotional intensity felt "intrusive" at times, that the proximity occasionally made her "uncomfortable," and that "getting drawn into systems and becoming part of that became scary at times."

Toward the end of the discussion session Reichertz reacted to the accomplishments of her students in using the Fictional Family technique, saying:

Isn't it astonishing to create an artificial family with all of you who already know each other well with very solid roles and functions with each other? Muriel comes in and it all gets intense. . . . Isn't it astonishing, amazing, and wonderful that you could do what you did? You succeeded in trusting one another amazingly well. You became "budding stars." You treated each other well. While developing authenticity you were being very careful and good with one another. It pulled all of you together quickly in a nice and easy way.

In response to a questionnaire filled out after the final session, some participants stated that they analyzed some aspects of their fictional family dynamics on their own or among themselves. It appears that the idea of incorporating an intervention where characters "freeze," not only to create dramatic tensions and conflict but also to examine the interaction and application to the client families, would add a useful dimension to the experience.

Most recommended that this analytical intervention should be carried out by the participants' professor. A disadvantage of this approach, as expressed by Reichertz, might be overexposure of the participants to their supervisor. She had provided an acting teacher to work with the students to expose them to a very different set of skills. In future groups, she said, she should not attend workshops at all because "there are only so many hats a person can wear."

Therefore an alternative might be to offer to the theatre director, well in advance of the project, a profile of the client families, including systemic structures, so that the theatre director might act as catalyst to evoke connections to client families. The students could then record these connections in their journals and discuss them with their social work professor.

In addition, situations analogous to those often found in client families could be set up as part of the family therapy training. Fictional families could be created for the entire year. In the first semester students would create fictional families from their own imaginations. In the second semester, they would work with situations based either on their particular client families or from situations commonly seen in family therapy practice. Among the examples that could be cited are the following: in families with weak and inconsistent parental leadership, the children try to tell each other what to do; in families with great tension between parents, the child may develop psychosomatic illness or behavioral problems to keep parents' attention on the child and avoid facing their own problems; a spouse may have had an affair; or one of the parents keeps a secret about one of their children.

Although these types of situations were not deliberately set up in this project, some of these typical samples did appear in the participants' scenarios, either enacted or written in their characters' diaries. For example, Wilfred Ferris's secret was that he had had an affair in the past and has a son whom he has never seen. Working through such experiences would offer participants the opportunity to experience what their client families are feeling. Both supervisors and students agreed that the Fictional Family proved beneficial in getting to know one another very well. Therefore it may be even more beneficial to implement this method during the first term to promote bonding.

The Fictional Family offers a variety of techniques that can be useful to family therapists in their roles of promoting communication and health within families. It can help them to feel comfortable integrating dramatic techniques with conventional interventional approaches. It provides a framework in which they can more confidently express themselves and thereby help their client families to be more expressive. By experiencing fictional characters, participants can build a deeper understanding of the variety of emotions experienced by their clients. By walking in another character's shoes, they can feel what their clients are feeling. During this experience participants sometimes resisted presenting confrontational scenes because they preferred to distance themselves from the emotional intensity the scenes would provoke. Exposing themselves in character emphasized the fact that clients were being expected to expose themselves in therapy while they, the therapists, could maintain their own distance.

Works Cited

Bandler, Richard, John Grinder and Virginia Satir. 1976. *Changing with Families*. Palo Alto, Calif.: Science and Behavior Books.

Blatner, H. Adam. 1973. *Acting In*. New York: Springer.

Cohen, Robert, 1978. *Acting Power*. Palo Alto, Calif.: Mayfield.

Gold, Muriel. 1991. *The Fictional Family in Drama, Education, and Groupwork.* Springfield, Ill.: Charles C. Thomas.

———.1994. "The Fictional Family in Actor Training: A Technique to Develop Characterization." Ph.D. diss., Concordia University, Montreal.

Hagen, Uta. 1960. *Respect for Acting.* New York: Macmillan.

Hoffman, Lynn. 1967. *Family Therapy Techniques.* New York: Basic Books.

Imber-Black, Evan. 1988. "Celebrating the Uncelebrated." *Family Therapy Networker* 12 (1):60–66.

———.1993. "Unlocking Family Secrets, Ghosts in the Therapy Room." *Family Therapy Networker* 17 (3):19–29.

Imber-Black, Evan, J. Roberts, and R. Whiting, eds. 1988, *Rituals in Families and Family Therapy.* New York: W. W. Norton.

Jennings, Sue. 1990. *Dramatherapy with Families, Groups, and Individuals: Waiting in the Wings.* London: Jessica Kingsley.

Johnson, David Read. 1991. Introduction to the special issue on the creative arts therapies and the family. *The Arts in Psychotherapy* 18:187–89.

Landy, Robert. 1986. *Drama Therapy Concepts and Practices.* Springfield, Ill.: Charles C. Thomas.

Leveton, Eva. 1991. "The Use of Doubling to Counter Resistance in Family and Individual Treatment." *The Arts in Psychotherapy* 18:241–49.

Papp, Peggy, Olga Silverstein, and Elizabeth Carter. 1973. "Family Sculpting in Preventive Work with 'Well Families.'" *Family Process* 12:197–212.

Roberts, Janine. 1991. "In Their Own Words: Working with Stories in Family Therapy, Treatment and Training." Toronto, May 1991 workshop pamphlet.

Satir, Virginia. 1972. *Peoplemaking.* Palo Alto, Calif.: Science and Behavior Books.

Spolin, Viola. 1963. *Improvisation for the Theatre.* Evanston, Ill.: Northwestern University Press.

Sternberg, Patricia, and Antonina Garcia. 1990. *Sociodrama: Who's in Your Shoes?* New York: Praeger.

Strasberg, Lee. 1987. *A Dream of Passions: The Development of the Method.* Boston: Little, Brown.

Ads and Ills:

The Social Body, Consumer Culture,

and Activist Performance

Mady Schutzman

I'm walking through the Galleria Mall into an obsessively attractive night-mare of expenditure. I haven't entirely forgotten my allegiance to the disaffected, but the ad industry has this uncanny ability to defy real dis-content through a purchasable product. Torn jeans modeled by Calvin Klein's contemptuous preppies. Revolutionary pantyhose donned by post-hip baby boomers. Coca-Cola's real thing for everyone alienated by Reaganomics, the post-cold-war national identity-crisis, and mediated electronic communities. I climb the circular stairwell that delivers me to the balcony level overlooking the glittering stalls below. I'm a bit weary, but Philip Morris reminds me that "We've Come a Long Way, Baby" mit-igating the feminist sensibility that tells me otherwise. I've always known that obsessive consumption of capitalist ideology in its material form would get me nowhere. But I'm compelled now, racing for a memory that will restore my identity, my feet tracking through the aisles of an Abraham and Strauss outlet as if to an ageless beat. My voice is lagging behind a new primeval passion, my formidable doubt is fading, over-powered by the convergence of childhood helplessness, clearance sales, and the scent of Uninhibited perfume. I am seduced through the gleaming corridors of Neiman Marcus to the glass counter of the cosmetics section to purchase that special thing. A clear but estranged voice emerges from my body. "All You Have to Be Is You," I say, staring ardently at the saleswoman. She doesn't falter for a moment and reaches for the product I know only by ad copy. She leans surreptitiously over the counter. "Avoid a Crisis," she whispers provocatively. "It's on sale." I am already swooning in the dream state I am about to possess. "I'll take it." She rings up $19.95 for Liz Claiborne's latest fragrance and $4.89 for a 16 oz. bottle of Sea Breeze antiseptic. I pass her the money with uncanny relief. For the time being, I have suspended all critical disbelief in the power of advertising and pretend, as if by nature, to be Woman, every woman, shopping.

How might activist performance intervene in hypermediated, image-based cultures that thrive on the suspension of critical thinking and the systematic pathologizing of the female body? In this essay I outline and analyze three workshop/classroom projects that employ performative techniques to disrupt the culture of mass consumption. All these experiments engage Theatre of the Oppressed techniques designed by Brazilian social activist and theatre director Augusto Boal. Each project, however, uses different kinds of stories as the sites of intervention, and investigates and unmasks different aspects of media culture. As will become evident, while the activist techniques fail to directly infiltrate the institutions of image making, interventions are successful when they focus upon the individual lives and bodies inscribed by the ads and ills of media culture, the right arm of the "social body." It is this social body that becomes the crux of the theoretical analysis concluding this paper: how does it breed and disseminate the gendered afflictions of not only popular advertising but of medical science and the mental-health industry?

After introducing Boal's techniques and the principles of capitalist realism against which they are pitted, I will focus on three specific projects. In the first, a collaboration with Women Educate Themselves (WET), individual and personal stories, evoked from advertisements selected by participants, were verbally shared then nonverbally staged as a site for dramatic dialogue. The work attended specifically to gender oppression in women's individual lives and did not confront the culture of advertising per se. The second project was conducted earlier in the context of a college-level course entitled Women and Popular Culture. Here we pursued the more ambitious goal of animating and dramatizing the ads themselves. The third project was an exercise in invisible theatre in which students enrolled in a political theatre class staged interventions at a shopping mall, advertising culture incarnate. Here the objective was to destabilize the advertising ideology that we as consumers have internalized, often unconsciously, by literally penetrating a public space in which these internalizations are cultivated and rewarded. The actors' failure to significantly perturb or even distract mall shoppers was revelatory.

These experiences raise numerous questions regarding the efficacy of activist performance—based on immediacy, presence, and interaction—in impeding, not to mention disabling, the ubiquitous contrivances of mass mediated culture, rooted in reproduction, absence, and disengagement. While not all of them can be answered here, by analyzing the ways in which the experiments failed the very dilemma of performative resistance in the current age of institutionalized repression is illuminated. The invasive strategies of capitalist realism become more and more explicit and thus new possibilities for interventionist techniques are simultaneously suggested.

Capitalist Realism and Theatre of the Oppressed

Approximately twenty-five students at California Institute of the Arts have enrolled in my Gender Advertisements course. Since it's an elective, they have enrolled of their own free will. However, the very notion of free will is about to be sorely tested as I bombard their sensual universe with over two hundred advertising images from contemporary popular magazines. At first they are overwhelmed; upon closer analysis they are aghast at the implicit gender formulations broadcast before them, how insidious and illusive they are, how adeptly the advertisers undermine consumer confidence and self-possession by radically warping the popular mirror through which they are reflected. Then comes the predictable and inevitable disclaimer; I have heard it before in every class on advertising that I have taught: "So what?" His voice is riddled with aggravation and humiliation, as if I have grossly underestimated his intelligence. "We all know that advertising lies to us. We aren't fooled by it anymore." Within minutes a surge of righteous distance and intellectual disaffection infects the class and ostensibly eliminates the previous swell of vulnerability and awe. A safe, cognitive *Aha* now ripples through the room as they agree that their critical interpretation of the ads deems them immune to the psychocultural effects. They join the ranks of very distinguished mass-media critics (Ewen 1976, 1988; Marcuse 1964; Goffman 1979), who, as if by virtue of their academic analysis and acuity, position themselves outside the cultural fog of representational politics. Mass consumers are portrayed, conversely, as hapless dupes, a crowd of indiscriminating dullards.

In fact, the general public is probably as aware of advertising hype as their patronizing fellow citizens in the academy. It may be that this very cultivated awareness (advertising "puffery" and "spin" are well documented by advertisers themselves) provides the psychological arena within which ad manipulation indeed thrives. That is, by recognizing that the ads are superficial renditions of reality, consumers come to believe that advertising's effects on us are also superficial; consequently, in believing we are "above" ads, we consume them with less resistance.

Michael Schudson writes about advertisements as "capitalist realism," the aesthetic right arm of the state through which a mass audience becomes attuned to the same commodities for sale and to the same symbols used to promote them. What is garnered by advertising is an epidemic of abstraction that "does not represent reality nor does it build a fully fictive world. It exists, instead, on its own plane of reality, a plane I will call capitalist realism" (1984:214). In capitalist realism people become incarnations of social categories. Through techniques of simplification and typification, optimistic prospects are the only prospects, and the visual discourse assumes the constancy of "progress." All troubles are absorbed and resolved within the world of the particular product and the style of life it guarantees. Advertisements work, in part, because they look more real than they are;

surface aethetics are overaccented, appealing to just the kind of cinematic intimacy that an alienated public finds alluring. And, finally, the imagery of capitalist realism appeals to sentiments already circulating and popular. It gets potential consumers nodding in agreement over their dissatisfactions and unmet desires before it offers for sale the reformative antidote. Within this fertile field of rampant consumer distress and longing, the industry markets a romanticized and mythic Present—available here and now—that prognosticates an ideal and luring forever to come. It fools people into believing they are exercising free will—making self-directed choices within a plethora of possibilities—when in fact they are complying with a culture of sameness devoted to the obliteration of diversity and criticality.

By midsemester in Gender Advertisements my students are mentally preparing themselves for that suspicious part of the course syllabus that requires "on-your-feet theatrical experimentation." The intention of this experimentation is to enter the ads and their ordained universe, and to alter them by at least making visible the tensions and conflicts obscured by advertising strategies. I introduce a warmup exercise from the Theatre of the Oppressed repertory. We move around twenty-five chairs in the room, cre- ating configurations that would give one particular chair power over all the others. One student sets up the chair with two bodyguard chairs buffering it from a mass of disorderly chairs strewn at its feet. Another student mod- ifies the first arrangement by lining up the "masses" in orderly rows. A third student places the endowed chair in the hallway, out of sight. We are in the midst of political analysis. We discuss how and why certain arrangements deny or grant different chairs power. We are talking issues of visibility and panoptic authority, order versus anarchy, isolation versus collectivity, and the erotic tension between danger and opportunity. With each composition of chairs, students identify different kinds of institutional power— classroom, church, prison, media—and how differently they function. Each arrangement vibrates like the nervous system of an explosive site, flashing forewarnings and possibilities, elucidating the ideological underpinnings that keep certain sites of power effectual. The apparatus that bolsters capitalist realism and its multiple and seductive faces (the advertisements themselves) are made visible and thus more vulnerable to critique.

One of many aesthetic forms of political critique, Theatre of the Oppressed (TO) is an exemplary body of dramatic techniques designed to maximize dialogue, collective problem solving, individual self-empowerment, and the disordering of socially sanctioned power structures. Boal is intent upon creating an environment in which people can rehearse how not to cope and accommodate social mandates. Rather, the goal is to eradicate the madness of isolation, to cultivate a "madness" populated by many, to engage a practice that will provide a map for living fully one's nonprescriptive social position. What makes TO especially potent is its politically conscious treatment of well-being and its therapeutically informed concept of politics. Theatre, and art in general, becomes a conduit between the social body and the individual body, between the institutional structures and biases of late-capitalist ideology and the thoughts and performances of its constituents. What TO makes evident is that the ills of the social body are consumed and internalized by individuals who come to hold *themselves* responsible for the recurrent psychological and physical deficiencies they suffer.

Paradoxically, this mistaken assumption of self-responsibility is itself one of the indoctrinary infusions of capitalist realism that is being internalized: advertisers deliberately incite feelings of deficiency in consumers while simultaneously implying that the source of their dissatisfaction is personal rather than social. Commodities, as representatives of capitalist tenets, are presented as the solution only, bearing no responsible part in the systemic cultural epidemic of discontent and malaise. Culturally constructed categories (such as gender) are made to appear absolute and natural and, subsequently, social forces are conveniently absolved of any accountability.

The pedagogical directives of TO instruct individuals and groups to question and discharge from their bodies those biddings of the social body that prohibit the fulfillment of personal or collective desires, needs, and pleasures. It is often necessary to spend much theatrical time in exercises that reunite participants with their long-forgotten or repressed desires, needs, and pleasures. Boal calls his work rehearsals for the revolution, and his revolution includes, if not depends on, therapeutic values of reflection, vulnerability, interdependence, collaboration, and the critical analysis of one's personal relationship to power.

Theatre of the Oppressed is immediate, live, improvisatory theatre requiring "actors" (training unnecessary), *spect-actors* (observer/participants rather than passive spectators), real locations, and pressing issues that threaten people's survival, quality of life, and/or sanity. Forum theatre (Boal

1985, 1992), the most popular form of TO, is a participatory group process in which spect-actors, audience members, intervene in *anti-models,* that is, scenes in which a protagonist is failing, for any number of reasons, to effect a critical change in his or her circumstances. The anti-model is the core scene of forum theatre. It is an anti-model rather than a model because it is not intended to be complied with or duplicated; rather, it is intended to elicit interventions and the playing out of alternative actions in relation to the antagonist of the scene. At any moment in the scene, spect-actors can yell *Stop,* replace the protagonist in the scene, and act out an alternative to the original, ineffectual approach. For forum theatre to work it is necessary to have the conflict embodied by a named protagonist who faces a crisis of either will, courage, knowledge, confidence, or support in an encounter with an embodied, named antagonist or group of antagonists.

After doing the chair exercise called the Great Game of Power (Boal 1992:150), the students in the Gender Advertisements class selected provocative advertisements and wrote stories from their own lives triggered by the narrative suggested in the images. All the stories revolved around events in which gender was perceived as the criterion of their (mis)treatment. We staged the anti-models, made interventions, and found some alternatives to the disempowering actions that characterized the scenes. As is typical in TO scenes, most of the interventions taught us what *not* to do, seeing the repercussions to be fateful. As spect-actors performed alternative behavior, the antagonists improvised accordingly, maintaining their original intentions. Oftentimes, they were actually afforded opportunities to oppress the protagonist in even more severe ways. Some of the spect-actors' alternatives provided the protagonist with viable choices that the protagonists believed they could access should a similar situation arise in the future.

I have tried several ways of applying Boal's activist, grassroots, culturally democratic, and dinosaurlike aesthetics to the slippery, postmodern, global aesthetic of ads. The contrast between TO's immediate and concrete approach and the illusive, indeterminate structural permutations of mediated power venues is the basis of the "failures" to which I have already alluded: it replicates the contradictions between individual activist struggles to affirm marginalized realities and the politics of capitalist realism. While the process in Gender Advertisements served the students well, it did not pro-

Figure 1   Figure 2

Line drawings by Maureen Selwood.

vide any clues as to *direct* activist interventions into mediated culture. We had transposed the scenes in such a way as to redefine both the target and context of the interventions, shifting from media culture itself to the sphere of the personal, albeit culturally informed. The following example, an independent workshop also conducted at California Institute of the Arts, focused from the very start on personal narratives.

Project 1: Women Educate Themselves (WET)

The women of WET[1] are walking across hundreds of advertising images spread across the studio floor. They each choose two that are particularly intriguing to them, that suggest some personal story in which gender dictated an interpersonal dynamic. In this workshop I was interested in exploring more deeply the psychic connections between the images and personal narrative. What was the relationship between the two images each selected? What specific elements of the imagery elicited personal identification? How, if at all, does awareness of the politics of gender advertising reframe the interpretation of one's own gendered behavior and self-image?

Roberta chooses two images from the Kikit campaign (figs. 1–2): "I consume it," she confesses, "because I see myself in it." She tells a story about

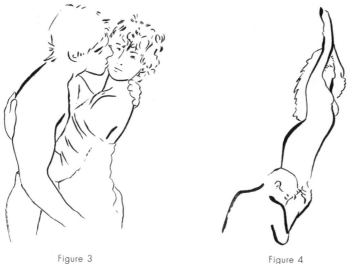

Figure 3   Figure 4

Line drawings by Maureen Selwood.

the power dynamic within her family, with her sisters and mother, her endless attempts to be heard, and the innumerable surrenders. Trying, giving
up, trying, over and over again. It is the seemingly overdetermined physical
intimacy in the ads that captivates Roberta and reminds her of the chronic
and fused aspects of familiar contact.

Kate selects L.A. Models (fig. 3) and a Pheromone perfume ad (fig. 4).
She talks about the notion of muted lust in her life. She identifies with the
ethereal, romantic vision in the ads; she sees her own power as a spiritual
and untouchable private resource. But within a sexual relationship with a
male partner Kate confesses that the passion overflows and violates the fan-
ciful dimensions of the sublime and produces a kind of ruthlessness. She
talks about sexual domination of and by her boyfriend that starts playfully
and then verges on cruelty. The group is spellbound and aroused, intuiting
with ease the logic binding popular imagery to personal narrative.

Overwhelmed with resonant choices, Dana meanders through the glossies
and eventually selects Facsimommy (fig. 5) and an ad for Gianfranco Ferre
boutiques (fig. 6). Margaret takes no time at all in choosing an ad that fea-
tures "Women's Bodies with Children's Faces" (fig. 7) and "Woman with
Mannequin" (fig. 8). Both Dana and Margaret speak of repeatedly servicing
others, of not wanting to, but not stopping either, terrified that the

Figure 5   Figure 6

Line drawings by Maureen Selwood.

consequences (which neither could articulate) would be intolerable. They identify with the dissociation that pervades these images: subtle but clearly substitutive shifts of presence from real to facsimile, woman to animal, woman to child, self to doubledself. Both speak of how one self within them seems to perform certain expected social and "feminine" duties while

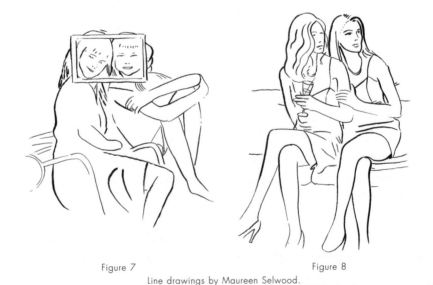

Figure 7   Figure 8

Line drawings by Maureen Selwood.

Figure 9   Figure 10

Line drawings by Maureen Selwood.

an-other self witnesses these performances with disgust, self-pity, and alarm. Adrienne choses Calvin Klein Jeans (fig. 9) and Secret, a deodorant ad (fig.10). Rather than share with the group what attracted her to these two images, Adrienne immediately launches into a personal story with great detail and intensity. Adrienne (transexual and white) tells of having engaged reluctantly in a fight with an African-American woman at a very rough high school where girls are set up to physically fight with one another. The two tallest and most robust women are chosen, a way of simulating, at least in physicality, the fights that the boys at the school perform publicly on a regular basis. Adrienne does not want to fight but does not know how to avoid fighting. She also has no idea *how* to fight. She enters the arena of dirt in the schoolyard circumscribed by primarily male voyeurs and hecklers and begins to attack savagely, without discipline—*boundless* was the word she used. Her opponent, no more interested in fighting than Adrienne, does the same. The brawl is wild and brutal, quite unlike the more sophisticated and regulated "sport" of fighting to which the boys adhere, and perhaps one reason why they so "boundlessly" enjoy it. Eventually, the two girls are pulled apart. Adrienne (for some reason she did not know) is held back by several students and taunted as if she were the one who provoked the altercation. In her reenactment, the crowd hoots and jeers.

In the above exercise, advertisements—those everyday sights to which we are overexposed and seemingly immune—serve as a visual venue through which participants identify interior desires that have been suppressed or obstructed. The implicit voices of fashion designers, focus groups, ad executives, company clients, celebrity spokespersons, and renown trademarks take explicit shape in the more familiar bodies of relatives, peers, employers, and teachers. Like a ventriloquist animating his dummy, language takes form, the implicit becomes explicit, ideology becomes materialized in living bodies. In the process of transmutation from the immaterial to the manifest, the silence and abstraction of the ads become vocal and palpable; bodies of power that were hitherto obfuscated and unapproachable become perceptible and confrontable.

In the WET workshop the participants were more interested in performing image theatre (Boal 1992, 1995) than forum theatre. In other words, rather than staging the scenes for interventions, we did a series of nonverbal exercises in which participants sculpt their own bodies and other's bodies into individual and group images. These frozen images are then *dynamized,* or brought to life, through a sequence of silent, movement-based, and interactive exercises.

We work on our feet, each person making an exaggerated image—a physical self-portrait—of the oppression they experienced in their own story. We identify families, or groupings, of similar or complementary images amidst the various portrayals and recognize the recurrence of rage, resignation, shock, and frenzy. We do the same with exaggerated images of the so-called antagonists of each scene. Through an analysis of the poses and physical attitudes in the context of the particular stories it becomes evident how certain forms of oppression mold individual bodies into vivid portraitures of *social* dysfunctionality and sickness. Through image theatre the social body emerges as a complex web of tensions (hierarchical positions, genders, classes, emotions, and physical posturings) hovering precariously in a state of volatile coexistence.

Lastly, we release the exaggerated postures and return to our everyday habitual bodies. We compare our habitual bodies with the distorted postures we have just identified. We recognize similarities; we literally see how we have accumulated a repertoire of chronic gestures, attitudes, and expressions that signify arrested desires, and that broadcast corporeally—and often unconsciously—the gender politics of the distressed yet sanctioned social body.

I used a different, less personal dramatic strategy to the gendered social body in a 1993 Women and Popular Culture seminar I conducted at a university in upstate New York. Here feminist and psychoanalytic theories rather than individual narratives were the starting point for the scenes and for the deconstruction of media imagery.

After students viewed hundreds of ads we discussed a number of aesthetic tropes used by advertisers to sell their products: (1) naturalization, the presentation of cultural attributes as natural attributes; (2) fetishization, positing the female body as a magical substitute for either the material process of commodity production or, in psychoanalytic terms, for the phallic power supposedly threatened by women vis-à-vis castration anxiety; (3) totalization, collapsing of difference into typologies, demographics, and sameness; (4) objectification, commodity impersonation, and/or devoiding the subject of the image of subjectivity; and (5) appropriation, mimicking attributes of others, particularly those perceived as antagonistic, in order to blur and borrow their power.

Groups formed around each of these five strategies, selected one exemplary advertisement, and staged the advertisement *literally*, that is, simulating the characters and mise-en-scène of the print ads as best as possible. The ads chosen included a woman dressed as a cheetah poised sexually on an array of leopard pillows, a woman leaping preposterously high into the air while playing a tuba and holding the soft drink that inspired all this gusto, and a woman on her back, flat and motionless, clad in the same colors as the barren field in which she lies.

This approach proved the most complex and informative, although perhaps the least effective in Boalian terms. The virtual scene was often impossible to actualize physically due to the capacity of photographic and computer technology to invent bodies, manufacture forms of "beauty" unhindered by the attributes of real bodies, and simulate transcendent environments.[2] Students presented frozen tableaux that elicited humor and an instructional opportunity to experience the physical illogic of the ads.

But the attempt to animate the tableaux and expand them into forum elicited ambivalence and frustration. One problem was that students could not locate their own gendered identities in scenes in which femininity was represented as hyperexaggerated and/or humiliating. In the scenes that we could stage, one problem to overcome was abstraction. How does one embody a two-page Apriori clothing advertisement featuring a woman (shown only from neck to knees) wearing a waffle-patterned dress posing beside an open, old-fashioned waffle iron? In other instances problems arose because neither the anti-models students were staging nor the protagonists they were playing represented meaningful circumstances in their own lives. As a result, the theatrical interventions were essentially irrelevant and superfluous.

The question that reoccurs in both the WET workshop and the Women and Popular Culture class is whether we, in any way, refashioned the culture of capitalist realism. Taking a humanist position, the answer would be affirmative, acknowledging that in the process of rehearsing proactive behavior we exorcise our passivity and reactive behavior. Such revisions can be formidable; the stirrings of popular culture have been known to function historically as "acts of war." In fact, the irrepressible and unpredictable uprisings, inventions, and appropriations of popular culture itself keep institutional forces forever busy working to standardize, neutralize, and devalue the rebellious undercurrents, and thus to steal away, through mimicry, some of their power.

In spite of this humanist rallying, something is perhaps awry in my orchestrated collision of theatrical activism and mediated culture. These two energetic enterprises emit such disparate frequencies, languages, modes of address; they gyrate in such alien and incongruous circuits of information travel. How can confrontational, carnate interventions of live theatre access, not to mention upset, a media culture characterized by disembodiment, bureaucratic specters, invisible hierarchies of power, and antagonists with disguised, shrouded, and mutable faces? How can the immediate and nonreproducible nature of performance counter the incessant and voluminous barrage of mass-reproduced images, symbols, and commodities that defy theatrical time and space? How can a theatre like Boal's that requires the antagonist to be a real person in a specific location at a given time even begin to address Kafkaesque chains of oppression?

These two projects made it evident that while TO techniques are invaluable in the classroom as pedagogical tools, the classroom—like any other institutional space in our culture—embraces the values of commodity capitalism. Nonetheless, the classroom was not the choice site for most effectively challenging media culture. It was necessary to move outside controlled space and time and to interact with consumerism in a space where it was overtly promoted and thriving. The immediacy of TO techniques begged for a less studied environment where spontaneous interaction with an unexpectant public was possible. If there is any cultural hub that embodies the abstract reality of advertisements and serves as a container for its values, it is the shopping mall. And there are plenty of those to choose from in southern California.

Project 3: Valencia Town Center

It is not a far leap from the culture of advertising imagery to the sterile yet deeply paradoxical culture of the shopping mall, public park and marketplace rolled into one, where the dutiful consumers of capitalist realism can now bodily perform its ideological biddings. In the greater Los Angeles area the mall is an essential site of public culture. Since street culture is virtually nonexistent, the mall is the primary space in which the public congregates. In certain fundamental ways, all malls are the same. They are villages of franchises in which one can take an afternoon and acquire clothing and running shoes, fast foods from Mexico or China, an array of ornaments and trinkets, toys and stuffed animals, T-shirts and mugs inscribed with personal names and credos, Hallmark cards, best-sellers, papier-mâché palm trees, silk flowers, camcorders, computers, TVs, and sound systems.

My mall of choice is the Valencia Town Center, conveniently located within two miles of my workplace and housing my favorite Italian restaurant in the Santa Clarita Valley. The main entrance is conspicuously marked by a thirty-six-horse carousel, garrishly painted in various shades of cheerfulness and blaring out tacky carnival music. Upon entering I feel absorbed into a colossal hangar whose steel infrastructure, massive beams, and elaborate interior scaffolding have all been dipped in the most insipid liquid candy. The spatial design is a bizarre hodgepodge of every style of architecture you could imagine, from Gothic to rococo, all drenched in a strangely luminous artificial light that struggles unsuccessfully to simulate the outdoors. The balconies are lined with magnificent live plants that curiously blend in with the painted trees of several offensive colonialist murals that line the two-story promenade. This place, an apocalyptic dystopia masquerading as another southern California paradise, is my—and many others—distinctive every-place and no place.

In spite of all the bodies and activity, there is a pronounced lack of vitality at the Valencia Town Center; within the spectacular contours of boundless materialism and choice, a flat and numbing monotony hangs in the air. What appears to offer a feast of diversity, on closer scrutiny offers only slight variations on nearly identical motifs; particularity is shamelessly effaced. This is the magic of capitalist realism embodied in the mall: an *illusory* profusion of choice stands-in for the *actual* politics of difference that simmers ominously beneath the slippery and deflective surface of prome-nade life. An epidemic of sameness ravages the appetites of consumers and leaves a suspiciously prosaic taste on our ideological palates.

The official code of conduct of Valencia Town Center, graciously pro-vided by its security service, states the following:

> Welcome to Valencia Town Center. In order to make your visit, and that of your fellow shoppers, a pleasant one, we kindly ask that you refrain from the following activity while shopping at Valencia Town Center.
>
> 1. Using physical force, obscene language, obscene gestures, or racial, religious or ethnic slurs which are likely to create a disturbance.
>
> 2. Annoying others through noisy or boisterous activities or by unnecessari-ly staring, by following another person through the Center or by using sexu-ally explicit language or conduct, or in any other way creating a disturbance.
>
> 3. Running, skating, skateboarding, bicycling, obstructing or interfering witht the free flow of pedestrian traffic or with patrons' view of windows and other tenant displays, or assembling for the purpose of disturbing the public peace.

The list goes on to spell out fourteen regulations of appropriate behavior that include the usual, and some not so usual, prohibitions in public spaces: yelling, screaming, singing; playing of musical instruments, radios, or tape players; littering and destruction of private property. Policy number 8, how-ever, is particularly vague and yet incisive in its mandate; it declares that "engaging in non-commercial expressive activity without the prior written permission of the management of the Center" is forbidden.

The students in my Political Theatre class decide to take on the Valencia Town Center. They are mostly interested in engaging shoppers in conversation about their experience of the mall. After a long discussion they conclude that by the time they had formally staged a theatrical scene, they would be whisked away by security. They reject guerrilla theatre for its hit-and-run tactic that would not foster the desired dialogue with shoppers and instead opt for invisible theatre (Boal 1985:143–47).

Invisible theatre is a rehearsed sequence of events that is enacted in a public, nontheatrical space, capturing the attention of people who do not know they are watching a planned performance. It is at once theatre and real life for, although rehearsed, it happens in real time and space and the "actors" must take responsibility for the consequences of the "show." The goal is to bring attention to a social problem for the purpose of stimulating public dialogue. The following narratives are drawn from students' descriptions[3] of their invisible theatre at the Valencia Town Center.

> PANDORA: The purpose of our project was to see how people in the Valencia Town Center would react to . . . [men] going into women's clothing stores and trying on women's clothing. . . . Our group was divided into two pairs. The first pair was the man who was trying on the clothes, Jesper, and his friend, Darin. The second pair was Dave and myself, the anonymous shoppers. The first place we went to was J.C. Penney's because it was the most crowded store we could find on a Tuesday evening.

Jesper is a lean, big-boned, and exceptionally hairy young man who stands approximately six feet two inches tall.

> JESPER: To start off softly I take a blouse and go up to the attendant and ask if I can use their changing room. She smiles jokingly but after looking at my seemingly frank and honest expression she explains to me that ladies are sometimes walking around half naked in there and that a man in there would not be appropriate. She politely directs me to the men's department. I thank her and we walk over there, grabbing a black and white turtleneck and skirt for me to put on. . . . This costuming had a slight ethnic look supported by my sandals. I put it on and walk around. Me and Darin discuss the look of it and get advice from Dave who politely

remarks that the turtleneck looks a bit stuffy. No one reacted except by looks, and still very slightly. In order to expose myself to as many people as possible, I walk back still dressed to the woman's department and grab a summer dress with lots of exposed chest. I am wearing only a thin summer dress and sandals and the only remark we get is from the girl behind the counter who smiles and says, "Can I help you with anything else?"

DAVE: I think the reaction, or lack of it, was revealing. . . . The next step is to move toward the more sacred women's items—lingerie and wedding dresses—and to make certain that our male subject presents himself in highly visible portions of the store, in the front where people in the mall can see, and at a time when a great deal of commerce is going on. I don't want to push it toward making a scene and distorting the nature of the piece. . . . If the lack of conflict continued, we would truly disclose the state of liberality or, more probably, the state of apathy, in the mall.

PANDORA: The next place we went to was a small clothing store called Rave. Jesper was allowed to try on a short flouncy mini dress with big yellow sunflowers. The salesgirl was even quite helpful and answered all his questions. And Jesper was allowed in the dressing room. He got some real funny looks, but that was all.

JESPER: I wanted to try on one more outfit. I tell her I need large or X-large but she has nothing bigger than medium. The salesgirl starts looking and gives me a tiny skirt and extremely short T-shirt to go with it. She implies that it might fit. I thank her and go put everything on. The shirt is so small that it almost splits open. The skirt is so short that I have to pull up my shorts not to see them. It is very hard not to laugh at what I see in the mirror and even harder to go out to the other people in the shop. I hold my breath and walk out. The shop assistant looks up from the back of the store and then looks down only to continue working. There is no reaction from the cashier either so I got back into the dressing room and put on my own clothes.

Dave, Pandora, Darin, and Jesper are frustrated at not being able to arouse even the slightest discussion but realize that herein lies a meaningful clue to their investigation of mall culture. They are rightfully skeptical about the seemingly indifferent and nonoppositional attitudes of the store staff and shoppers. How can gender roles be so culturally contentious (in spite of increasing promotion of cross-dressed and unisex looks in the couture industry) and yet elicit such reticent responses when challenged in public? Perhaps this reticence is, in fact, a regulated response generated rather insidiously by mall policy and culture itself. Jesper did experience some antagonism from passing male shoppers who censured him with hateful, contemptuous glares. This relatively mild reaction is likely a censured one as well, inspired by an atmosphere that encourages hyperneutrality. The mall aura is a shock absorber that mutes and condemns conflict, disturbance, and emotional responses. Consumers are there, in part, to avoid being subjected to any marginal, provocative, or atypical conduct, to experience a safe place where their prescribed emotional, psychic, and moral equilibirum will not be tested in any way. They are there to experience the blissful absence of social discord and accountability characteristic of capitalist realism.

The policy that my students so desperately wished to challenge—the prohibition of expressive "noncommercial" activity—was more widespread and trenchant than they imagined. They concluded that in order to be heeded they would have to exaggerate and intensify their presentations to highly sensational (hysterical) and/or offensive (perhaps even criminal) levels. They decided against this choice as they recognized the dangers of pathologizing their own actions in the attempt to become visible. The irony here is complex and troubling: in the attempt to do invisible theatre in the mall, to become visible at all (enough to be responded to), the action would have to get so big as to become hypervisible, thus unbelievable as invisible theatre, and consequently dismissable as unreal or "just theatre."

This became evident with another group of students in my Political Theatre class who called themselves the Consumer Hysteria group, a foretelling title that amused me given my extensive research on female hysteria and the media. They worked in pairs and planned to stage invisible theatre scenes that would exaggerate different emotional states: (1) a screaming dispute between a straight couple at the centrally located mall fountain; (2) uncontrollable tears when a woman cannot find at Sears a remote control for a toaster for her ailing grandmother; (3) relentless and boisterous laughter from the balcony as two students stare down mockingly at the shoppers below. As with the first group, their actions initially got no response other than peripheral glances. They too realized they would have to intensify their performances and, unlike the first group, they all did so. They reached nearly grotesque proportions before being approached by security, and even then the guards merely stood by with reproachful stares. The sobbers and laughers had pushed to such a point of distortion that they felt they had cast themselves as zoo animals, exhibiting ghastly deformations of the original emotional behavior. Even the loud arguing couple did not manage to draw an audience. One elderly man asked the woman (who was doing most of the screaming) if she was all right. The more "impassioned" response from the crowd came when Michael, the man in the argument scene, raised his voice and took a step toward Lisa: the crowd quickly backed away from the action, leaving the invisible actors to deal with their "private dispute."

Hysteria and Criminality

Let's consider the ramifications of activism contingent on the kind of sensational or spectacular representations that the invisible theatre performers felt were an imperative in the mall environment. As indicated earlier, both hysteria and criminality—as aesthetics and symptomologies—become relevant here. While hysteria no longer bears substantial weight in the applied lexicon of medical science, it has, in fact, become a relatively popular paradigm among cultural critics for analyzing cultural phenomena of late capitalism (not unlike Lasch's [1979] use of narcissism and Deleuze and Guattari's [1983] use of schizophrenia). In a previous work (Schutzman 1994) I theorized hysteria as the normalized "pathology" of consumer society, particularly among women who are ceaselessly subjected to the mediated iconography of the female body. They must reconcile the discrepancies between their personal experiences of self and their consumed representations of female experience. Hysteria can be understood as an epidemic of culturally fabricated femininity; hysterical symptoms are the overdetermined signs of distress predicated on the suppression of voice and of subjectivity that accompanies this impossible reconciliation.

When the experiences of an individual or collective are dismissed, negated, shamed, or pathologized, they are necessarily transformed in the direction of perversion. In the case of hysteria, expression begins to take on symptomatic qualities of desperation, hypersensitivity, mockery, and exaggeration (to name just a few; the documented symptoms of hysteria number in the hundreds). But these hysterical reactions—suggesting a seeming inability to sustain rational, controlled, or coherent self-representation—do *not* signal a shortcoming or inherent malady of the persons who exhibit it. Rather, they are culturally determined responses to social and political inequities and biases, many of which are manifest in ads. Nonetheless, in our late-capitalist consumer society they bear the stigma of a personally and psychologically based disorder of epidemic proportions among women. Advertising asserts these "hysterical" qualities as essential, biologically based attributes of women, thus a cultural fiction is portrayed as a natural or scientific fact.

These stigmatized symptoms, however, beg to be read as more than mere signs of women's victimization at the hands of advertisers. "Through hysterical symptoms women are, in fact, articulating the problematics of sexual difference imposed upon them by a false construct of female identity. These symptoms express female silencing and invisibility *while simultaneously breaking that silence and visualizing that invisibility*" (Schutzman 1994:1–2). In other words, hysteria is also a form of protest (albeit with restricted access to symbolic resources) that seeks to harness the spirit of insubordination within the belly of the commercial beast; hysteria screams, caricatures, and exaggerates because nothing less than spectacular, gross, and offensive displays (on the part of women, minorities, disenfranchised others) seem to be heeded.

The application of a maligned hysterical or other pathological diagnoses to aesthetic performances is invariably employed in relation to socially restricted groups: to the poor, to ethnic and racial minorities, to women, children, lesbians, and gays. These marginalized (not marginal) groups naturally reciprocate to their stigmatization with creative variations of frenzied, rageful, self-indulgent, overdetermined, attention-getting, and spectacular behavior. Subsequently their conduct is typecast in the mainstream media, in medical classifications, and in legislation as immoral, sick, and criminal, respectively. The cycle of cultural ghettoization is reinforced over and over.

As I've already implied, the "offensiveness" of our work becomes subject to the stigmas of the criminal as well as the hysterical. To a certain extent theatre artists who do not distinguish the criteria of their art from the criteria of their political judgments would have to concur with Jean Cocteau's assertion that "art should follow the example of crime" (Cocteau 1988:33). How could it not? The only way to literally, performatively deconstruct mall culture is, first, to physically enter it and become part of it and, second, to violate it.

We are immediately faced with the issue of ethics. If we try to work in complete adherence to the mall's official definitions of right and wrong (as elusive as they might be), we compromise our goals by making art that reproduces the very structures and ideological purposes we desire to overthrow. Once we begin to locate the structural paradoxes, twisted language, and internal contradictions, we find a stage. But this stage will always be subject to arrest.[4]

I do not mean to imply that all forms of burlesque, melodrama, satire, slapstick, and caricature become ineffectual on a basis of some omnipotent dogma that deems them all hysterical or criminal. As indicated earlier, such forms of popular theatre have been, at times, efficacious in assailing the progenitors of social misery, injustice, defamation, poverty, and abuse. But as Joan Holden notes in her article "In Praise of Melodrama," it has become necessary for progressive, innovative theatre artists to find ways to integrate the imagery and strategies of melodrama with those of deconstruction and critical theory. Holden calls the new hybrid "postmodern melodrama" (1990:280). The broad, loud, visual, and emphatic gestures and language that characterize political melodrama must be stretched not only to deflect the stigmatization and morality but to incorporate a self-critical awareness of its place within the arena of debate. It needs to include some of the fluidity, ambiguity, fragmentation, polyphony, and deconstruction that characterizes postmodernity and inescapable mediated culture without undermining its political agenda and call for collective action.

One major unanswered question is whether such representational flexibility is possible without snapping the very political and activist muscle we are trying to exercise. We wonder whether, if we are anything less than obscenely obvious and bold, we will even be heard. If we are obscenely obvious and bold, will we not be dismissed as hysterical and offensive? Is there a way to perform the dilemma itself?

Ads and Ills

An intriguing trajectory has been cast. In exploring how theatre, particularly Theatre of the Oppressed, can intervene in the image world, I am necessarily seduced into the very political meaning of exhibitionism and spectacle.

Given the obvious associations with hysteria, I am, in turn, obliged to confront how these performative tropes share and borrow meaning from the world of medical science and mental health. *Health,* however ambiguous the term may be, can serve as an incisive nexus for investigating the notion of the individual body as a sociocultural object, as a product of the social body.

The medical and legal sciences have employed physiognomies and typologies for centuries to serve as their own set of models and anti-models, signifiers to the public at large of how to appear and *not* to appear to avoid being labeled unhealthy or immoral. Studies done over a hundred years ago citing correspondences between mental health and a discernible "look" (Gilman 1977)—although they have been critically refuted—have not been entirely rejected by practitioners as clinically unsound. Contemporary researchers continue to come up with new ways to render illness, criminality, moral or affective temperament by sight,[5] or by one's interpretation of another's performance, as was the case with hysteria.[6] The fashion and advertising industries, at the service of capital, promote similar bundles of visual barometers of the healthy and, consequently, the unhealthy person. One frighteningly polemical 1994 ad for Look and Company Music shamelessly celebrates the importance of looking:

> *Look* at life in a new way. *Look* at what you've been doing. *Look* at how you've been acting. *Look* at yourself in the mirror. *Look* at your neighbor. *Look* at your partner. *Look* at your friends. *Look* at the world as your oyster. *Look* at what we're saying. *Look* at us. *Look* on the bright side. *Look* at your job. *Look* beyond the obvious. *Look* what matters in life. *Look* harder. *Look* who's talking. *Look* who's doing. *Look* who's making a difference. *Look,* no one said it would be easy. *Look* what the future has in store. *Look,* it's only your career.

Other ads define the consumer, particularly how she feels inside, by virtue of how she looks on the outside, as a visually readable performance. An example of this kind of ad was produced by Nike. Its 1994 campaign entitled "Love in Six Acts" included a six-page spread in which six different emotional states—lust, fear, disgust, euphoria, greed, and "truth"—were represented by the diverse body languages of six different women. Vitabath advertisements present a similar correlation between looks and interior experience by having different women appear as manifestations of three different scents. The women are called "fanatics"—sensual fanatic, intellectual fanatic, and psychological fanatic—and each demonstrates rather clichéd physical gestures representing the special quality they are at once embodying and selling. These looks provide a mythic template for instantaneous assessments of people's interior landscape. We are then seen in relationship to this template, and our experiences of our selves become transformed by how others see us. Put another way, mental health in contemporary popular culture is defined, in large part, by the image of the facade, the fabrication, the *Look*.

By assigning everything and everyone a visual valence that functions as a quick calibrator of social merit, consumers are saved the bother of having to question, probe, interact, encounter difference, evaluate experience and/or experience the process of making evaluations for oneself. Subtlety and discretion become tedious and time-consuming distractions. The very notion of health in Boal's Theatre of the Oppresed depends precisely on the activation of interaction, encounter, and self-evaluation, those factors that clearly frustrate and upset the smooth operation of mediated culture. But interaction first demands visibility and exposure. That is, the protagonists of TO must deal with the politics of visibility, how and when their biddings for acknowledgement, inclusion, and self-representation will, in fact, be respected.

As we have seen, the notion of seeing and visibility has been usurped by advertisers as an act of categorizing and dismissing rather than incorporating and encountering. The issue of activist intervention in media culture becomes something of a fierce semiotic war over the meaning of visibility itself. The revisioning of "vision" within capitalist realism facilitates corporate goals of realizing healthy profits, not healthy citizens. Their kind of vision—or antivision—comes along free of charge whenever we engage in the process of consumption. It shows us that we are free to avoid reflection, questioning, or unwanted interferences into our routines. We are free to surrender to an intimacy with artifice. We are free to look at ourselves resolved by airbrushing, photographic studio lighting, cosmetic surgery, and narcissism. We are free to exhibit symptoms of anorexia, obesity, hysteria, violence, and self-denigration, and to thus mark ourselves as targets for social cleansing. In this way, advertising fulfills its ambition to be "capitalism's way of saying I love you to itself" (Schudson 1984).

It is fortunate that in spite of the totalizing and hierarchizing tactics of ad imagery, the visual messages of advertisements regarding health are riddled with contradictions. For instance, anthropologist Robert Crawford (1984) points out that while the advertised/performed body is the site of health, health is alternately envisioned as self-control or discipline and as release or abandon. On the one hand, we are inundated with images that teach us self-denial: construct a firm body governed by order, diligence, labor, and regulation. On the other hand, we are warned that we might jeopardize our health if we deny ourselves the pleasures of abandon and gratification: indulge yourself, relish the abundance and freedom of capitalism. The oscillation between these two oppositional mandates is evidenced in a social body that endures the waves of recession and inflation: conservative, frozen stockpiling rejoined by excessive, reckless spending. For the individual body, particularly the female body employed to broadcast this polarity, the oscillation might be understood as what Susan Bordo (1993) cites as the injurious and toxic mandate to purge/regulate and then binge/release.

I refer above to Crawford's exposition of contradictions as fortunate only in hopes that the duplicity may become an arena for dialogue, for generating ideas for further projects that bring performative techniques into confrontation with media culture. Rather than getting lost trying to stage the elusive abstraction of ads, or entering individual images as if they were divorced from the culture of mass reproduction, or performing hysterically to mallgoers performing their indifference, Crawford offers another starting point: two stark and contrasting *looks*/performances that disarm capitalist realism of some of its luring mythic abstraction and romantic oversimplification. The binging and the purging scenarios can perhaps be recognized as two anti-models between which we swing incessantly and yet blindly. Perhaps a next project would seek to "stage" (visibly or invisibly) these two poles (and the often invisible movement between them) to better recognize the infrastructural space that allows for such radically unhealthy embodiments of nonintegration, denial, and sickness. It may be that this transitional arc is a potential site where a different consciousness can be forged, and where countermediated or remediated interventions can be made. By staging scenes in which we are flailing between antivisions, we may discover something healing—something urgently called for—precisely in that nauseating undulation between the two. And if we are to consider such movements toward health as inextricably linked to politics, then we will be joining Boal on a very long, performative, and uncertain road toward change.

Postscript

In the process of composing this article I conducted several workshops with an organization called Reach LA.[7] They had just hired four youth educators—two Latino women, one Asian woman, and one African-American man, all between the ages of fourteen and seventeen—to learn Theatre of the Oppressed techniques so that they, in turn, would conduct workshops with their peers on issues of violence, health education, and safe sex. The newly hired educators asked their friends to participate in the workshops so that there would be enough people to stage scenes; for several months I worked with approximately fifteen teenagers in a small studio space in downtown Los Angeles.

The focus of these workshops was not image culture or advertising, and yet the confrontation between Boalian performative techniques and media culture could not have been more profoundly manifest in the workshop. The youth were living embodiments of the media culture I have tried to somehow isolate, locate, or stage in order to unsettle theatrically. Their attention span was extremely short; they had no working concept of analytical or critical thought. They were intimate with advertisements, movies, television, and video games in an affective but not cognitive way. They could copy *what* I did as TO facilitator but could not remember *why* I had done it, thus greatly limiting, or so it seemed, the pedagogical value of what I was teaching. Exercises that required either rigorous analytic concentration due to their complexity and/or those that did not involve lots of physical activity led to inattention, sudden attacks of hunger, hyperactivity, and/or despondency.

In attempting to accommodate their particular skills and limitations, I went through more exercises in three days than I usually do in weeklong workshops. But I also learned that I could repeat those same exercises many times over without complaint. In other words, in order to achieve depth of understanding, it was most effectual to do the same exercises for short periods of time, over and over again in the course of the training. Although their attention span increased only slightly, their absorption of meaning increased immensely.

While this work veers somewhat from the advertising emphasis of this essay, it has suggested to me that using Boal's techniques with American youth may be an effective and significant platform for exploring some of the issues and questions raised here. For instance, the inability of these young trainees to absorb the philosophy and criticality of TO possibly reflects the inability of shoppers to absorb the interventions of the invisible theatre students at the mall. This has suggested to me that daily performative actions (of perhaps the same invisible theatre pieces) at the seemingly impenetrable mall might prove efficacious, just as continued repetition of the TO exercises eventually penetrated the teenagers' high-speed MTV-informed sensibilities and eventually grabbed their attention and interest.

Notes

1. WET is an informal organization of female students, faculty, and staff at the California Institute of the Arts. The students were by far the most assiduous participants of WET activities. They asked me to work with them on issues of sexuality and representation using TO techniques. The workshop described was conducted in March 1994.

2. Of course, theatre is also capable, to an extent, of such invention, manufacture, and simulation. But as live spectators, at even the most magical of proscenium spectacles, we more readily bear in mind the process of fabrication and the apparatus employed to create theatrical illusions and to transport us into states of suspended belief. Advertisers are particularly adept at blurring if not entirely eradicating this apparatus; by willfully veiling the modes of production, they endow their images with a truth function that makes that which has been aesthetically and ideologically orchestrated appear unequivocable.

3. Pandora, Jesper, David, and Darin were students at California Institute of the Arts when this invisible theatre project was enacted.

4. It may be interesting to note that in British slang, "to shop" means to arrest or imprison. Shoppers at a mall engage in collective self-imprisonment. The question remains: How do we stage jailbreaks among criminals who don't want to leave prison?

5. I recently learned of a study group in San Francisco working on computer-generated images that can provide a standardized spectrum of appearances (facial proportions, muscular tensions, etc.) for determining whether someone is healthy. Also, the *DSM IV,* the bible of medical diagnoses, offers symptoms for various disorders (for example, histrionic personality disorder) that can be read only by a subjective witnessing of another's performance. No physiological or psychological testing can measure the supposed affliction. As for typological diagnoses of criminality, see late nineteenth-century Italian author Cesare Lombroso, best known for his work on the "female offender."

6. Hysteria has never been proven to have any physiological base. Even one hundred years ago when hysteria was supposedly a serious epidemic among women, it was founded on subjective readings of performance rather than scientific evidence. It was not until 1987, however, that hysteria was eliminated from the *DSM,* the official diagnostic manual of the American Medical Association. The classic hysterical symptoms were parceled out to other more clinically substantiated mental disorders. The change in classification suggests that contemporary medical practitioners recognize the elusive, indeterminate, and visual or exhibition-based qualities of the ailment we call hysteria.

7. Reach LA is a youth-driven HIV-prevention organization utilizing the media and performing arts for innovative AIDS education. Reach LA serves adolescents in the South Central, East, and Central Los Angeles areas.

Works Cited

Boal, Augusto. 1985[1979]. *Theatre of the Oppressed.* Trans. Charles A. McBride and Maria-Odilia L. McBride. New York: Theatre Communications Group.

——.1992. *Games for Actors and Non-Actors.* Trans. Adrian Jackson. London: Routledge.

——.1995. *The Rainbow of Desire: The Boal Method of Theatre and Therapy.* Trans. Adrian Jackson. London: Routledge.

Bordo, Susan. 1993. *Unbearable Weight: Feminism, Western Culture, and the Body.* Berkeley: University of California Press.

Cocteau, Jean. 1988. *Diary of an Unknown.* New York: Paragon House.

Crawford, Robert. 1984. "A Cultural Account of 'Health': Control, Release, and the Social Body." In *Issues in the Political Economy of Health Care.* Ed. J. B. McKinlay, New York: Tavistock.

Deleuze, Gilles, and Felix Guattari. 1983. *Anti-Oedipus: Capitalism and Schizophrenia.* Trans. Robert Hurley, Mark Seem, and Helen R. Lane. Minneapolis: University of Minnesota Press.

Ewen, Stuart. 1976. *Captains of Consciousness: Advertising and the Social Roots of the Consumer Culture.* New York: McGraw Hill.

———.1988. *All Consuming Images: The Politics of Style in Contemporary Culture.* New York: Basic Books.

Gilman, Sander L., ed. 1977. *The Face of Madness: Hugh W. Diamond and the Origin of Psychiatric Photography.* Secaucus, N.J.: Citadel Press.

Goffman, Erving. 1979. *Gender Advertisements.* Cambridge, Mass.: Harvard University Press.

Holden, Joan. 1990. "In Praise of Melodrama." In *Reimaging America: The Arts of Social Change.* Ed. Mark O'Brien and Craig Little. Philadelphia: New Society.

Lasch, Christopher. 1979. *The Culture of Narcissism: American Life in an Age of Diminishing Expectations.* New York: Warner Books.

Marcuse, Herbert. 1964. *One-Dimensional Man: Studies in the Ideology of Advanced Industrial Society.* Boston: Beacon Press.

Schudson, Michael. 1984. *Advertising, the Uneasy Persuasion: Its Dubious Impact on American Society.* New York: Basic Books.

Schutzman, Mady. 1994. "The Aesthetics of Hysteria: Performance, Pathology, and Advertising." Ph.D. diss., New York University.

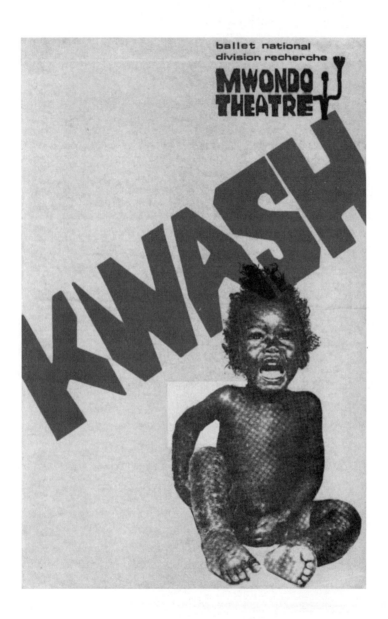

Poster by Denis Franco.

Kwash and Other Ventures

in Contaminating Theatre

Jill Mac Dougall

Serendipity has played a major role in my involvement in theatre as a public health communication medium. Little in my early background— training as an actress in a French classical theatre school or cofounding experimental theatre ensembles, first in France and later in Zaire[1]— predicted this. I became involved in the field in the late 1970s while work- ing with the Mwondo Théâtre of Zaire. Fifteen years later, after returning to North America via Quebec to complete graduate degrees in *art drama- tique* and then performance studies, I seized the opportunity to use theatre in public health education while training health educators in theatre at the University of Montreal and teaching an acting course in a Philadelphia nursing school. Until 1993, when I began organizing conference panels on the intersections of theatre and public health, I considered this work as peripheral excursions away from my theatre projects and scholarship. I have since come to see how experimental theatre and improvisation laid the groundwork to an evolving praxis of theatre in health education.

The material of this article is intertwined in a personal and professional journey where serendipity continues to play a major role. This research essay describes a past trajectory and a theoretical path in the making through two case studies:

- *Kwash,* a production on childhood nutrition by the Mwondo Théâtre instigated by pediatricians and dieticians in Lubumbashi, Zaire
- Workshops in the use of theatre in public-health communications conducted at the University of Montreal for health professionals from Francophone countries

The concluding section touches on more recent acting workshops with nurses in training completing their associate degree at Pennsylvania State University. The issues of agency, context, and message that emerged from the *Kwash* experience continue to influence my teaching methods and to drive my research on theatre in public-health communications. This work suggests a methodology of reciprocally contaminating performances as a healthy principle toward producing change.

K w a s h

The Mwondo Théâtre

Founded in 1969, the Mwondo was the first professional Zairean company to use national languages and the rich verbal arts of the region to produce works that centered on local social problems and that toured in Zaire, Africa, and Europe.[2] Originating in a teacher-training high school in Chibambo, a Bemba village set on the banks of the Luapula River, the company later moved to Lubumbashi, center of the country's copper mining industry. Despite the presence of two Westerners, the shift from a rural to an urban context, and its subsequent international tours, the Mwondo remained a grassroots company, performing in Lubumbashi Swahili and other languages of their popular audience. And despite the fact that all its productions were driven by a sociocritical and activist mission, the troupe enjoyed the approbation of Mobutu's neocolonial dictatorship for many years. This was due to multiple factors, not the least being that the company constituted a *vox populi* in the national *authenticité*[3] campaign.

Because of its apparent official approval and its evident popularity, the Mwondo was approached in 1977 to work on an educational campaign against malnutrition undertaken by local doctors. The doctors were working in the hospitals and clinics of Lubumbashi that fell under the aegis of three mainstays of the urban center: the university, the national railroads, and the national copper industry. Alarmed by the increasing number of children afflicted with kwashiorkor[4]—a disease caused by severe protein deficiency—the doctors turned to the Mwondo to spread the word on what constitutes good nutrition in Lubumbashi and neighboring towns. The ostensible reasoning was that the rise of cases in the city's clinics could only be due to negligence or ignorance on the part of the children's caretakers.

Why kwash should be on the rise or why parents employed by the mining companies should suddenly become negligent or ignorant was hardly apparent. Kwashiorkor had been a rare phenomenon in the experience of these urban clinicians, something that might fester in deprived hinterlands of poorer African countries but did not belong in the wealthy copper capital of Zaire.

Excited by the prospect of a paid contract that would allow the company to survive during the three-month research and production period and by the opportunity to collaborate in an undeniably useful project, the Mwondo actors set out to learn everything about childhood malnutrition from local health educators and began conducting interviews with their neighbors to draw lessons about the popular conceptions of kwash. With the doctors, we approached the problem of malnutrition as primarily educational: a translation of biomedical causality into "local knowledge" that would subsequently lead to a shift in nutritional habits and, hopefully, the eradication of the disease. That the rise of malnutrition in the urban center's children corresponded to the first years of an economic crisis in Zaire—a crisis that would reach epic proportions in the next two decades—can only be seen a posteriori. What did become rapidly apparent was that *Kwash*—this production that in all earnestness sought to educate and not to critique or provoke—was the most potentially revolutionary piece the company had ever created.

Musikiye (Listen)

There were two phases to the initial part of the process: collecting data from health educators and talking to parents about their reading of kwash symptoms and their ideas on keeping children healthy. The lessons in health education consisted of lectures and slide shows on the causes and signs of childhood protein deficiency and its prevention. The ABCs of a well-rounded diet and sources of protein in locally available produce were emphasized. At the top of the list were meat, fish, eggs, milk, and soy—a product that dieticians were attempting to introduce in place of the protein-devoid corn or manioc flour as daily staple—followed by kidney beans, manioc leaves, and edible insects. The symptoms and progression of kwashiorkor illustrated by the slide shows were more dramatic than the lectures: children crying in hunger, children whose hair and skin had turned orange, children with dead eyes, emaciated limbs, and swollen bellies.

At the end of the lessons what prevailed in the conversations between the dieticians and the actors—many of whom were parents themselves and certainly not from the privileged class—was a sense of bewilderment. Why, in a culture in which children are considered the primary wealth and in a geographical region where meat, grain, and vegetables are readily available, should children suffer from malnutrition? Could it be due to food taboos against eating eggs or to superstitions concerning the origins of the disease?

The Mwondo actors interviewed child caretakers—mothers, aunts, fathers, older siblings—in their neighborhoods concerning the symptoms and causes of kwashiorkor. Here the disease's manifestations were considered primarily as signs of neglect and social breakdown. Joining biomedical views on infant malnutrition, the first cause cited was premature weaning. Deprived of her mother's milk, the baby's hair turned red because she was jealous of the younger sibling the mother was nursing. This was a metaphor that both dieticians and psychologists should readily understand. Other reasons given for the child's deterioration were being abandoned by irresponsible relatives or left without a primary provider. Protein deficiency per se did not figure in these explanations of kwash. But neither did beliefs in sorcery or, when questioned about what children need to eat, did food taboos.

The biomedical and social data were all very concrete and seemingly complementary. Our task appeared simply to put together a show that would combine these two takes in a straightforward message. The Mwondo set out with its usual method of treating information received as material for improvisation and dramatic structuring. Having listened themselves for a time, the actors now wanted their audience to sit up and listen.

The actors opted for a simple story and a narrator who could dialogue with the spectators. They also wanted to lend what they called a *Highlife* spirit to the performance. This term—coming not from Zaire's traditional or renown pop music, but drifting in from Nigeria, Ghana, and neighboring Zambia—evoked urban nightlife, from clubs to illicit bars. The urban beat was direct, lively, compelling to the audiences in the mining towns where the play would be performed. This concept combined with *babatoni,* the music of neighborhood kids who fashioned banjos and drums out of oil cans and gave street shows imitating Highlife bands.

Each of the ten performers, who constituted the narrators, musicians, dancers, and actors of *Kwash,* wore black vests and pants slit up to the knee. Chorus line dance formations with broad, synchronized gestures and direct address to the audience in the songs punctuated the narrative. Moving back and forth between this direct address and dialogue between characters elaborated before the eyes of the audience, the fiction was overtly framed as theatre, a story enacted in the present.

In the opening song the cast moves to the edge of the stage and, with stylized gestures, invites the audience to witness the story about to unfold:

> *Musikiye wa ndugu wa penzi*
> Listen, dear brothers and sisters,
> Once there was a family with children
> One got sick, very sick
> So thin, yet swollen, so red, so changed.
> What could be the reason?
>
> Witness, dear brothers and sisters,
> It's late at night,
> A mother is sleeping next to her children,
> Where is the father of this family?
> Listen, he is fumbling at the door.

When cited in the song, the actors playing the mother, the two children, and the father step out of the chorus and take on attributes and attitudes of their roles. The mother wraps a bright orange broadcloth over her black pants, straps an "infant" on her back, and lies down. The children roll up their pants legs and lie down, a toddler cuddling near his older brother. The father grabs a beer bottle and begins pounding at an imaginary door.

The drama opens with a crisis. Gritting her teeth, the mother determines not to let the father in, but the eldest child—about six—is awakened by the wails of his younger brother and opens the door. A brawl ensues and the mother storms out with the baby, leaving the father to fend with the two boys who huddle together, terrified.

Without a clue in daily childcare, the father decides to confide his sons to his older sister the next morning. The aunt is a widow, mother of a large family herself, and a market woman. Occupied with her business, she in turn leaves the children in the care of her own children. The teenage cousins resent the intrusion of the younger boys and, especially, the fact they have to share their food. The eldest distributes the meat according to age hierarchy and leaves the two little intruders with the leftover *bukari* (corn or manioc mush).

On a pure starch diet and with little resistance to opportunistic disease, the younger child quickly falls ill. The musicians sing *"Kwa nini kwashiorkor?"* (Why kwashiorkor?), which asks, "What is wrong with this child, why doesn't he play, why is his belly so fat and his arms so thin?" The aunt is too busy to notice that the little one is wasting away. As for the voracious cousins, they are rather pleased there's one less at the table. The six-year-old brother, who at first tried to comfort and defend the toddler, is himself locked in a struggle for scraps of meat and dregs of sauce. During one last horrendous meal where the older hyenalike cousins are devouring all the meat, the youngest child appears to be sleeping. The chorus sings a traditional Lunda lullaby: "*Wova rinkind,* Mama, hear the wind blow. Papa's coming too, hear the wind." The song shifts to Swahili to announce that the child has in fact died and to renarrate the incidents and causes leading to his death.

"He won't wake up," says the older brother when his aunt returns home. She shakes the child and then wails to announce the death. The others join her in a mourning scene. The child is wrapped in a shroud and lowered into the "grave" over the edge of the stage. As the mourners move back, they begin to grumble among themselves and eye each other suspiciously. How could this have happened and who is to blame for this sudden death?

The Trial

At this point the narrator interrupts the action and turns to the audience to ask who or what they think is responsible for the death of this child. Without any hesitation, a man steps forward to say it is the mother's fault for having abandoned her children. The actress playing the mother, still sobbing with grief, steps out to defend herself: "I couldn't take it anymore. . . . Could you? This man who spent all our money on beer and who beat me, . . . he's the one who killed my son." A male spectator shouts out his approval of this verdict. The father steps forward to say "Listen, I didn't know what to do, I am not a rich man. . . . Sure, I drink . . . a little. That's no reason for her to abandon her children!"

A woman in the audience focuses the blame on the aunt who neglected her nephews. The aunt steps forward to defend herself, claiming she already had more than she could handle as a single mother of a demanding family. The aunt lashes back at the mother, who in turn cries out her anger. The women scream reciprocal accusations until, ultimate insult, they thrust their posteriors at each other and stomp off. The debate takes a comical turn but, although the audience is laughing, it is not deterred from earnestly locating the person responsible for the death.

One woman in the audience suggests the older cousins are to blame. They were, after all, responsible for the household in the parents' absence. The elder cousin steps forward with a "who me?" look. He blames his uncle for having dropped the youngsters on the family and his mother for having left him and his siblings to fend for themselves.

The characters are now all accusing each other in a heated cacophony. At a culminating point the shrouded figure on ground level rises slowly. There is a stirring in the audience, who notice this before the characters. The actor jumps up on the stage in the middle of the fray. The relatives gasp and pull back. He points an accusatory finger in a panoramic sweep englobing stage and audience, then speaks: "One child is lost, what about the other?" During the trial, no one has paid attention to the older orphan huddling in a corner. "Who are you going to blame when the next child dies?" After a pause, the narrator intervenes to ask, "What can you do to prevent this?"

Contaminating Messages

What was emerging from the forum debate was a reversal of the African proverb "It takes a village to raise a child" twisted into "It takes a village to destroy a child." However, the intended objective was not to locate social causality or individual blame, but to focus on the basic prevention of kwash.

The closing number of the show was a very lively song enumerating the foods that would keep growing children strong and healthy. After these didactic songs the Mwondo narrator and a nutritionist stayed to answer questions.

Kwash was produced in numerous venues accessible to the targeted working-class audience, which included men, women, and children. It was performed for free on weekends in public arenas and at the work place in hours allotted off from the job. It was presented in the red-plastic auditoriums of national and private companies and in the soccer stadiums of the mining towns where two minivans served as dressing rooms and as supports for the plank stage. Here hundreds of children stood in the field made muddy by the rainy season and the adult workers sat in the bleachers above the official podium where the managers were seated.

The children were perhaps the more ardent resonators of the nutritional messages, because they would quickly learn the lyrics and return to the following show to bellow them out with the actors. The adults seemed much more preoccupied with the social implications of the disease. Consistently, the moment where the spectators were invited to intervene was the most animated of the performance. Audiences felt connected to the family drama and quite readily stepped in to express their opinions. Many did stay for the nutritional lessons and frequently demonstrated that they were fully aware of children's basic nutritional needs.

The more interesting responses often occurred after the official closure, when the audience was preparing to leave and the actors to pack up. Mothers would share stories of their own family dramas—and also their struggle in trying to make ends meet—with the actors. Identifying with the father of the play, men would take actors aside to explain their situation. After one performance sponsored by Renault, the French car manufacturer that maintained a small assembly plant in Lubumbashi, a man stormed onto the stage and thrust his pay slip in the narrator's face, saying, "This is what I make. How can I feed meat to my kids two times a week with that?" The actors, whose salaries were less than the autoworker's, could not provide the answer.

We had exploited the two-way medium of live theatre, but the message spinning back to us was much more powerful than well-intentioned lessons in good nutrition. *Kwash,* the only Mwondo production undertaken that had not been designed as a social critique, was proving the most subversive.

Health, we discovered, is a revolutionary issue. Although taken aback, the company considered it a sign of success that the production was stirring up so much controversy. The doctors, however, did not.

The doctors and clinic directors who had instigated the project had followed little of its progression, outside of an official opening for an audience of clinicians and health educators. They were enthusiastic about the content and form of the piece, but they had never witnessed its impact in a popular venue. Having obtained the means for the project and approved the product, they considered their role complete. In fact, they never requested a follow-up report and might have remained oblivious to the audience's reaction had I not run into the head of pediatrics of the National Zairean Railways in an informal setting. She was delighted to hear of the wholehearted participation of the audience, and especially of the children's enlistment as message bearers of the ABCs of kwashiorkor prevention. But when I continued, still enthusiastic, to talk of the rumblings about paychecks and market prices, her face turned ashen. "They're not supposed to do that . . . they can't do that," she spluttered. For the company the emergence of the socioeconomic issues did not necessarily diffuse the nutritional lessons, whereas for the doctor this was a dangerous perversion of the message. In fact, she looked terrified.

This totally spontaneous reaction was in itself revelatory of the two basic contradictions underlying our enterprise. First, the show was financed by the corporations that could be challenged by the workers' increased awareness of their economic deprivation brought out in a seemingly innocent show about malnutrition. The pediatrician had good reason to fear a negative reaction since these same organizations financed her clinic. Moreover, most of the performances were held on the property of the company and, frequently, in the presence of the managers. In this setting, lessons of how workers should care for their children smacked of the paternalistic. If we had told the workers they should feed their children imported caviar daily instead of eggs and soy, the message could not have been more provocative.

The second basic contradiction lay in the fact that, although the creators of the show were present as mediators and as listeners, the medical practitioners who had instigated *Kwash* had no desire to listen directly to an audience who might deform the message. Their objective was to prescribe sound nutrition, good behavior, and to avoid the messy social causes of the disease, which we all knew were implicit but were powerless to change. The clinicians must have suspected that their premises were simplistic, that local superstitions and igno-rance of nutrition were not to blame for the disease, and that the drama's focus on family breakdown was bound to provoke the audience. But it is eas-ier to putatively dismiss popular metaphors equating the red hair of the afflict-ed child to anger and jealousy than to face why the infant was weaned too early. It is more comfortable to say, "I've heard eggs are taboo," than to face the conditions of the economically deprived.

The most naive premise of all—which the creators shared to some degree with the doctors—was: message sent equals message received. That the clini-cians had, in fact, recognized the social causes of kwash was evident in their soliciting the Mwondo in the first place. Having provided the list of remedies and having confirmed the accuracy of the data, the doctors hoped that because the actors were of the same social class as the audience and because the delivery was "culturally appropriate," the message would pass directly to the spectators. Instead of bypassing the socioeconomic problems of kwashiorkor, the performances seemed to highlight them. The pediatrician's insisting "they're not supposed to . . . they can't" revealed a desperate wish to maintain control over the audience, to prescribe a singular remedial message for direct ingestion, rather than to accept the dialogical nature of the live medium.

This experience inclined me to think the company should have con-ducted theatre workshops with the doctors, if only for them to discover the circulatory power of communication theatre offers. In fact, I would have the opportunity to work with healthcare providers years later in a very dif-ferent setting: in North American universities. As for *Kwash,* it continued to stir up local audiences for a few months and did, undeniably, sensitize them to the problem of childhood nutrition. For the company, it opened the way to further commissions from local and world health organizations during the 1980s, to productions dealing with such topics as family plan-ning and, later, AIDS awareness.

In spite of the fact *Kwash* never toured outside of the Lubumbashi area as other Mwondo productions had, it augmented the international reputa-tion of the company. Although we were not aware of this at the time, Kwash was part of a global theatre for development movement.[5] International funding for public health projects were, in part, what allowed the Mwondo to survive through the 1980s, years after funding from the Zairean state dwindled and then disappeared.[6]

The University Setting

Having returned to North America via Quebec, I again happened on an opportunity to work in theatre and public health, and this time directly with doctors, nurses, and health educators. In 1990 I conducted the first of three intensive workshops in theatre facilitation for Francophone health professionals, at the University of Montreal. The following year I began regularly teaching Fundamentals of Acting as an arts-credit course to nurses in training who were completing their associate degree at Penn State. Although the participants and the ostensible purposes of the two classes were quite different, the processes—with their problems and discoveries, their setbacks and rewards—proved remarkably similar. And although a fifteen-year hiatus separated these from the Zairean experience, *Kwash* and the issues it raised continue to inform my teaching of theatre in the field of public health. What follows is a composite description and analysis of the three workshops I conducted in Montreal.

The chance to work with health professionals first presented itself when Patrick Brunet, an audiovisual expert teaching in the communications department at the University of Montreal, approached me to design the theatrical component of an interdisciplinary program in family planning/community health he was coordinating. Brunet, who was familiar with the work of the Mwondo, which he had filmed years before on tours in Zaire and France, felt that theatre was a crucial medium in public health campaigns.

Financed by the United Nations and the Canadian International Development Agency and conducted through the departments of communications, demography, health care management, and preventive medicine at the University of Montreal, the annual ten-month program aimed to train health care providers and educators from Francophone developing countries in the design, implementation, and evaluation of family health programs. The curriculum included core courses in communications theory, demography, healthcare management, epidemiology, statistics, and specialized classes in either a health or communications profile. Theatre facilitation was one of several optional workshops, others being audiovisual, graphic and print design, and advertisement composition.

I devised a manual with a reading packet and sample syllabus, and in the fall of 1990, 1991, and 1992 I conducted intensive workshops (the requisite forty hours over a week and a half) in using theatre for what the program defined as *santé familiale*. The trainees—six to ten per workshop—were doctors, nurses, midwives, directors of family-planning clinics, health educators, and journalists specializing in public-service communications. A little less than half were women. Although the program focused on Francophone West Africa and was destined to relocate to the University of Dakar in Senegal after five years, participants also included citizens from the Antilles, Southeast Asia, and the Maghreb.

The trainees came from radically different cultural and political contexts and occupied variant positions in the social hierarchy of their countries, from midwife to doctor to bureaucrat in the ministries of health or communications. All held university degrees, were fluent in French as well as at least one of their national languages, and could read English. Many, having participated in numerous training enterprises at home or abroad, constituted a sort of caste of international public health workshop professionals. Their field experience—that is, working on a grassroots level as healthcare practitioners or educators—varied widely from rural doctor or urban midwife to radio journalists or ministry personnel working from offices.

Despite their cultural/linguistic diversity, educational, firsthand experiential, and social-status discrepancies, two factors united the participants: their current context and a common goal. All shared the experience of transient living in a foreign country, where surviving on a tight budget in anonymous apartments—away from their families and friends—and in the notorious Canadian cold, created both bonding and tension among the participants. What the trainees had most in common was a commitment to mother/child health, which implied a commitment to family planning.

As theatre facilitator I was delighted to have the opportunity to work directly with healthcare practitioners but ambivalent about the efficacy of a communication program so distanced from its target audience. This distance was as much the geographical or geoeconomic gap that separated the trainees' home countries from North America as the discrepancy in social status that might separate the trainees from the very people they were supposed to be reaching. The main problem lay in convincing the participants of the necessity of engaging with their target communities and offering them tools to do so in a context that had very little to do with conditions they would encounter back home. A tangential problem lay in actually getting them to work on their feet as actors and facilitators.

I could have bypassed these problems if I had treated theatre as a one-way medium. Designing technically well-made messages—however theoretical in producing behavior changes these might be—was the major objective of the other workshops in audiovisual and graphic communications. It would have been possible to develop minimal play-writing skills and to turn out a written product at the end of the workshop, but I saw little point in even doing a theatre workshop if it did not exploit the very specificity of the live medium and its interactive potential. Moreover, the workshop was entitled *Stage d'animation théâtrale* (training in theatre facilitation), which implied the process of group work and active interventions rather than the production of finished works. Breaking through the abstract nature of conceiving an interactive theatre for a totally virtual context and actually engaging these health professionals in the present moment of an acting workshop was the true challenge of the course.

Confronting the dilemma of context and agency directly, the syllabus proposed that the trainees would be the acting subjects of the intensive workshop, their experiences the raw material, and their goal to acquire facilitating tools they could share with actors and public health educators in their praxis. The first half of the workshop was devoted to opening up elementary creative channels (nonverbal communication and listening skills, focus on the action and acting partners rather than self-representation, creating trust and permission to play in the group, and "writing in space" techniques) and to investigating theories of theatre's transformative power and the medium's use in public health projects. The second half of the course moved toward applications: enacting narratives from the participants' experiences and developing scenarios on family-health issues. As the workshop progressed the trainees were increasingly involved as facilitators, directing warmup exercises and staging their scenarios with the other members of the group. The last day of the workshop consisted of a performative synopsis presented to an invited audience of faculty, colleagues, and friends. This, along with a concept to be applied in the participant's milieu—a theatre-intervention project or a script outline stipulating the objective, form, and issue explored, the producing partners, and target audience—constituted the ostensible objectives of the intensive workshop.

During the first phase of the workshop, mornings were spent in acting exercises and theatre games I have developed over the years, drawing from a repertory of multiple borrowings and my own experience as an acting coach and facilitator. Based on readings provided before the workshop began, the afternoon seminars touched on the ritual and social potential of theatre. Four theoretical lines were discussed, including Aristotle's notion of catharsis or purging the community of nefarious passions—a theory that fascinated some trainees—and Soyinka's (1975) concept of drama and ritual as related to the revolutionary ideal[7]. Brecht's alienation effect—the casting of social reality as uncanny, aberrational, and subject to change— was another theory that intrigued the trainees. Boal's praxis-based Theatre of the Oppressed (TO),[8] which invites the spect-actor to intervene in the course of the drama and to rehearse for "real life," capped the succinct theoretical overview. During discussions of TO's dialogical approach, which was central to our workshop, trainees inevitably brought out Paulo Freire's pedagogical theory, with which most of the participants were familiar. Implicit in Boal's and Freire's theories was direct participation and a warning against vertically designed messages.

Theoretical readings and discussions served not only to justify the proceedings in an academic setting for a primarily intellectual clientele but also to displace the notion of drama as a scripted and static entity, predetermined by priests of "high culture." If Western theatre had been the object of widely diversified theories on how to affect the audience, it must be much more than a formula for a "well-made play." And if these nonactors were to venture onto the stage of our class, any ideas of elite art or corporatist boundaries had to be jettisoned.

Preliminary readings and discussions on theatre as a social world and an immediate exchange also included documented case studies that explored three models of live popular theatre and health education in Africa:

- Mass message theatre, through a giant puppet show used in an AIDS-awareness campaign in South Africa (Friedman 1991)
- Interactive performance, through the Zairean Mwondo Théâtre's *Kwash* production as described above and documented in a videotape and through the Atelier Théâtre Burkinabé's collection of forum-theatre

scripts, published by the Burkina Faso Ministry of Education, scripts on family planning and hygiene that used the TO forum-theatre format in a rather normalizing wrong-way/right-way fashion, inviting spectators to correct the behavior of the promiscuous teenager or the negligent parent

- Long-term theatrical interventions, through the grassroots workshops of Ahmadu Bello University, in rural Nigeria, where drama students collaborated directly with villagers to produce performances on problems pertinent to the community (Ahmadu Bello and Kidd 1982).

These case studies were enriched by the participants' sharing of experiences in the use of performance in public health campaigns they had witnessed, which included a Haitian *carnaval* crew's musical comedy on sexually transmitted diseases and a Laotian shadow-puppet show on vaccinations. The examples were analyzed in view of their apparent capacity to use theatre as a two-way medium rather than a channel to prescribe messages. I hoped that the variety of experiments would suggest other ideas to the trainees and that the critical perspective would inform any theatrical ventures they might collaborate on back home. Tangent to these testimonies of live performances was the fact that theatre is ultimately dependent on the immediate community: in our case the community was the one we were creating in the *hic et nunc* of the workshop.

Generally, the participants enjoyed juggling with theories and critiquing imagined theatrical ventures. When asked to actually construct performances that would constitute a concrete object to critique, they were more hesitant. Just getting up to move rather than sitting anchored to their desks seemed a plunge into dangerous waters. Since many were used to public speaking, this was not a problem of inhibition. In fact, those who were most demonstrative in the theoretical discussions proved the most wary of the physical exercises. The problem lay rather in momentarily stepping beyond the word and the public persona, in simply giving oneself permission to play and trusting the others.

From the outset the participants differed in their willingness to put themselves in the vulnerable position of an active subject caught in a quandary resembling that of their patients rather than a superior dispensing messages from above and outside. Although acquainted with each other, they had little experience in openly sharing personal experiences, let alone playing together. Many of the initial exercises I proposed involved dropping the mask of the clinician or the educator to communicate non-verbally with their acting partners. After formal introductions I asked the trainees to present an image of their home in one or two silent frames. The presentations ranged from attempts at anagrams (that is, corporally repro-ducing words) or shaping the country's topography (a mountain, a lake), to personal memories of eating a meal or cradling a baby, images that struck universal chords of home. The nonverbal communication phase included the classic mirror exercise—the objective of which is that the gesture organ-ically take over the direction of both partners—and a series of "blind trust" exercises where the subject is led blindfolded through the space by her partner's voice or guided through an imaginary obstacle course created by suggestions from the group such as "Don't trip on that stone," or "Duck, there's a branch."

For a few trainees, being deprived of words or trusting in the group was at first painful. For one, it proved impossible. A radio journalist from Benin, sent by his government to become a proficient health educator, was paralyzed by the nonverbal exercises and not about to give up personal con-trol. He dismissed the workshop as unproductive and childish. After all, he objected, he could not report back to *mon Ministre*—an abstract telos that apparently regulated his every move—that he had spent his time in Canada playing games. He wanted a quick formula to produce behavior change rather than a critical awareness of the dubious nature of message produc-tion, a commodity to peddle back home rather than engagement in a collective process that might actually develop the basic communication skill of listening to others.

This resistance was fortunately rare. Most of the trainees moved rapidly into the spirit of "the play is the thing" and created a team. For some the nonverbal communication exercises proved liberating. These were the qui-eter trainees who were often, but not always, women. The most eloquent example was a Laotian doctor whose French was very hesitant. Because of his language difficulties, nonverbal communication proved a survival skill that brought him out of the isolation he had experienced in other classes.

One of the exercises I proposed was to mime daily activities at home. Quite far from home and in the neon-neutral space of a university classroom, the trainees' projections of their customary professional and personal life were highly idealized. In this context, working at triage or taking a pulse seemed a joy. None appeared so serenely confident in the inherent value of their life work as the Laotian doctor. His activity was tilling the soil rather than dealing with patients. Puzzled by this, I asked what it meant. Prompted by his acting partners, he explained in faltering French and a newly discovered body language that part of a doctor's or anybody's job in Laos was to participate in growing crops.

The initiatory phase developed not only basic ensemble cohesion and a taste for theatrical play, but reflexive awareness. Discrepancies between contexts, those between the trainee's present in Montreal and their life at home, were revealed through image theatre. I asked the participants to act out their returning home in the evening in Montreal as compared to the same daily ritual in their usual environments. Their pictures showed enormous differences in interpersonal contacts, which had as much to do with the trainees' peculiar situation as with cultural frames. Images of home depicted the subject rushing in to be greeted by the children, the spouse, the cook, the nanny (or the mother or niece who served as such). In Montreal the subject rushed for the mail, then, usually disappointed, returned to books and notes, or turned on the television, or eventually called a fellow trainee.

Images of "back home" were juxtaposed to their current home. Montreal, and North America as a whole, was depicted in a harsh and stereotypical light. I asked the participants to sculpt images of the city using their partners as clay. What surfaced were pictures of homeless crawling the streets, an aging society where the elderly are pushed out of the family and abandoned in nursing homes, where youths are lost to drugs, where unemployment and poverty run rampant, where violence is a permanent subtext. When I pointed out the radical differences in the cozy versus hostile images of the two environments, the trainees began to reflect on the subjective coloring of their projections.

The first impulse was always to portray their social reality at home in a romantic light. I asked the participants to sculpt images of the family. These were at first idyllic snapshots of a harmonious family with numerous children, happy parents, a supportive community. I asked why, if the family was such an unconditional blessing, had the participants committed their professional lives to family health and birth control. Subsequent images depicted a woman struggling to walk with numerous offspring clinging to her neck and her legs, a man conversing with a woman in a bar while two other women with ailing children waited outside and begged for money from people passing by, a man standing alone with his empty pockets turned inside out.

Strategies and Scenarios

The second half of the workshop was devoted to role playing, writing personal narratives in space, constructing scenarios for forum theatre, and designing a concept for use in the trainee's home context. If I was quite open to whatever intervention plan the trainees might design in relation to their target audiences, I was very insistent on placing the trainee at the center of their forum-theatre stories. I was leery of facile solutions to the problems of subjects who were not there, and especially of the wrong-way/right-way model we had critiqued in the Burkinabé experience. It was crucial the subject assume the role of a vulnerable protagonist in which she or an assistant from the audience could intervene to reverse the drama.

In this second phase I sought to move the trainees to center stage, both as directors of scenarios drawn from their personal experience and as facilitators organizing the workshop. The participants began to reveal the frustrations they had experienced in trying to convince their clients to use birth-control methods, in dealing with an inordinate number of patients in dire circumstances, or in attempting to dialogue with the cumbersome, obtuse, impersonal national and international apparatus that ultimately determined their funding. As I invited them to direct warmups or stage their narratives, the trainees were at the same time acquiring facilitating skills. Through role-playing the healthcare provider and the patient, they also began to perceive the persona they projected from other vantage points.

One particularly lively improvisation provided a role-play opportunity and an introduction to forum-theatre intervention. The scene depicted was a triage center in a West African metropolis. A group of very impatient patients is swarming around a triage nurse doing her best to cope. One patient, played by a male nurse from Guinea who had a remarkable gift for clowning, expressed his plight as "J'ai le rhume en bas" (I have the flu down below). The patient is continually rerouted to the back of the line because he is too embarrassed to express himself clearly to the female nurse. He eventually leaves the clinic carrying his gonorrhea with him.

The patient was portrayed with comic pathos that had nothing of the grotesque. Kito—as the man with the flu down below was later dubbed— kept looking desperately to the audience for help every time he was sent to the back of the line. The trainees found the performance funny not only because of the actor's mimicry but because they all recognized the difficulty of patients expressing themselves when it came to sexual matters or simply of speaking a language other than the clinical personnel. I pointed out that—because it would serve no purpose, not to mention make for a dreary performance—there was no point in replacing the protagonist who would become miraculously assertive or articulate in French. I suggested instead they focus attention on the triage nurse. At the same time, I told the three actors playing the other patients waiting in line to determine for themselves precisely what the medical problem that had brought them to the clinic was and that this be grounded in a personal-illness episode in their corporal memory. Moreover, they should express their problem aggressively in their native tongue or any language other than French. The man with the flu down below was to act as before.

The scene that ensued resembled a seething mob, a Tower of Babel pushing and shoving poor Kito out of the way and totally overwhelming the triage nurse. Here we had a role-play where the participants could actually "rehearse for real life," where they became active subjects rather than judges of others' behavior or dispensers of prescriptive messages that they wistfully hoped would bring about change. The woman playing the triage nurse was replaced several times to enact strategies for dealing with difficult clinical situations and recalcitrant patients. At the same time, playing the roles of the patients with a personal "as if" memory allowed the practitioner to step into the patient's shoes and to observe the clinical world from the other side.

To prepare forum-theatre interventions I invited the trainees to stage stories where they had felt personally wronged. Lorraine—a nurse, health educator, and family-planning program director from Burundi—proposed a narrative from her experience in which she applied for an international health program in Belgium. Her *Stage en Belgique* (*Training in Belgium*) later evolved into a collective scenario entitled *Stage au Canada*. The trainee had applied for a workshop in Europe years before and had been bumped off the list in favor of a candidate who was, she claimed, the mistress of the deciding bureaucrat, who was himself a relative of the minister of health. Lorraine told her story first in images and playback theatre,[9] sculpting and then casting roles as she went along. The scenes followed the protagonist filling out endless administrative forms, preparing for and executing a written test, walking out of the exam room with her rival, who bragged about handing in a blank paper, going to receive her outstanding note, then meeting with the bureaucrat, who announced she was rejected.

Whatever the subjective coloring to Lorraine's interpretation of her dismissal, her story was quite plausible and clearly depicted an abuse of power with which all the participants could identify. We isolated the scene where the candidate encounters the bureaucrat to see what strategies she could use to reverse the decision. The participants replacing Lorraine used a variety of tactics. An appeal to reason in view of her qualifications, a plea for pity, an attempt at flattery, nothing seemed to sway the actor playing the bureaucrat, who was confident in his protection. This actor had agreed that his objective was to get rid of the pesky woman as soon as possible and not to give in unless he was genuinely affected. As different tactics failed, he became smugger and more secure. There was a consensus that the best way to counteract this abuse of authority was to appeal to a higher power; the problem lay in locating this power.

We tried creating a scene where Lorraine solicits the help of the Belgian examiner. He defers to the ministry explaining that, in spite of her test results, he has no control over the final decision. The hierarchical chain of protection seemed to block any retaliation. Finally, one woman, who had never intervened before, said she wanted to replace Lorraine during the scene in the director's office. She was at first disarmingly friendly, almost diffident, putting the man off guard by graciously accepting her rejection and stating her earnest intention to reapply the following year. Then she complimented him on the choice of the rival candidate, subtly suggesting she knew what good friends they were and she was sure his wife would also like to know this. The actor/character blanched at the mention of his wife. He began fidgeting around with papers and murmuring that perhaps the ministry could accommodate an additional trainee. Reaching for the phone, he said in a strained voice that he would call the minister immediately. The newly empowered candidate said no, this wasn't necessary, that she could wait until next year. Tables turned, the antagonist wound up pleading with the woman to reconsider her decision. Following this scene, which delighted all, one man claimed, "But your tactic is just blackmail." "No," shrugged the woman, "simply appealing to a higher authority."

Critiquing this intervention, the participants began to see that the purpose of forum theatre was not to provide pat answers but to create a safe space for people to try out solutions, to practice assuming the role of a directing subject, and to observe and listen. Parallel to this came an understanding that the facilitator's role was also listening, provoking, and waiting for the opportune moment to create this opening rather than attempting to direct the outcome according to a master plan or transmitting a normative message.

The rationale for placing the participants in vulnerable positions and encouraging them to struggle their way out is that no change can come about without the subject's consent and will. In the workshop process per se, this premise was fully recognized: theatre as a means of collective investigation, of penetrating and challenging reality from the inside, flourished. Most agreed that reversing roles, stepping back to look at how the practitioner is perceived, learning to critique and laugh at one's own foibles, and especially to allow the message to circulate in the group had been a liberating exercise. Yet the temptation to use theatre as a management device rather than a two-way communication process resurfaced when preparing term projects. Although the trainees readily recognized that the art of facilitation was first to listen to how the participants viewed a topic and then to create a safe space to practice change, when given the choice between an indeterminate interactive process and a scripted message, most chose the latter.

I could understand their hesitations, since the desire to control reality within the microcosm of the play stems as much from a need for security as actors and writers as it does from the health educator's wish to find the magic formula. The group generally chose to present better-prepared and closed skits rather than forum theatre, which required them to improvise and rely on the intervention of spectators who might or might not follow the thread they had devised. The group decided to present the drafts of their scenario outlines in an afternoon seminar and then choose one or two to perform at the public workshop closing the class. They could then later revise their written concepts indicating how they might materially produce this at home, in what setting, with what company, for what target audience, and with what funding.

The trainees proved surprisingly skillful in creating characters with some depth—many of whom were fashioned from class improvisations—and all showed they had acquired a sense of the theatrical. But their scenarios tended to fall back on a classical structure of exposition, crisis, resolution. In our earlier seminars we had critiqued the three pitfalls of presenting message-oriented scenarios: (1) the pedantic approach, which reduced the play to a series of lessons with no dramatic content; (2) the moralizing approach, which locates an individual scapegoat to bear responsibility for the disease or social neglect; (3) the happy-ending approach, which dissolves the problem rather than stimulating the will to change. An indication of how successful the workshops were in creating a feel for the dramatic and visual dynamics, the flat-lesson approach—with charts and talking heads giving lectures in the why and how of birth control to passive clients—was quite rare. The tendency to moralize or to wrap up the story with a happy ending was more frequent.

One example was the story of the man with the flu down below, who was incorporated into a more complex scenario on condom use and the prevention of sexually transmitted disease. *La Maladie honteuse* (*The Unmentionable Disease*) portrayed a healed central character who magically convinces his fiancée to be tested, to forgive his transgressions, to marry him and ride off into an HIV-free sunset to raise a (reasonably sized) family, and to live happily ever after. In the collective critique we looked for ways to bring the scenario closer to reality and perhaps to create a window where the audience might intervene. It was suggested that the hero trick the fiancée into being tested, and that she, upon discovering the truth, resolve to break up the relationship. Yet, as she is packing her bags, she hesitates. The audience could then dialogue with the character, offering reasons for and against her leaving.

Among the scenarios that did provide an opening for spect-actor intervention during the closing workshop, one was entitled *Chez moi, jamais* (*Never in My Home*). The dramatic narrative was starkly simple: (1) a mother of five children attempts to broach the subject of birth control with her husband; (2) he declares "never in my home" and that he is rich enough to take care of all his children; (3) despite the supposed privacy of the conversation, numerous in-laws, ancestral voices, and even peers descend on the woman, urging her simply to obey her husband and avoid conflict; (4) again pregnant, the desperate woman ingests a homemade abortive agent, which kills her.

As the wails of the grief-stricken relatives are about to begin, the writer/director interrupts the action, saying this didn't really happen because something shifted earlier. The drama is "rewound" to the first scenes and audience members are invited to suggest strategies or replace the woman striving to state her position vis-à-vis the patriarchs, her mother, or her peers *before* the tragedy incurs. After one or two of the workshop participants replaced the protagonist, several volunteers from the audience, both men and women, stepped into her role to confront staunch antagonists. Here it was not a question of producing a family-planning message—which would have been preaching to the choir anyway—but of creating a dialogue and practicing alternative persuasive strategies. The creator of *Chez moi, jamais* determined to follow up on the project with clients of a woman's health center in her country where women wishing to halt repeated pregnancies could perform not only the role of the protagonist but that of the antagonists. It is in the slippage between the roles and the active listening that the subject begins to picture the forces alive in her daily reality and, perhaps, to grasp an opportunity for change.

Cross-contaminations

If the trainees did for the most part recognize that their role was to create that opportunity and not to dictate a lesson, the course accomplished its goal. Although I did hear from a few participants who returned home to organize health-education interventions with actors, I cannot measure the long-term effects of the workshops. As a theatre practitioner I am predisposed to think that the propagation of theatre is in itself of value. As a facilitator, I tend to measure success in the immediate results of one workshop, one performance, one exchange in the present moment. Most gratifying are the moments of discovery—conflictual or communal—when there is a shift in the perception of a problem or a new approach emerges. I measure the immediate success of the workshops in the trainees acquiring a sense of their own expressive powers, of visual and dramatic impact, of thinking on their feet in the improvisational moment, and of their ability to open up to what is happening in that moment rather than retreating behind the bulwarks of their preconceptions.

Since conducting these international workshops at the University of Montreal, I have had ample opportunity to observe this occurring in acting classes and workshops I've conducted in the United States. Issues of contaminating theatre have been especially relevant to the acting course I developed over five years teaching with Penn State at a nursing school in Northeast Philadelphia. The students of Frankford Hospital School of Nursing are as diverse as those of the University of Montreal international workshops. Most are from local working-class stock, but their education and life experience varies from coming directly out of high school to having raised a family or served in the armed forces. These are women and men—predominantly from the Irish-Catholic neighborhood, followed by African-Americans, then a burgeoning international minority from India, Africa, and the Caribbean—who have committed to a nursing career for both ideological and material reasons.

Conducted over ten weeks four times a year, these classes have allowed me to refine the structure of an acting workshop for health professionals, as well as to recognize the limits of working within a university setting. Being frequently caught off balance by the students, these classes have continually compelled me to challenge my own set recipes. Structured in two parts—initiation into acting skills and applications in public-health theatre—this course uses improvisational and interactive techniques to develop performances based primarily on the students' narratives. These stories revolve aound problems they encounter in their personal and professional lives. Since in addition to a demanding courseload many of the students have young children and part-time jobs, the repertory of problems is extensive, a gold mine for improvisations. Many work in nursing homes in difficult material conditions, an environment that has figured frequently in the role-plays or narratives the students stage.

More so than in the short-term workshops I conducted in Montreal, this course proved successful in developing teamwork and thinking-on-your-feet skills, as useful in nursing as in theatre. Through their enactments the students have also been able to test coping strategies, to try out others' roles, to process reality in a different way. In the open-ended improvisations where students are invited to replace the protagonist, subjectivity circulates and ideas percolate.

The application of these interactive techniques in their term projects—a brief performance focusing on a public health issue designed for a specific audience—has proved less successful. As in the Montreal workshops, when asked to devise a presentation centering on a pertinent problem, the students tended to retreat to the safety of closed theatre and simplistic messages. Although they have experienced the pedagogical value of active participation and have recognized that change can only be produced by a willing and active subject, when they take on the mantle of the educator, the initial impulse is to use theatre as another platform for lecturing, preaching, prescribing behavior that will lead to the best of all possible worlds.

For example, a topic frequently chosen is teenage pregnancy, not only a burning issue in the wider social context but prevalent in the students' clinical experience and, for some, in their own personal experience. In the sharing of case studies the students revealed the gap between reality and projecting a public health message, between themselves and the others they hoped to reach. One story emerging in a small group preparation session—but never theatrically exploited—was that of a woman who had come to a clinic for her eighth abortion. "My God," said one of the students, "she had her first at thirteen. My daughter is twelve."

These preparatory sessions were awakenings for myself and the students, but the resulting scenarios were often formulaic and facile responses. These skits might show the travails of a high school dropout in her third pregnancy contrasted with the sterling accomplishments of the girl who said no. I asked what they thought would happen if they showed this to a group of teenage girls struggling with issues of sexuality and birth control. The students agreed they would probably meet with hostile silence or mockery unless they allowed the spectators to reshape the scenarios by intervening directly or acting as dramaturges. In that case the actors/educators might learn from the audience, but they risked being overwhelmed.

When asked in their wrap-up analysis of the class to name advantages and disadvantages of interactive versus straight-message theatre in public health education, students have responded that role-play and forum-theatre "spect-actor" intervention can effectively raise awareness and offer new ways of viewing a problem, but that the health educators risk losing control over their message. Although they recognized the improbability of actually producing the prescribed change and entertained no illusions of controlling the audience—beyond the hope they would remain quiet during the presentation—they at least wished to have control over *their* message.

Here, stated starkly, was the recurrent fear of contaminating the health educator's message that I first encountered in the *Kwash* experience, and then again in the Montreal workshops. Viewed conjunctively these experiences inform each other. Conducting workshops in the confines of the university laboratory allows the participants to explore a variety of techniques and to grasp the reciprocally transformative potential of the two-way medium. If the facilitator trusts in the outcome, the safe space of the closed workshop creates the trust the participants need to overcome self-consciousness, to disturb set ideologies, to truly listen to the other.

What the workshop cannot do is meet the challenge of working in the field, where the spectators may, as they did in *Kwash*, retort with their own messages. Ideally the workshop needs to move beyond the utopia of the classroom to intervene in real-world sites. In the acting for nurses class the closest we come to an immediately concerned public site is through inviting fellow students—peers from outside the workshop—to intervene in performances revolving around issues pertinent to their collective situation. These have ranged from the gender bias male nurses experience to alcohol abuse among student nurses. Here the audience will not allow the actors to dispense putative and facile lessons. At the same time, the actors/educators realize that "cross-contamination" does not deform the basic information they wish to convey, which is probably shared by the audience anyway. It may, however, seriously invade the well-intentioned message and shake the confidence of its bearers.

Although both acknowledge their inevitable dependence on their interlocutors, theatre artists share with health educators the overt desire to control their performances and the secret desire to manipulate their audience. There is a natural propensity to transmit constructed truths and to pay only token attention to the people addressed. Yet it is the ability to question one's own truths and to allow contamination by other views in the performative moment that allows reciprocal understandings, the creation of new meanings, and the collaboration necessary to begin to address common problems.

Notes

1. After the fall of the Mobutu regime in May 1997, the nation that had been known as the Republic of Zaire since 1971 was renamed the Democratic Republic of Congo.

2. Throughout the 1970s the Mwondo performed in Lubumbashi, in Kinshasa, within Shaba and Kasai Provinces ("bartering" performances with local artists), in neighboring Rwanda and Burundi, and in international festivals in France (Nancy World Festival) and Nigeria (with the Ballet National du Zaïre at the Lagos FESTAC).

3. The state's authenticity campaign that flourished in the 1970s was based on the principle of seeking inspiration in national roots to escape colonial acculturation. Theoretically this implied turning to popular culture—where traditions were very much alive and continually reinvented—and to encouraging indigenous languages, art forms, and material culture. Although this did occur to some degree, *authenticité* as an official policy quickly revealed itself as another form of cultural alienation and as a means of justifying the despotism of the regime and the economic oppression of the vast majority of the population.

4. The name *kwashiorkor* is derived from a Ghanaian term meaning "red child," referring to the rusty tint of the hair, a frequent symptom of the affliction.

5. In the 1970s many Anglophone African university drama departments were instigating projects engaging local populations in treating specific problems. For critical overviews on African theatre for development, see Etherton 1982, Mlama 1991, Kerr 1995. See also Epskamp's work (1989), which explores theatre for development in Asia and Latin America, as well as Africa. For particularly probing case studies on theatrical interventions in public health and the issue of vertical messages, see Ahmadu Bello Collective and Kidd 1982 and Conquergood 1988.

6. The Mwondo was assimilated into the Théâtre National Mobutu Sese Seko in 1975. The theatre received token salaries from the state for a few years, but no funds to produce or to tour, for which they relied on international backing. In addition to their public health projects, the company pursued their research in fusing traditional performance and modern scenography. In 1991 they toured France with *Satonge,* a production financed by the French Cultural Services.

7. In Soyinka's view, live theatre and ritual share the ideal of social transformation: "the matrix of creativity, most especially in the dramatic

mode, embraces at all times—both in individual and communal affec-
tiveness—the regenerative potential of society" (1975:87).

8. For more information on Theatre of the Oppressed and its relationship to Aristotelian and Brechtian systems, see Boal 1985. For more
information on the techniques and formats of TO, see Schutzman in
this volume and Boal 1992.

9. For more information on Playback Theatre, which allows narrators
drawn from the audience to cast and direct their own stories, see
Salas 1993.

Works Cited

Ahmadu Bello Collective and Ross Kidd. 1982. "Plays for Farmers:
Popular Drama Workshops in Northern Nigeria/ *Théâtre à la ferme:
Ateliers de théâtre populaire dans le nord du Nigéria.*" *Théâtre
International* 6 (2):21–44.

Atelier Théâtre Burkinabé. 1988. *Recueil théâtral, piéces de théâtre forum.*
Ouagadougou: UNESCO, Ministère de l'Education Nationale,
Presses Africaines.

Boal, Augusto. 1985. *Theatre of the Oppressed.* Trans. Charles A. McBride
and Maria-Odilia L. McBride. New York: Theatre Communications
Group.

———. 1992. *Games for Actors and Non-Actors.* Trans. Adrian Jackson.
London: Routledge.

Conquergood, Dwight. 1988. "Health Theatre in a Hmong Refugee
Camp: Performance, Communication, and Culture." *TDR: A
Journal of Performance Studies* 32 (3):174–208.

Epskamp, Kees. 1989. *Theatre in Search of Social Change.* The Hague:
CESO.

Etherton, Michael. 1982. *The Development of African Drama.* London:
Hutchinson.

Friedman, Gary. 1991. "AIDS in South Africa, Puppet Power." *Links* 9
(1):20–22.

Kerr, David. 1995. *African Popular Theatre.* London: James Currey.

Kidd, Ross. 1982. *The Popular Performing Arts, Non-Formal Education and Social Change in the Third World: A Bibliography and Review Essay.* The Hague: CESO.

Mlama, Penina Muhando. 1991. *Culture and Development: The Popular Theatre Approach in Africa.* Uppsala: Nordiska Afrikainstitutet.

Salas, Jo. 1993. *Improvising Real Life: Personal Story in Playback Theatre.* Dubuque, Ia.: Kendall/Hunt.

Soyinka, Wole. 1975. "Drama and the Revolutionary Ideal." In *In Person: Achebe, Awoonor, and Soyinka.* Ed. Karen Moreil. Seattle: Washington Institute for Comparative Studies.

Notes on Contributors

David Dan has several career interests—writing, theatre, and clinical social work—and looks for opportunities to bring them together. He has a background in theatre and social work. For nearly fifteen years he has served as therapist and director of community mental health projects. He has published widely in the field and is the recipient of the 1993 National Magazine Award for Public Interest awarded by the Columbia School of Journalism. He is currently coordinator of Children's Services for Community Health in Philadelphia.

Muriel Gold is a theatre producer/director and a university acting teacher, and has served as artistic director of the Saidye Bronfman Centre, in Montreal. She has taught acting to special populations and conducted drama-therapy workshops with survivors of domestic abuse. She has given numerous conferences and workshops and published articles on the multiple uses of the Fictional Family method, which is described in her book *The Fictional Family.* She is currently editing an anthology on how the method has been applied in a variety of fields.

Joan Holden has been principal playwright for the San Francisco Mime Troupe since 1967. Her plays and collaborations for SFMT include *The Independent Female, or A Man Has His Pride; The Dragon Lady's Revenge; False Promises; Hotel Universe;* the *Factwino* trilogy; *Steeltown; Spain/36; Ripped Van Winkle; Seeing Double; Back to Normal; Offshore; Coast City Confidential,* and *Soul Suckers from Outer Space.* She has translated and adapted classic plays and modern comedies for the Eureka Theatre, the American Conservatory Theatre, the Berkeley Repertory Theatre, and the San Francisco Shakespeare Festival. With Daniel Chumley she has participated and collaborated on plays in Israel, the Philippines, and Hong Kong.

She has received a Rockefeller Foundation Playwright's Fellowship, the Bay Area Critics' Circle and Edward R. Robbins Playwrighting Award, and the Bay Area Media Alliance Golden Gadfly Award.

Kwaleleya Ikafa, a Zambian playwright and a civil engineer for a mining company, wrote and directed numerous plays, from musical comedies to media dramas. For many years he wrote a weekly newspaper column about theatre in Zambia. His work on the social ramifications of AIDS in his country include the Zambian radio series *Nshilakamona*. In 1993 he was transferred to South Africa, where he continued serving as civil engineer for a Zambian mining company while undertaking theatre projects with the new theatre-for-social-change movement in Johannesburg.

Jill Mac Dougall is a translator of plays from the Francophone world, director, facilitator, and performance scholar. She has cofounded activist theatre companies in France and Zaire and worked as acting coach and production coordinator for national companies in Zaire and the Ivory Coast. She has trained health educators in acting and interactive-theatre techniques at the University of Montreal and Pennsylvania State University. She has published numerous translations (*UBU Repertory/TCG* series), as well as reviews and critical essays (*Anthropologie et sociétés, Theatre Journal, TDR, Women & Performance*), and a book on national identity politics, *Performing Identities on the Stages of Quebec* (1997). She is currently teaching with the Pennsylvania State University and serving as artistic director of the National Women's Theatre Festival in Philadelphia.

Maureen Martineau is a longtime member and artistic codirector of the Québécois activist company Théâtre Parminou. For nearly twenty years she has served regularly as performer, playwright, and director for the company which has produced throughout Quebec and Canada, as well as in Europe and Africa. In 1985 she received a grant from the Canadian Arts Council to conduct research on theatre in Eastern Europe, specifically Hungary, Romania, and Czechoslovakia. She has also trained with the Berliner Ensemble on Brechtian styles of stage production. She has recently established a school within the Parminou that offers courses in creative theatre techniques for a wide variety of groups, from street kids to primary-school drama teachers.

Mady Schutzman is a writer, theatre artist, and feminist scholar. For eight years she codirected the Experimental Theatre Project, which developed politically conscious art in nontheatrical settings. She is a freelance practitioner of Theatre of the Oppressed techniques and has focused on their relationship to feminist theory and media culture. She is coeditor of *Playing Boal: Theatre, Therapy, Activism* (1994) and has published work in *TDR, Errant Bodies, Women & Performance, Oxalis,* and *Home Planet News.* Her current work, *The Real Thing: Performance, Hysteria, and Advertising,* will be published in 1999. She currently teaches at the California Institute of the Arts, where she is also assistant dean.

Mele Smith served as a Peace Corps volunteer teaching in Nepal before returning to the United States to complete a master's degree in public health in New York. She worked for the New York City Department of Health, where she coordinated the Smokefree Coalition, which successfully advocated legislation banning vending machines and free tobacco samples. Since 1991 she has been serving as health educator in the Tobacco Free Project of the San Francisco Department of Public Health.

Lucy Winner is an associate professor of theatre at the State University of New York/Empire State College, which specializes in alternative and flexible training for adults. She teaches and directs programs at the intersection of theatre, education, and public health. She has worked in activist and educational theatre and has taught and performed in schools, hospitals, theatres, prisons, settlement houses, and streets, and was a founding member of the Rhode Island Feminist Theatre in 1973. Winner founded and directs the Theatre for Adolescent Survival Project and currently cochairs the Association for Theatre in Higher Education Advocacy Committee's task force on the expanding role of theatre and theatre education.

Stanley Yoder is a medical anthropologist and public health researcher who has conducted research on local knowledge of illness and medicine and on the development and evaluation of community health projects and media effectiveness in a dozen countries in Africa. He has served as senior research director at the University of Pennsylvania's Annenberg School for Communication and as international consultant for development agencies. He has published numerous articles on traditional healing and international health issues in anthropology and public health journals. He is the editor of *African Health and Healing Systems* (1982) and *Knowledge and Practice in International Health,* a special issue of *Medical Anthropology Quarterly* (1997).